P9-ARP-305

1993 32

The author at the summit of Popocatepetl.

NEW WORLDS TO CONQUER

By

RICHARD HALLIBURTON

Author of The Royal Road to Romance

and The Glorious Adventure

ILLUSTRATED

PROPERTY OF
COLBY SCHOOL FOR GIRLS

INDIANAPOLIS
THE BOBBS-MERRILL COMPANY
PUBLISHERS

10435

Copyright, 1929
By The Bobbs-Merrill Company

Printed in the United States of America

F
1409
H18

10435

PRESS OF
BRAUNWORTH & CO., INC.
BOOK MANUFACTURERS
BROOKLYN, N. Y.

To

David Laurance Chambers

CONTENTS

CONTENTS—*Continued*

ILLUSTRATIONS

ILLUSTRATIONS—*continued*

FACING PAGE

ILLUSTRATIONS—*continued*

FACING PAGE

ILLUSTRATIONS—*continued*

FACING PAGE

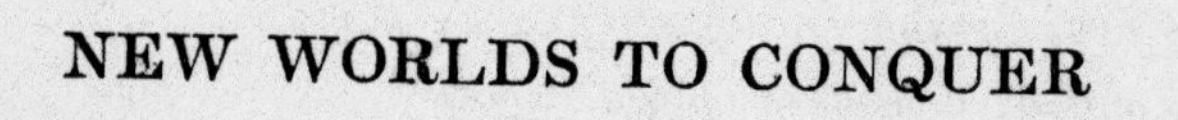

NEW WORLDS TO CONQUER

NEW WORLDS TO CONQUER

PROLOGUE

THE NEW WORLD

"Behind him lay the gray Azores,
Behind, the gates of Hercules;
Before him not the ghost of shores;
Before him only shoreless seas.
The good mate said: 'Now must we pray,
For lo! the very stars are gone.
Speak, admiral! what shall I say?'
Why, say 'sail on! sail on! and on!'"

SAIL ON—the *Niña,* and the *Pinta,* and the *Santa Maria.*

Straight into the West, farther and farther into the wastes of ocean, Columbus grimly steers his course.

September passes. October finds the fleet in tropical seas.

Flocks of gulls and pigeons are seen flying overhead, all headed in the same direction—surely to some land where they can rest.

Land must indeed be near. The admiral orders his crew to keep a sharp lookout.

At ten o'clock that night he believes he sees a light. Impatiently, anxiously, on the quarter-deck of the *Santa Maria,* he peers across the sea for another sign.

At two o'clock the clouds that had been obscuring the moon had cleared, and in the sudden illumination, there, not two leagues away, Rodrigo of Triana, a common sailor aboard the *Pinta,* had seen a line of white surf breaking on a tongue of sand. With a cry of *"Tierra! Tierra!"* he had rushed to the ship's cannon and fired the shot that announced the most momentous discovery in history.

Taut with excitement the three caravels lay to, waiting for dawn to reveal to them the golden shores of Cathay.

Cathay! Had not this been their destination? Had Columbus not promised them marble harbors, and elephants, and all the wealth of India?

At last day broke. But as the sun rose their spirits sank. Nowhere could they find the ivory towers, or the silken banners flying, or any of the glory they had dreamed of. There was only a flat, sandy island, thinly forested, and a group of savages, naked and astonished, staring from the shore at the miraculous ships.

Only a flat and sandy little island, forgotten and denied—but the birthplace of all the Americas.

This island Columbus named San Salvador, in honor of the Savior.

Yet no sooner was it named than it fell into oblivion; and has never existed as a reality in the minds of the very people—the Americans—who owe it so deep a reverence.

After more than four centuries of neglect, I rediscovered it in the modern manner—by seaplane, the seaplane *Santa Maria.*

The island, twelve miles long and six wide, is one of the Bahama group—the most seaward of them all. East of it there is no land till Africa. West of it the coral architects have built three thousand reefs and keys that stretch in a labyrinth of sea and shoal four hundred miles to the southern coasts of Florida.

In order to approach the island as Columbus approached it, I had my pilot make a wide detour, and turn about, and hold our course above the sea, straight into the West.

We hugged the waves, not thirty feet above them. At two o'clock in the afternoon I observed a dull gray line upon the horizon.

The land grew clearer. Near this spot Columbus saw the light on shore.

We streaked ahead—leaving the flagships behind—overtaking the *Pinta* two leagues off the northern point.

At the left was the line of white surf breaking on a tongue of sand.

Columbus could not disembark at once, even with the daylight. A coral reef lay between him and the land, so that he had to round the northern cape and sail along the western coast until he found an opening and a safe anchorage. Then arrayed in all his red robes of office, sword drawn, the flag of Ferdinand and Isabella unfurled, he was rowed ashore at a point known to-day as Riding Rocks, to meet the bewildered "Indians," and take possession of the island in the name of the sovereigns of Spain.

In the wake of the caravels, my own *Santa Maria* sped past the north point of San Salvador, turned south and followed down the western coast along the threatening coral reef to Riding Rocks. As we circled and descended, preparing to land, the inhabitants in the near-by village, all negro, rushed out to stare at us. The natives Columbus found on the same spot were scarcely less awed at the sight of his three magical ships than the modern San Salvadorans at the sight of my seaplane.

We drifted within fifty feet of the beach, for the sea was perfectly calm. When in four feet of water I plunged overboard and waded ashore to greet the excited Indians.

Then my roaring sea bird bore me back again up toward the clouds. The island became a blotch of lake and land five thousand feet below. The western seas and isles and keys, Española, Jamaica, Cuba, stretched endlessly on to Mexico.

Across these waters, among these islands, the *Niña,* and the *Pinta,* and the *Santa Maria* sailed on, exploring, discovering, seeking, always seeking, the shores of Cathay.

Though ten more years and three more voyages were to be spent in quest of this elusive East, Columbus was destined never to behold it, destined to find only defeat, and poverty, and prison, and death, instead.

But he had planted a seed that was to yield a fabulous harvest; he had set fire to the imagination of his century. He did not find the land of his own desire, but he gave to the other restless, adventurous heroes of that epic age, new dreams for their fancies, new fields for their energies—new worlds to conquer.

CHAPTER I

THE CONQUEST OF MEXICO

Twenty-seven years after Columbus' discovery of America, Hernan Cortez and four hundred Spanish adventurers out on a plundering expedition found their way past Cuba into the Gulf and landed at its western end on the shores of a country as unfamiliar as the moon. Strange natives in overwhelming numbers opposed them, but with one of the most audacious gestures in history, Cortez, lured on by the rumors of Aztec treasure, burned his ships behind him, and defying all hell's devils to stop his rapacious quest for gold, plunged blindly and recklessly into the conquest of Mexico.

The record of this conquest is one of the world's immortal stories. With the assistance of a few horses and blunderbusses Cortez and his handful of followers annihilated the Aztec Empire—an empire more civilized in some respects than Europe itself.

His exploit stands as the greatest single achievement in the military annals of Spain.

Later, by four hundred years and more, on the shores at Vera Cruz where Cortez landed, a new invasion was about to take place, and a new march to Tenochtitlán (Mexico City), the ancient Aztec capital. The invader was not an all-conquering Spanish knight this time, but only a harmless American—myself—who had been spellbound by reading Prescott's *Conquest of Mexico* and had gone from San Salvador to Vera Cruz in order to follow the heroic captain's trail. I wanted to recreate in imagination his exploits on the spots where they came to pass. Three hundred miles of wild and difficult country lay before me—hot sun, heavy rains, deserts, mountains—and so, lest my courage fail and my interest flag, lest the hardships and unknown dangers of the way break down my resolution, in imitation of Cortez I burned my ships behind me.

True, they were not literally ships, but I pretended they were. I gathered bits of driftwood from the sand, and set a match to them. They were the "ships"—ships that meant subjection to the old familiar life of safety and monotony. Through the spiral of smoke I could look out upon the sea where, beyond the northern horizon, lay the United States, put away in favor of new worlds. Behind me loomed the mountains of Mexico, with snowy Orizaba, a white far-off cloud in the sky, brooding over the deeds it had seen in this land of blood, and beckoning me, as it beckoned Cortez, toward the fascinations of a land unknown.

In further imitation of Cortez, I was going in quest of gold—but it was the gold I'd thrown away, like most young men, when I was twenty-one. If I were to regain it, if once more I were to feel an enthusiasm for a romantic enterprise and find excitement in following Cortez's phantom banner, I must be able to dream again, to tell myself stories, and turn back clearly in my mind's eye to that glorious century when almighty Spain ruled the world.

Away went every bond that might hamper this spirit and make my search for gold on the trail of the conquest tedious and practical. I would rid myself of every possible burden. One can't do much dreaming when there's a baggage train to look after. I'd exchange my folding bath-tub for a pistol and cartridges. I would wear a flannel shirt and stout breeches. I would try to lead the simple life, to be a vagabond again, to follow Cortez, with a staff for my sword, a sombrero for my helmet, a burro for my prancing steed, and my own father, the best of companions, for the conquering army.

Photograph by Brehme, Mexico City

Popocatepetl and the Sleeping Woman from the top of the Aztec pyramid at Cholula. In the shadow of these glorious mountains, on this high and holy altar, for a thousand years the inhabitants of Mexico, Christian and pagan, Aztec and Spaniard, have worshiped the power that composed such a universe.

Photograph by Brehme

From Cholula, Cortez's route led westward across the pass between the giant volcanoes which stand guard over Mexico City.

Thus light-laden and light-hearted I struck the path of the Conqueror, and tramped away from our sunken ships toward the marvels of Mexico.

It had been with some difficulty that I had persuaded the *père* to join my expedition. He insisted he didn't enjoy hardships, that Mexicans were all bandits, that *tortillas* and *frijoles* gave him indigestion, that I would expect him to climb a lot of silly mountains, that he would look ridiculous riding on a burro, and that Cortez was a pirate and blackguard anyway who shouldn't be encouraged.

But I persevered and at last got him to Vera Cruz. There I outfitted him like a true conqueror. He had the biggest sombrero in Mexico, with bull-fight scenes painted on the brim, and a short leather jacket with huge silver buttons. I tried to array him in spurs, mandolin and a Mexican sash, but he absolutely rebelled and *would* wear commonplace corduroys unromantically held up by suspenders.

Our first disagreement arose over baptizing our burro. I felt the only proper Christian name for her was "Virgie," and would listen to nothing else. The *père* would have none of it. So throughout the miles we were accompanied by the animal, I called her Virgie, and he called her various names —all uncomplimentary.

The first day of our expedition we plodded up the barren, uninhabited coast nearly twenty-five miles to the point where the Spaniards turned inland, cursing the same sand and scorched by the same sun as they, ignoring all modern roads and following only the route, no matter how rough, indicated by an authentic conquest map.

From this point Cortez seemed to choose the way of most resistance. He led us straight up the slopes of a high mountain range that parallels the coast. The day we reached the pass we had to fight our way through endless obstacles—deluges of rain, almost impassable trails, flooded streams, hours in wet clothes, no shelter, no food, no rest. The bullfight scenes all melted from my father's sombrero and the sunshine from his countenance. It is no discredit to his good sportsmanship if I admit that I overheard him once or twice muttering wingèd words at Cortez (who, if we are to believe his chroniclers, had an even worse time of it in this wilderness than we did). Poor Cortez! Poor Papa! But there was no retreating. The hulks of the sunken ships lay rotting on the beach at Vera Cruz.

Reaching, after incredible hardships, the city of Tlaxcala, two hundred miles from the coast, Cortez came face to face with a most gruesome native custom—that of human sacrifice.

In ancient Mexico the gods of the Aztecs were bloody gods indeed, for they were moved by nothing but the gift of human hearts. In each city of the land, on top a towering moundlike temple called a *teocalli,* before the blood-splashed images, living victims by the thousand were stretched, their breasts carved open by the priests, and their hearts, still beating, torn out to be cast with supplications at the feet of the insatiable deity. Having witnessed this fearful butchery, Cortez seized upon the suppression of it as a moral argument to justify henceforth his rapacious conquest.

With a new crusading ardor added to his old passion for gold, the commander now moved on toward the Aztec capital.

The route lay via the city of Cholula, twenty-five miles to the south, and then westward again over the great pass between the giant volcanoes of Ixtaccihuatl (Is″-tak-si-wa′tl) and Popocatepetl (Po-po″ca-te′pet-l), which stand guard above Mexico City. This route was especially chosen by Cortez because Cholula was the Sacred City, the Mecca, the Jerusalem, of the empire. Here, by the hundred thousand, pilgrims came to worship and take part in the ceremonies.

In this city, in honor of the supreme Aztec god, a stupendous *teocalli,* the largest monument ever built in the Americas, had been reared. On top of its flat, truncated summit, over an acre in extent, the holiest temple of the Aztecs stood, enshrining the image of the deity. And before this temple six thousand human hearts were offered up each year—sixteen every day—so that the butchery was never-ending.

As Cortez and his little army approached this holy place he saw the Great Pyramid looming far above the city's other towers. He marveled at its huge pile, fourteen hundred feet along each side—almost twice the base dimensions of Cheops Pyramid—and a hundred and eighty feet high.

It was Sunday when the *père* and I left modern Tlaxcala behind and pushed on south with Virgie in Cortez's footsteps. Cholula drew in sight, and the same old mountainous *teocalli.* From the plateau on its summit the Aztec temple itself has long since departed. In its place we saw a white cathedral, white and shining, lift up its Catholic towers against the clouds.

Six o'clock was striking as we climbed the last of the broad stone steps that wind in gentle sweeping curves up to the table-top of the vast and grass-grown monument—and turned to look back toward the west. Surely, nowhere else in the world, not even at Delphi itself, is there a scene so likely to fill one with religious awe and reverence for the gods as this scene. The most hardened Philistine must be moved by the majesty of Popocatepetl and Ixtaccihuatl before him, and Orizaba behind, unearthly, immaculate poems of grace and snow and clouds and violet mystery—Popo, the smoking, the terrible volcano; Ixtaccihuatl, the white-draped, sleeping woman; Orizaba, the highest and loveliest thing from Mount McKinley to the Andes. Higher than the highest Alps these mountains are. Half a mile and more Popo soars above Mont Blanc, and Popo's pale-veiled sister sleeps two thousand feet above the Matterhorn, while the peak of Orizaba, 18,225 feet high, would grace the very Himalayas with its miraculous, infinite beauty. And in the purple shadow of these intimates of God, on this high and holy altar, for a thousand years the inhabitants of Mexico, Christian and pagan, Aztec and Spaniard, have worshiped the power that composed such a universe.

On this particular afternoon the church on top the pyramid was open, and packed to suffocation with pilgrims who had come to say their prayers. It was the date of some special fiesta, and the bells and candles and gingerbread gewgaws strewn over the poor sanctuary irritated one with their obtrusive tawdriness.

But it took small imagination as the sun sank toward Popocatepetl's rim, leaving all the sky and the clouds in one crimson glow, to forget the garish church behind me and remember only the ancient shrine. I needed merely to half-close my eyes to see the sacrificial ceremony at my side—not the casual before-breakfast butchery of a few slaves, but one of the sacred festivals in honor of the creator, in which a carefully selected young citizen was offered to the deity.

In my mind's eye I could see the procession approaching. For a year before this tragic day the favored victim had been a religious hero, arrayed in splendid dress, attended like a prince, and honored by all the nation as a divine representative.

Now the term of his glory was ended; the fatal hour of sunset was at hand.

Slowly, miserably, the chosen of the gods climbs the long stone stairs, surrounded by the chanting priests, and followed by ten thousand worshipers.

The summit where I stand is reached. The sacrificial stone beside the image of the god is ready. There is no time to lose. The sun is all but touching Popocatepetl's snows.

I see the victim seized, his jewels and royal garments stripped away, his body stretched, chest up, on top the jasper block.

Five priests in scarlet robes press down his limbs and head. A sixth is poised, knife in hand, above the waiting breast. Ten thousand people hold their breath.

Popo, in homage to the Aztec gods, is pouring forth a shaft of smoke into the highest heavens. The sun has dipped into the crater crest—a half remains—a rim—a final signal gleam.

The knife descends; there is a scream. The executioner stabs open the writhing breast, inserts his hand into the wound and tears out the still-palpitating heart. He holds up the gory offering to the blood-red sky, and then casts it at the feet of the inexorable deity, while all about, the multitudes lie prostrate in humble adoration. . . .

Clang! Bang! Clang! The hideous iron bells in the tower of the church, with sudden devilish clamor, dashed aside the fearful dream, and jerked me back to the age of plaster saints.

CHAPTER II

POPO AND PAPA

Of all the books I own, there is one book which is my particular prize possession. It is not the threadbare copy of *Don Quixote* that I carried in a knapsack all over Spain, nor the *Odyssey* that was my companion for a year in Greece. These old friends rest proudly on the shelf of honor, but even they bow down before this one incomparable book of my heart—my begrimed, passionately beloved *geography* book I studied in school at the age of ten.

What a glorious book! What maps! What pictures! It was the magic carpet of my boyhood on which I floated away from the boredom of my school desk to the far-off fairylands. Its author understood the dramatic appeal of the sea. His frontispiece was a picture of Columbus' sail-spread caravels. He understood the romance of great mountains, and gave extravagant space to full-page pictures of the Matterhorn and Etna, to Vesuvius and to Fuji, and a dozen more. And one by one

I've climbed them all—the mountains I met on the pages of that book, when I was ten years old.

It was here, facing the chapter on Mexico, that I first saw a picture of snow-clad Popo soaring royally into the clouds, and read the lilting, rolling name of this far-famed volcano. And it was then that I first resolved some day to climb it.

Years passed, but not my inclination toward Popo. The spectacular sunset behind the volcano's cone that my father and I had seen from Cholula's Pyramid, caused my admiration for the mountain to sweep over me anew. Popocatepetl—the very name was enchanting, a name that every schoolchild who ever studied a geography book in any land you please has caught and remembered to the end of his days.

Nor is the great mountain all name without a history. To be sure it has not the murderous record of the Matterhorn. Few, if any, climbers have perished on its slopes. Its eruptions, however frequent, have not overwhelmed the cities at its base as has Vesuvius. It is too high and too aloof to be climbed by crowds of pilgrims as is Fuji. It isn't the biggest as is Everest. And yet with the possible exception of Vesuvius it has witnessed more bloodshed, more romance, more tragedy, than any other mountain on earth.

All the vivid history of Mexico has revolved in Popo's shadow. To the Aztecs it was the supreme wonder and glory of their world. As Popo watched, Spain won and lost the largest empire in history up to that time. Kings and presidents in rapid succession have looked upon it from the capital near-by. And Popo, which alone has witnessed all this epic pageantry, alone will continue to watch over Mexico's fate, her one god that is not false, her one dictator that will keep faith, her one permanent thing of everlasting beauty which time will not destroy.

Whatever initial stand my father had taken before leaving America against "climbing a lot of silly mountains" with me in Mexico (he was referring very specifically to Popo which he knew I had definitely in mind), began to weaken even as we approached Vera Cruz by water and caught sight of Orizaba. Its pale unearthly beauty moved him profoundly. He'd forgotten how stimulating and challenging a snow-clad mountain was, and how biting clean the wind three miles above the sea. He'd forgotten the thrills of a dangerous ascent, the exultation of conquest over so vast a natural force, the feeling of spiritual liberation from the world as one attains the pinnacle, the feeling of being winged and free.

Later, when we had reached Cholula and stood on top of the Great Pyramid and saw the sun go down in a flaming sky behind Popocatepetl's snows, he clung to our observation post till the last light had faded, heedless of my own impatience. The picture of the beckoning silver cone so broke down whatever resistance he had left that if I had not quickly made plans for a Popo climb as an excursion from our pursuit of Cortez, he would have done so himself.

In Cholula we found a young Indian named Jesús (or Haysoos, as he called it) who had accompanied previous climbers all the way to the summit.

We commandeered him immediately, and once more picking up Cortez's trail, which now led over the high saddle that links Popo with Ixtaccihuatl, moved upon our mountain.

All one day along what is still only the thinnest and steepest of mule-trails we tramped up the eastern slopes—Jesús, the *père,* the *fils* and Virgie. Nine thousand, ten thousand, eleven thousand feet we climbed, shaded by huge and ancient pines that may have shaded Cortez's men when they passed this way. Popo always at our left, the White Woman always at our right, so close, so cold, we felt compressed between two glacial walls which like the Symplegades might crush us in their vast embrace unless we hurried past.

At the summit of the trail Cortez and his soldiers could see the Aztec capital, the city of gold, in the distance, and tumbled eagerly down the west slope of the saddle. But our invasion turned aside to find a camp higher up the mountain side.

All that afternoon the rain had poured upon us mercilessly. When we halted beneath a pine grove for the night both my father and I were stiff and shivering from five hours in cold wet clothes. But there was no sign of weakening from *him.* However much I may have cajoled him into coming to Mexico to join me, and with whatever secret reluctance he may have marched the two hundred and fifty miles up from Vera Cruz, *this* adventure was his very own. From the moment he surrendered to the call of the snow, all irresolution was cast aside. His will to conquer Popo grew into an eagerness I had not seen him reveal in many months. Little trifles like cold and dampness were not going to stop him now.

Soon after dark the rain relented and the night-sky became radiantly clear. We got a fire started and slept beside it until two hours before dawn. Then the *père* spurred us into action.

I reached for my equipment, and immediately

Popocatepetl, the *père,* the *fils,* and Virgie.

Ixtaccihuatl, the pale-veiled Sleeping Woman, two thousand feet higher than the Matterhorn.

found that while I had been sleeping, disaster had overtaken me. During the night the fire had crept out to my boots, which I had left to dry near the coals, and burned the feet off both of them. The parent, having helped me repair the boots with strings and sacks as best he could, decided I was far too careless to be the leader of this particular expedition in which so much satisfaction to his immortal soul was at stake, and that *he* was going to direct the grand assault. Did I have the camera loaded for photographs of the crater? Did Jesús have the flask and the flash-light? All aboard then —to the pinnacle—and no surrender. The rare and freezing morning wind sent a surge and a challenge through our blood. A million brilliant tropical stars flooded the icy slopes with luster. An old moon slipped down the mountain's silhouette. The Popocatepetl dream had come to pass.

Our trail, straight up the great blunt cone, was deep in lava ash which for countless centuries Popo has been pouring down its slopes. Climbing ankle-deep in this sandlike substance, our progress was painfully slow, especially for me with my sackcloth boots. Our hearts were pounding furiously, and our halts growing more frequent.

But the *père* asked no favors. His enthusiasm gave him wings. He led us to the thirteen thousand mark—past the summit of Fujiyama—on to fourteen thousand feet. Here the snow began in earnest, and the wind and the dawn. We dug into the ever-steepening slope, noticing at the same time how the sky was reddening behind the peak of Orizaba one hundred miles away, and how the Sleeping Woman, pale and snow-draped across the forested saddle, was beginning to awaken.

On up we crawled foot by foot, past the summit of Mount Ranier—the horizon was bursting into flame; past Pike's Peak—the lights of the capital had faded; past the Jungfrau—a huge red disk sprang from the earth-clinging mist; past the terrible Matterhorn—Popo's ice-armored pinnacle glittered with the shaft of sunrise; past fifteen thousand—past Mont Blanc—past sixteen thousand—my boots went to pieces and fell off!

There was no help to be had. I was left standing in my stocking feet in eighteen inches of snow three miles above the sea.

My father felt there was only one solution.

"You must take my boots," he shouted above the wind.

"Then how will *you* climb?"

"I'll go back!"

"I'll go back"—go back, when he was almost there; go back, when he was about to be perhaps the only man fifty-odd years old ever to reach the summit of this spectacular mountain, go back and abandon his suddenly rediscovered youth. I knew how much Popo meant to him. This was the one mountain he had most wanted to climb—and he was seated on the wind-whipped slope unlacing his boots to give them to his son who had carelessly gone to sleep at the crucial moment and let his own burn up.

I revolted with all the force I had against this gesture. But he had made up his mind that I was the one who must carry on, and with him there was no contending.

Feeling unspeakably selfish I laced on the paternal footgear. My father seized his climbing stick, bade me a brave good-by and left me. I watched him struggling down into the cloud-filled void below, with the sack rags flapping about his unshod feet, his body bent to the wind, his Popocatepetl tryst all failure and frustration. And he'd never come this way again. . . .

Stung by remorse over the situation I turned once more toward the slope and trudged on upward —Jesús right beside me.

We could take only three steps forward at a time now through the knee-deep snow, and then rest for as many minutes, breathing as if we'd raced a mile. As we reached seventeen thousand, with only eight hundred more to go, a blast of extra-savage wind, screeching down from above, came suddenly at us as if shot from some bow of Popo's guardian gods. We were both blown over by it, and my sombrero, worn as protection from sun-and-snow-burn, was torn, despite the buckled chin strap, right off my head. Without it I knew from hard experience on Fuji and the Matterhorn that my face and eyes would be completely cooked, for the sun was now high in the sky and beating upon the snow rampart with a dazzling glare. I *must* recover the runaway, or endure unrelieved exposure for another four hours.

Jesús and I plunged after it, but the sombrero seemed possessed of the devil. It would wait until we had dragged ourselves through the deep snow to within a foot of it, and then with demoniac perversity take flight for another dozen yards down the ice bank, prevented only by its lightness from slithering five thousand feet.

Ten times we staggered in pursuit. Ten times it flew away. In twenty minutes we had lost all the altitude gained in the entire previous hour.

Then the beastly hat repented and lay still. Jesús, reaching its final resting place, fell prostrate

Photograph by Brehme

All the vivid history of Mexico has revolved in Popo's shadow. And Popo will continue to watch over the nation's fate, her one god that is not false, her one dictator that will keep faith, her one permanent thing of everlasting beauty.

Photograph by Brehme

A black and ominous void appeared below me. I seemed to be at the edge of the universe looking into an infinite hell that smoked and swirled and reeked with the sulphur of burning souls.

on top of it, and didn't move for half an hour—nor did I, except to put it on.

Another hour was required to regain the point where the blast betrayed us. Climbing—recuperating—climbing—recuperating. My camera came to weigh two tons, each foot as many more.

Grimly we floundered on. This mountain *had* no summit. We were climbing to the moon up a ladder made of ice. The earth had floated far away. There was only wind and light and space, and a shimmering whiteness before my eyes, and a sweet drowsiness in which I felt my mechanical legs sinking into the snow and struggling out, and heard a violent knocking somewhere inside.

Then all at once the shimmering disappeared, and a black and ominous void drifted before me. I now seemed to be at the edge of the universe looking into an infinite hell that smoked and swirled and reeked with the sulphur of burning souls. I stood still before some mighty apparition. . . . Somebody was speaking. . . .

"El cráter, señor. Muy grande."

The crater! I was on top and staring into the crater! On top!

One clear look about me, and I forgot the conflict with the mountain. I stood on top of the earth—nearly eighteen thousand feet—heaven close above, hell close below. The wind raged about the crater crest, but its stimulation now offset its sting. The cold dug through me, but now I could stand it, warmed by the exhilaration of a battle won. My head throbbed, my legs trembled with exhaustion, but I forgot all that, now that the monstrous crater, smoking and sulphurous, evil and threatening, gaped a thousand feet below me. I was breathing a maddening wine of frozen fire that made me want to shout, to sing, to laugh, to fly across the chasm to the Sleeping Woman, to plunge headlong into the crater, to fall on my knees.

I must find Jesús and have him fall on his knees with me. I did find him, lying in a wind-protected crevice making a large meal of beans and *tortillas*.

To punish such a lack of reverence I put him to work holding down the camera tripod against the onslaught of the wind. Thus supplied with a steady base I aimed the machine at the snow-rimmed crater, determined to prove to my father waiting anxiously a mile below, that I had beheld his promised land.

But my haste to take the pictures and escape before the blasts annihilated me, was too desperate. I made three exposures of the crater—and each time forgot to turn the film. I aimed at Ixtaccihuatl's summit six miles away—without adjusting the focus; at the sea of clouds that had formed beneath us—and jambed the plunger. Then, just as I was about to start all over again with a new stock of film, I allowed this reserve supply to drop from my numbed fingers and roll over the crater precipice. I gave one howl of despair, snatched up the cursed camera, fled with Jesús from the pinnacle and flung myself down the iceberg's slopes all the way back to camp as though Popo's demons were in hot pursuit.

CHAPTER III

POPO'S SURRENDER

IN THE meanwhile we had by no means lost sight of Cortez.

Once I had rejoined the *père* and recuperated somewhat from my mountain climb, we returned to the trail and descending the western slopes once more tramped on in pursuit of the Conqueror.

With the goal of their long march at last beckoning in the distance, Cortez and his army hurried forward. They soon found that the capital was built on a fortified island in the middle of a lake (long since drained), and that the only approaches other than by boat were three magnificent stone causeways linking it with the shore.

Straight down one of these the little company, drawn on by the city's huge *teocalli,* tramped with fast-beating hearts.

Behind them, our own invasion followed. We tried not to see the trees, or the telephone poles, or the filling stations, which now line the still-existing causeway. We tried to see only blue water on each side—and Montezuma, the Aztec emperor, with his spectacular cortège approaching from the city.

Unhappy Montezuma! Daily, hourly, the couriers tell of the Spanish advance. He decides he may as well invite them into his capital since with invincible tread they are coming anyway.

Cortez is received. But he soon proves himself a most ill-mannered guest. He exasperates his Aztec hosts to the point of revolt by his ruthless seizure of their gold. And then he seizes Montezuma himself.

The city's patience bursts. In self-defense the Mexican warriors mobilize and fall by the thousand upon their now bitterly hated guests.

Cortez realizes he has overshot his mark. Escape, not conquest, now becomes his chief concern. And escape offers itself when with the coming of darkness a furious rainstorm disperses the swarms of Aztec assailants. He prepares to slip out at once with all the treasure he has seized, and try to reach the mainland.

Midnight arrives. It is still pouring rain. The barracks doors open softly in the inky darkness. Cortez, all his soldiers, two thousand Indian allies and the treasure train move through the gates with muffled tread.

Scarcely have they stirred when a shout from the native sentry raises the alarm. Straightway some priest rushes to the war drum and sounds the war cry through the rain.

In a moment thousands of howling Aztecs, faintly visible in the night, reassemble and charge upon the flanks of the Spaniards who in growing confusion are now streaming along the narrow pitch-dark street toward the causeway.

My father and I, following Cortez's campaigns around the City of Mexico, go hurrying after them.

There is but one authentic spot from which to observe the flight. This is beneath El Arbol de la Noche Triste—the gigantic cypress tree, the only living witness of the celebrated retreat, which stands to-day, guarded as one of the most sacred monuments in the nation, at a point where the western causeway joined the mainland.

Reaching this tree we can picture the wild confusion. The causeway is intersected by a thirty-foot canal. The Spaniards are not prepared to bridge this gap, and suddenly, coming to it, find themselves hemmed in by deep water on three sides.

Seeing their enemies thus trapped, the Aztecs charge down the causeway with triumphant fury. In the black night and the rain the entire company becomes one horrible, stampeding mass of disorder.

The retreating rear drives the forward ranks over the edge into the canal, or over the sides into the canoes of howling warriors who drag the unfortunate Spaniards aboard, and off to the hideous sacrifice. . . .

In this hysterical struggle for self-preservation, the "Conquerors" (how ironical the name seems now) push enough of their own men, Indian allies, prisoners, gold-laden porters, horses, wagons, cannon, into the breach to fill the gap entirely, and over this screaming, writhing, horrible mixture, the ruins of an army pass.

One half of Cortez's forces, by trampling the other half to death, reached our cypress tree alive. All the two thousand Indian allies, every single piece of baggage and artillery, all his horses, all the millions in treasure—perish.

This would have been the proper time for the usual military commander to quit and go home. Not Cortez! Without guns or ammunition, with the mutilated remains of his fugitive little army cursing the sight of him, with his whole conquest a hopeless, helpless wreck, Cortez made up his mind to face about and reconquer the City of Mexico.

Once more fortune favored the brave. No sooner had he announced his purpose to his flabbergasted soldiers than several hundred new recruits supplied with cannon arrived from Cuba.

Immediately Cortez re-besieges the capital, captures control of the lake with his own boats built in the nearest forest, and simultaneously seizes the heads of the three causeways.

Then along the raised stone roads the cannon begin to sweep. Foot by foot, day by day, the artillery is pushed nearer the city.

Seeing their prison walls move in, the Aztecs are fighting like demons, but they are helpless to free themselves from the ring of iron. Slowly they are being squeezed into a constantly decreasing space. And now, when there is no escape, and the great plaza has become their only island in a sea of ruin, Cortez gives the signal.

The steel constrictor closes. The Spaniards charge into the dense-packed square. Forty thousand starving Indians are put to the sword, and when that bloody day is over Tenochtitlán is no more.

I looked up from the pages of Prescott's heroic history which all afternoon I had been reading, seated on the balcony in the topmost tower of the Great Cathedral. The roar of the Spanish cannon has died away, and Tenochtitlán has faded. It is

Photograph by Brehme

The Great Cathedral at Mexico City, built on the site of the ancient *teocalli,* and overlooking the plaza where Cortez annihilated forty thousand Aztecs.

The crater of Popocatepetl, two miles in circumference and a thousand feet deep. In o
enveloped the mountain, accompanied by a photographer and a forty-pound panorama
blasts of wind. At dawn, with the temperature below zero, the photographer loaded the
The desired photograph was made, though

The picture of Popo published in my schoolboy geography book. It was this view that first introduced me to the volcano.

take this picture the author made a second ascent, at night, through a blizzard that had
Once on top, nearly eighteen thousand feet, a heavy tripod held its own against the
chine with a roll of film three feet long, aimed at the gigantic crater target, and fired.
cost of badly frost-bitten hands and faces.

With the possible exception of Vesuvius, Popo has witnessed more bloodshed, more romance, more tragedy, than any other mountain on earth.

Hernan Cortez. His conquest of Mexico stands as the greatest single achievement in the military annals of Spain.

the twentieth century again—and of the sixteenth nothing remains. Nothing remains but the venerable cypress tree de la Noche Triste—and the imperishable Popo, hanging at that moment, above the city's towers, clear and cold in the eastern clouds.

I gazed reminiscently at the beautiful, dreadful mountain—Popo—that had mocked me on its crater crest, addled my brains, blasted my photographic hopes and driven me, half-dead, from the summit. Oh, well, thought I, seeking consolation, was not Cortez himself driven half-dead from the Aztec capital with a loss of all *his* treasures?

But that failed to prove consoling, for I realized I'd just been reading of Cortez's magnificent come-back—while I sat there weakly accepting defeat at the hands of Popo's guardian blasts, and ready to run home to Tennessee without any photographs, without any gold. No, the spirit of my conquest of Mexico bore faint resemblance to Cortez's.

Very well then, damn it, I'd climb Popo again!

This sudden decision rather stunned me. However, there really was nothing else to do. My conscience would never be able to face Cortez's scorn henceforth if I allowed an arrogant Popo to deny me the photographs I sought of its pinnacle and to gloat over my expulsion.

PROPERTY 10435 OF
COLBY SCHOOL FOR GIRLS

And so I carried out my decision. I turned about for another battle with the triumphant enemy, reënforced not with fresh troops and new cannon, but with the best photographer in Mexico whose skill and energy gave me every reason to believe that *this* attack on my own particular Tenochtitlán would succeed.

This time I would have to fight without my chief ally. My father, under pressure of his affairs in the United States, had been called home.

And it was a fight far more savage than the first attack. Burdened with three hundred pounds of professional artillery, an assistant and four porters, we progressed so slowly up the mountain that in the late afternoon I decided to keep right on with my expedition and climb all night. Then we would be sure of having the machinery on top by morning.

At fifteen thousand feet our assistant, something of a novice at mountaineering, gave one groan and collapsed in the snow. He was done for. In the midnight darkness we distributed his forty-pound share of equipment and pushed on.

Scarcely had we left him behind when a new difficulty enveloped us—mist, so dense and so laden with frost that it covered whatever it touched with icy flakes. In ten minutes every one of us was a snow man, clothed in ghostly white, climbing like a driven spirit up the ghostly mountain. Our staffs became great icicles six feet long. Little icicles hung from our chins and noses. The wind was lashing this arctic fog past us at fifty miles an hour and we still had two thousand feet to go.

In the teeth of such obstacles, of which the impenetrable night was not the least, all six of us lost heart. But I had reached a state of stubborn unreasonableness brought on by angry resentment against fortune, and plowed deeper and deeper into difficulties. I remembered Cortez's determination to persist despite everything, during his second assault of Tenochtitlán, and vowed that by the unholy ghost of the Conqueror I was going to the top.

The porters, clad only in cotton clothes, were by no means so resolute. Seeing how they were suffering under their covering of ice I had to send them back. And further distribution of equipment was impossible. We must abandon everything they carried—the movie outfit, the Graflex and my own camera. The photographer, however, did not desert me. Truly faithful he continued to struggle on with the panoramic machine, I following with the thirty-pound tripod.

When the two of us *did* reach the top, we found

our worst fears realized. The fog was overwhelming. Even so, I was unwilling to give up hope. Perhaps if we waited with prayer and fasting, the rising sun might scatter these evil forces of mist.

One hour, two hours, as the first streaks of day drifted through the fog, we clung on. Presently the sun broke above the horizon, and almost at once, to our unspeakable joy, the mist began to lift. Thick as it was, it could not resist the onslaughts of the Mexican sun.

Popo's guardian gods had at last relented. The very elements (except the incorrigible wind) now appeared in perfect photographic arrangement—black sky, fresh deep snow piled on the rim and clinging to every ledge on the walls of the clean-swept crater, all flooded in dazzling brightness.

There was no blundering this time when we put our panoramic camera in place, no failure to focus, no double exposure. The heavy tripod held its own against the blasts. The photographer loaded the big machine with a roll three feet long and ten inches high, aimed at the gigantic crater-target, and fired.

And the picture that resulted? Glory to the Gods! Peace be unto Cortez! It was perfect!

Several copies of the three-foot Popo photograph were made for me. One of them I later pasted in my old geography book, right opposite the picture of the Popo I had "climbed" in my boyhood, to remind me in later years when I had grown old and become a cynic, that once upon a time in the far-off days of my youth I had told myself a story, and behold—it had come true!

CHAPTER IV

THE WELL OF DEATH

SLOWLY into the deep black pool, the shadows of the moonlight crept. Upon the water's surface far below stirred the spirits of the Rain God's brides and his phantom warriors, released on magic nights like this from their prison of wave and shell. Across this awesome pit the night wind brought the wild perfume of the forest flowers, the chanting of the hidden cicadas, and a ballet of the fireflies to dance before these lonely spirits of the dead. This was the enchanted hour. This was the sacred place. This was the Well of Death.

To see it I had journeyed from Tenochtitlán a thousand miles by land and sea into the heart of Yucatan.

It was a journey well rewarded, though to those who do not know the history of the Well and are not favored with an inner eye, the reward is but a deep-sunken pool of water in the forest. But when one reads the record of this pool, and looks on moonlight nights into its somber depths, one realizes that here has been drama, terrible in its intensity; that here lingers inexhaustible romance.

Long ago—more than five hundred years—a race of people called the Mayas, the most cultivated race, by far, of all the aboriginal Americans, inhabited the peninsula of Yucatan. Why they chose this country for their abode is one of the real archeological mysteries, for it was, and still is, a wilderness, flat, parched, sterile. Though it rains frequently enough, there is no water. The peninsula has over fifty thousand square miles, but not a single river, not even a small stream, for the entire surface of the land is composed of porous limestone through which the rain filters soon after it strikes the earth.

How then have people lived there? Through the kindness of nature in allowing the limestone surface sometimes to cave in and leave deep pools, locally called *cenotes* (che-nó-tays), varying in size from twenty to two hundred feet in diameter with a drop of seventy feet or more to the water level.

When the first Maya tribes migrated into the country, they came upon a place blessed with two *cenotes* scarcely a mile apart. A settlement was made there and because of the great water supply inevitably thrived, receiving the name of *Chi* (mouth) *-chen* (wells) *-Itza* (the tribal name), or the City of the Itzas at the Mouth of the Wells.*

The two *cenotes* soon took on an individuality each of its own. The smaller one had sides sufficiently gentle of slope to permit stone steps to descend, and thus it became the water supply for all domestic and agricultural purposes. The other, larger one, defied all attempts at access. Almost two hundred feet across, its walls are sheer, even undercut, permitting only the most tenacious and acrobatic vegetation to cling to them. The water at the bottom is a dull, dead green that lies silent and secretive, seventy feet below the brink. The very aspect of the pool is so gloomy and so mysterious that the dullest imagination could easily picture fearsome monsters and supernatural beings inhabiting it.

It was in the murky depths of this pool that the Mayas placed the abode of Yum-Chac, their god of rain. To him it was necessary from time to time, lest the country lose his vital favors, to offer virgin brides and attendant warriors by hurling them to their death into the pit.

The ancient Itzas were of great faith. This gruesome rite attracted thousands of pilgrims

* Pronounced *Chee-chen-Eetza.*

from all the Maya World. The moment the poor little maiden or the unhappy escort was flung from the brink, these pilgrims likewise threw down, as offerings to the Rain God, all manner of treasures. So national was the character of this ceremony, and so profoundly did it affect the aboriginal mind, that this city became the religious center of the empire, the Cholula of the Maya World, with the Well of Sacrifice the most sacred place of all.

The sanctity and ceremony connected with the great *cenote* are not mere legend. Nearly a hundred skeletons of delicate young girls and sturdy young men have been dredged from the sediment at the bottom, another seventy feet under water, and a veritable museum of all the Maya treasures, dropped into the Well by the pious, has been recovered.

This, then, was the "pool in the forest" I had come so far to see.

Nothing could have been more dull and uneventful than my journey from Merida, the capital of modern Yucatan, to the ruins. After three dusty hours across unbroken flatness I began to doubt that such a colorless country could produce anything beautiful, and to wonder why I'd paid any attention to the extravagant tales I'd heard and read about these Mayas and their Sacred Well.

But even at the station, fifteen miles from Chichen, where one leaves the rails to travel by motor-bus, the scene changed dramatically. With sunset a full tropical moon had risen from the arms of the bush-jungle, and spread over the monotonous landscape a romantic radiance. Through this sea of summer moonlight the white road flowed, fringed with the clutching forest, a forest hypnotized into deathlike stillness by the eerie glow. There was scarcely a house or a person to be seen. Then, unexpectedly, we turned a sharp corner—and I almost fell out of my seat staring at the great pyramid that suddenly rose up, gleaming, straight ahead. Over a hundred feet high, two hundred feet square, faced with smooth stone terraces, approached by sweeping steps that climb up to the shrine upon the summit, this spectacular temple, softened, whitened, chastened by the moon, told me I had come to Chichen-Itza.

And before I'd recovered from the daze of seeing *this* spring forth from the shadowy wilderness, the motor catapulted me, quite alone, into an ancient plaza that was all but surrounded by temples and monuments scarcely less startling and less beautiful than the pyramid. All were radiantly white, all tremendous in size, all rich with carving, all, considering the fact that they have been the prey of the voracious jungle for five hundred years, unbelievably intact.

Straightway I abandoned the bus which fled from this ghostly place back to "civilization." There was no shelter other than the stones in sight, but I was too enchanted by the magic change from the stark, mud-housed Yucatan of the present to this gorgeous carved-stone city of the past, to think about to-morrow.

Shedding my duffel-bag, I scrambled up the ninety ladderlike steps, reached the top and looked back down the slope out over the shimmering jungle. On one side was a majestic palace, likewise raised aloft on top a terraced base. The Temple of a Thousand Columns had removed its roof to reveal painted pillars to the moon. And from out the black forest, in every direction, a score more of carved stone monuments rose white and phantom-like against the stars.

And there, leading from the bottom of the serpent-balustraded steps that swept dramatically down the north side of the pyramid, stretched the Sacred Road, the great stone causeway that ran a quarter-mile through the aisle of trees to the very brink of the Sacred Well.

In silence I stared out over this vast graveyard. The moon lighted the temple-dotted jungle for miles on every side across this utterly flat land of Mayab. Not the smallest hill broke the horizon that lay in a perfect circle around the axis of my pyramid. There was not a light, nor a hut, not the bark of a dog. The tropical heat lay heavy on the earth. Even the wind kept still lest its whisper break the phantasy of the moment and remind me that the spectral temples were of stone, not clouds, the jungles of wood, not dreams, and that I was real and awake, and not one more shade drifting among the Maya ghosts that walked forth from their tombs on this extra-mundane night.

What strong and vivid lives these ghosts once lived! What brilliant records of their existence they have left behind! The manifestations of their handiwork which still exist must make them the proudest of all the ghosts among the ancient races that dwelt in the Western Hemisphere. They were the Greeks of early America. They were possessed with an intellectual and creative fire that burned hot and deep and long. With chisel and hammer, masonry and mortar, they built in stone, carved in stone and wrote in stone, with such rare and enduring skill that, after five hundred years of jungle burial, the ruins of their civilization are emerging to claim their place among the wonders of the world.

Where did these extraordinary people originally come from? Nobody knows. What happened to them that they should desert their noble cities and swiftly, silently, disappear? Nobody knows that either. The mystery of their disappearance is scarcely less astonishing than the record of their existence.

It was almost midnight by now. I had dreamed on top the pyramid long enough, for there were other things to be seen. Close at hand the great stone door to the summit-temple revealed a black cavern within. I crossed the threshold past the carved demons that stand guard, and found myself in a faintly visible windowless room of solid stone. The bats disturbed at such an unusual hour squeaked indignantly about my head, remonstrating against my invasion of a habitation that had been their private property for five centuries.

Looking back through the moonlit entrance I could still see the Sacred Way framed by the dark door-facing. From this very room where I stood, as the hour of dawn broke over the land, the sacrificial procession of the ancient Itzas moved toward the grim *cenote*. Here the heaven-blessed maiden was brought, the loveliest of all the maids of Mayab, robed in riches, garlanded in flowers, to be sacrificed to the Rain God lest he parch the fields with drought. Here the bravest of the nation's youths was waiting to escort the little victim on her tragic journey and attend the Rain King in his court. And here, too, the priests, resplendent in their ceremonial attire, their turquoise masks, their feathered diadems, filled the room with incense, chanted their sacred ritual and blared their conch-shell trumpets, announcing to the waiting thousands pressed about the Sacred Well that the great hour had come—that Yum-Chac was about to receive his bride.

From this room, down the sweeping stairs, on to the raised stone road, the Pontiff of the Feathered Serpent leads the glittering throng. The king and his noblemen splash the causeway with their robes of gold. The great warriors, the throngs of chanting priests, the acolytes with their incense, the temple maidens with their fragrant flowers, follow slowly toward the yawning Well. The music, singing forth the glory of the gods, joins the vast procession—the caracoles and the flutes, the muffled rumbling drums. Then last of all, followed by the doomed attendant, the catafalque of gold and jewels moves on the shoulders of the *nacon* bearers with slow and measured tread. And inside this royal litter, curtained from the multitudes that line the way, the pitiful little bride, dressed in her wedding gown, rides forward to her destiny.

In the semi-darkness I follow the procession down the steps, across the spacious plaza, along the Sacred Way. Feathered serpents, battered and time-worn, thrust their stone heads through the walls of bush and vine to look with stony eyes at the midnight visitor. Spangles of the moonlight, dancing through the arch of trees, brighten my path along the storied road—silver—shadow—silver—shadow—straight to the dark waters of the pit.

The quarter mile of corridor has stopped abruptly. The jungle falls away to either side. An altar of stone, the Altar of the Last Rites, now blocks the path. Beyond that, and below, a dark, still, fearful chasm. . . .

I climbed on to the ruined platform and peered over the brink. Down, down, full seventy feet the breakneck walls fell sheer, and at the bottom, a dead sheet of metallic water, two hundred feet across, lay motionless.

At this altar, as the sun breaks over the treetops, the sacrificial procession halts. From this altar, the High Priest, amid a solemn stillness, raises his arms over the sacred waters, and prays to the unseen deity waiting in his palace of rock and wave to accept the sacrifices. One hundred thousand worshipers, awed with the drama of the moment, stand in deep ranks, silent, at the rim. The catafalque is carried forward, the maiden lifted from her couch to the altar's edge. The escort in his gleaming armor is waiting at the brink. Once more the chant begins—the drums are pulsing—back and forth the *nacons* swing the tortured girl—the rhythm quickens, the arc grows wider—louder the chant, faster the drums, louder, faster—one swelling roar—the little bride is hurled far out into the dark abyss; and like a streak of fire, sword aloft, the Maya warrior plunges after her. . . .

Falling, turning, the maid and the man lurch forward, the white wedding garments and the helmet's scarlet feathers fluttering for a moment side by side, until their bodies strike the leaden waters seventy feet below with a dull and far-off boom that echoes from wall to wall across the hungry pool. The ripples spend themselves against the rocks . . . a moment of hushed watchfulness . . . the sacrifices do not reappear . . . they have been received into the palace of their Lord . . . the bride is safe in the Rain God's arms.

But that was five hundred years ago. Now at this midnight hour all is still and desolate. The priests, the pomp, the pulsing drums have gone. The altar is in ruins, a little garden of grass and stones. The multitudes who rained their offerings of jade and gold into the Well as the victim sank, have melted, and ramparts of greenery displaced them at the brink. The music, too, has vanished, though the natives say that on moonlight nights like this they hear it even now, strange and wild, and far away. Of all this ancient spectacle only the Well remains, still awesome, still evil, still inscrutable. The pitiful bones of Yum-Chac's brides and of their brave young guards have been dredged from the gloomy depths. But their ghosts linger on, drifting through their watery tomb, weary of the Rain God's court, hungry for the sunshine and the sky.

Midnight had come and gone long since. The moon had climbed to the zenith of the heavens and hung straight above the center of the deep-sunken mirror.

For half an hour in the thick, hot darkness, I had sat upon the altar's steps, the only living human being in this vast field of death, held by the melancholy beauty of the night and utterly surrendered to the bewitchment of the Well.

All about me, white and cadaverous, the stones of tumbled temples, buried beneath their pall of silence, stared through the clutching jungle at the stars.

Close at hand the jaguars prowled among the palaces seeking their own images on the painted walls.

A great bat lurched across the moon—or was it a feathered serpent, Kukulcan himself, flying back from exile to haunt his ancient sanctuary?

Somewhere a lizard stirred the leaves. . . . Furtively I looked about me, realizing that in the darkness the boa-constrictors would be abroad creeping forth from the ancient tombs and slinking down the leafy avenues.

The wind had begun to blow gently through the trees, and when they gently sighed I was not sure but that I heard the misty music, the muted conch, the ghostly caracoles, and the chanting, thin and far away, of the Rain God's phantom worshipers.

To escape these perils and these mysteries I crawled to the far side of the altar—to the very edge. There was a faint splash deep down in the pool—perhaps some scaly monster stirring in his sleep, or a water-spirit ascending from Yum-Chac's halls. I peered with straining eyes into the chasm. But it had grown quiet again. A stone from the débris near-by, tossed over the rim, sent back a hollow startled sound as it struck the surface far below. And when the ripples caught the glitter of the moon, they spread in silver circles across the ebon shield. I found it hard to look away, so insidious was the lure of these grisly waters. They half-repelled, half-fascinated. There was death and cruelty in their sunken gaze. But there was haunting beauty, too. They whispered to one to come to them, though it might be destruction, to enter their cool paradise, though they promised no returning, to rest untroubled in their arms, though their embrace might be the last.

I stood up to resist a morbid urge to leap into the gruesome pit. But the siren waters only beckoned the more invitingly. *"Come—in our sea-green corridors the Rain God lives—the Maya warriors guard him—the Maya brides will greet you at the gate, and sing for you, and there will be an end to pain and wandering—an end——"*

Already I heard their chanting, soft and low, and leaned, leaned forward toward the source. Yet even as I yielded, some instinct, elemental and primeval, deep down in the subconsciousness, fought against the power of the sirens, against the fascination of the Well of Death. *"No—no—not now,"* the instinct warned; *"sunken logs—hidden rocks—dark slimy fingers to drag you away——"*

"—Away to the caves of the Rain God's court," sang the waters, *"and a coral world——"*

"—And in the darkness you'll never climb the sheer rock walls back to this earth——"

"—You'll never, never desire to climb when you see the deeps where the Rain God lives," chanted the far-off choir.

In the struggle between these two voices, the voice of Reason slowly began to dominate, until I became willing, for the moment, to obey the instinct and not the impulse. Faint and cold I drew back from the brink and crawled, with pounding pulse, to the protection of the trees. A parrot in the branches just above, startled by my moving figure, shattered the silence with a sudden piercing shriek. My hair stood on end . . . there were strange cries and cackles all through the woods . . . long clawing hands reached forth from the darkness . . . the shadows moved and whispered . . . in them I saw misshapen monsters creeping closer, and grinning, ghoulish specters watching from across the pit . . . I would flee from this haunted spot before the jungle spirits stole forth to murder me.

But when I rose to escape down the Sacred Way, the *tunkul* drums came soft again, again the conch-shell's clear, far music. They held me to the spot, held me to the moonlit Well, unable to force myself away, yet not daring to surrender to those

A great pyramid suddenly rose up, gleaming, straight ahead. Over a hundred feet high, two hundred feet square, faced with smooth stone terraces, approached by sweeping steps that climb up to the shrine on the summit, this spectacular temple told me I had come to Chichen-Itza.

I took one deep breath, hung for an instant on the brink, and then plunged, seventy feet, into the Well of Death.

A movie camera records the second plunge, and the ascent. The angel-pantomime which brought such disastrous results is photographed in the first two pictures.

dark and deadly waters. . . . If it were only morning, so I could see the rocks, the floating logs. . . . Perhaps when morning came . . .

The morning was not very far away. The faintest wisp of gray was already showing in the east. A bird chirped very softly, then another, and another. Soon all the jungle was astir. In the tropics, the dawn, like the night, comes swift. It spreads over the treetops; it rushes up the sky, pursued by the relentless sun. A flaming blue and red macaw streaked across the pit, and I knew that it was day.

This was the very hour when the sacrificial processions moved from the temple, the hour when the Rain God's bride, escorted by the chosen warrior, approached the Well. I could picture the girl, pale with terror, yet believing with childlike faith that Yum-Chac would rescue her and honor her for ever. I could picture the Maya warrior marching forward unafraid, but with none of the girl's illusions as to their fate, with no prayer other than that his death beside the bride might be bravely faced and quickly over. He knew that the water would be bitter dark, that his armor would drag him down, but there must be no sign of his lack of faith in Yum-Chac's benevolence. Head up, plumes flying. The little bride must not know that it was a broken body and slow strangulation ahead of her, and not everlasting bliss. The multitudes must not doubt that he was proud to follow the maiden into the Rain God's court. He must leap exultantly to Death, must dive at the High Priest's august command into Eternity.

His resignation to their fate became my own. I crept back to the altar and looked down into the daylit depths. I could see, now, that there *were* no protruding ledges, no floating logs near-by. Reason, that had conquered temptation in the darkness, thus lost its best arguments . . . and the sun was about to burst above the wall of trees. It was the moment when the high priest stood in prayer over the waters, with the *nacons* and the maiden and the doomed escort in his flaming armor waiting for the signal gleam beside him—beside me—here at the altar's brink. . . .

Nearer and nearer the edge . . . yearning to draw still nearer the great green serpent's eye. I must go to the Rain God's realm waiting far below. . . . In my imagination I see the *nacons* lift up the bride . . . the warrior, resolute, is poised . . . and I know that when he leaps into the void that I'll leap too. The music swells . . . the signal sun has spoken . . . the girl is flung far out into the pit . . . the warrior is leaping after her. . . .

I took one deep breath, hung for an instant on the brink, and then plunged, headlong, into the abyss.

CHAPTER V

HIGH-DIVING

For several seconds that seemed an eternity I felt myself hurtling downward, conscious only of the upward rush of wind—and then there came a fearful shock and roar as if the biggest cannon in the world had exploded at my feet. Icy blackness engulfed me; icy demons dragged me down, down into bottomless seas.

I began to strangle. Instantly the instinct of self-preservation that had been overpowered by temptation at the altar's edge surged into action with a total disregard for Sacred Wells, dead Maya warriors and beckoning virgin brides. I felt my limbs struggling against the water spirits' clutches. I shook the demons loose, lunged upward through the fathoms and pushed my gasping, bursting face at last into the air.

Immediately I struck out for the nearest wall of rock, fifty feet away. It offered not the slightest refuge. Somewhere, somewhere, there must be a ledge, a vine, a crevice. Anxiously I swam beneath the overhanging cliff until I spotted a clump of dark shrubbery growing at the water's edge. The bush had found a tiny beach, and on to it I dragged myself.

For several seconds I sat there, dazed and faint and shivering, but with my senses full alive. This was no fantastic dream from which presently I might awaken. It was painfully real. My head throbbed. The clammy water of the Well streamed from my clothes—*clothes!*—for I was almost fully dressed—light sweater, shirt, linen trousers, socks, boots! Only my coat and sombrero had been left with the duffel-bag back at the Temple of Kukulcan.

The boots, though of the moccasin variety, were thick-soled and came half-way to the knee. And now, logged with water, they seemed to be made of lead. My wallet, carried in a hip pocket, was a total ruin, Mexican paper currency, cards, stamps, notes, all limp from their sudden baptism. A package of cigarettes floated around in another pocket. They'd never be the same again. I felt for my tin watch. It was there! And on extracting the poor drowned thing with dripping fingers, I found, contrary to the usual testimonial in regard to cheap watches in such circumstances, that it was *not* running, but had stopped when its owner took to high-diving—at six-thirty to the dot.

The next move of importance was to get out of the pit before I shivered myself to pieces. Any cry for help would be useless. The natives were all known to be superstitious anyway regarding the infamous *cenote,* and I could well imagine that if one *had* been in hailing distance and heard a cry at this impossible hour coming from the bottom of the Well of Death, he would promptly betake himself with all possible speed in the opposite direction.

Had the circumstances been otherwise, I might have enjoyed the prospect from my ledge. Familiarity with the Well did not by any means blunt astonishment. It was as mysterious and sinister seen from below as from above. The water had recovered from its violent agitation and returned to a normal deathly calm, gazing up at the sky, through the great cylinder of rock that encompassed it, with its usual leaden stare. Near-by the frogs croaked mightily, and the interminable cicadas chanted away in these gloomy depths as lustily as their cousins in the jungle overhead.

But these observations were not getting me back to earth. And so I took to examining the walls and noted that right above me there seemed to be a band of greenery reaching entirely to the top. Removing my soggy boots I began, in stocking feet, to wiggle up through the accommodating bush, consoled with the indisputable fact that if I tumbled back into the water from half-way up I could get no wetter than I was already, or receive any shock to which I was not already well accustomed. Slip and slide I did, many times, but each time managed to hold on.

After half an hour I had climbed only fifty feet; my clothes were in shreds; arms and legs were trembling from strain. Yet twenty feet remaining seemed so few—and I had come to a small tree curving out from the walls which promised and provided a means to the end.

Reaching the brink I limped around to the fatal altar and sank down on it, depositing a puddle of very sacred water upon the sacred stones. Listen though I might, I heard no more *tunkul* drums, no caracoles, no chanting phantom worshipers. I heard only the painful pounding in my ears, and felt nothing but the cold, the cuts and the bruises.

Enchantment was gone. No longer did I yearn for Yum-Chac's sea-green corridors.

All I wanted was a cigarette.

But in less than two days I was back at the altar again, standing on the brink, preparing to jump into that damned *cenote* a second time.

It happened this way.

The afternoon following the Sacred Well episode I returned (in borrowed shoes) to Merida and was invited to dine that night with Mr. Arthur Rice, the dean of the foreign colony and an enthusiastic student of ancient Maya civilization. Knowing of his intense interest in Chichen-Itza and the Sacred Well I related to him (leaving out the throbbing *tunkul* drums and other such unarcheological nonsense) my encounter with the *cenote* that morning.

"But it's seventy feet, man!" he exclaimed.

"It seemed like seven hundred feet to me," I admitted. "Thought I never *would* reach the water. Seventy feet isn't anything, though, to professionals. I've seen them do a hundred feet at county fairs into a bath-tub. And Steve Brody jumped off Brooklyn Bridge—that's twice seventy. It all depends on how you land. I landed all over myself and of course got knocked about unmercifully. I'm thinking of going back and doing it properly."

"You're *what!*" exclaimed my host.

"Oh, not entirely for the fun of it. I left my rather valuable moccasin boots on the ledge at the bottom of the pit—went to every shop in Merida this afternoon looking for another pair and can't find anything even remotely similar. If I travel any deeper into the tropical wilds they'll be absolutely necessary. And jumping is probably the only means of rescue—certainly simpler than trying to climb down that wall. Climbing up was hard enough."

"May I go along and watch?"

"Certainly. Let's go to-morrow."

When, on the appointed hour, we met at the railroad station, Rice was carrying an amateur moving-picture outfit.

"Thought I'd bring this along and 'shoot' you when you fall in," he said to me. "Now you've *got* to jump."

Back at the ruins the cinema machine attracted a group of curious native workmen who, when they learned the cause of our visit, decided to join us and witness what they felt sure would be another sacrifice to the God of Rain.

The situation did look disconcertingly similar—a crowd of Itzas moving from the temple down the Sacred Way in advance of the "victim."

However, I must have my boots.

Reaching the Altar of the Last Rites, my companion moved around the rim to the opposite side and set up his camera. I took off coat and shirt, but, as I had planned to go feet first this time, kept on trousers and heavy socks to break the sting. Also I retained the watch, hoping a second shock might start it again. Passports, wallets, paper currency and cigarettes I turned over to Mr. Rice;

in fact, willed them to him on the spot in case Yum-Chac decided to add me to his retinue after all.

Everything was ready. It was agreed I was to count one—two—three as a signal to the "movie operator," and jump on three.

I walked to the edge, took a deep breath——

"One—two—t——"

"Hold on—hold on," came a shout from across the chasm. "My film's snarled."

Delay. Then a second tightening of resolve.

"One—two——"

"Señor—wait—wait!" One of the native wardens on this side was rushing forward in Spanish to prevent the launching until I had received written permission from the authorities in Mexico City.

But I didn't wait. I jumped. It was the only means of avoiding further molestations.

My companion had suggested in advance that for the benefit of his "movie" I might register a few emotions as I fell—rapture, for example, or wistfulness. These proved a bit difficult moving at such high speed. But I knew some imitations and decided to offer these.

First I'd be an angel—and I flung out my arms as wings. About that time I hit the water, the angelic equilibrium so completely destroyed by the calisthenics that my face struck almost as soon as my feet. There was such a shower of stars and such violent wrenchings as I submerged into the Rain God's element a second time I was sure I'd broken my neck and would see Yum-Chac and his Maya captives at last.

No such luck. The clumsy plunge only knocked me deaf and speechless for three days after.

But I *did* get my shoes!

CHAPTER VI

THE LAND WHERE THE CORALS LIE

"The deeps have music soft and low
When the winds awake the airy spray:
It lures me, lures me on to go
And see the land where the corals lie."

On looking about for a means of departure from Yucatan, I found a very ridiculous little two-masted sailboat with the beautiful name of *Xpit.* Pronunciation *Speet.* Her captain informed me that shortly she would sail south to Puerto Barrios in Guatemala. I didn't want to go to Guatemala, but it was as good as any other place in reach; so I booked passage. The distance was six hundred miles. *Quién sabe* how long it would take. I'd have to sleep on deck where the crew slept, and eat the crew's food unless I brought my own. The captain was a negro; likewise all three of the seamen. The thirty-ton boat was dirty and dilapidated beyond description. One could scarcely have found a less pleasant or less secure vessel. But her very unseaworthiness gave a voyage aboard her a certain sporting charm. One of Columbus' own caravels, the *Niña,* was scarcely larger—and look what *she* did!

Also I had a companion to share the adventure with me, and the companion had a sense of humor. Besides these advantages my duffel-bag contained a pile of books, a writing tablet and a bottle of ink. With such equipment what voyage could be other than agreeable?

Kit, the companion, had heard, back in the United States, of my Cortez expedition in Mexico, and jumping to the conclusion that I was having an amusing summer, asked if he could join me in Yucatan for the duration of his short vacation.

I was agreeable. Although some years younger than myself—not yet twenty-one in fact—and though hopelessly inexperienced in the knapsack manner of travel, Kit had the saving graces of enthusiasm, energy and a happy heart.

I found him in Merida when I returned from my second encounter with the Sacred Well. Scarcely waiting for the paralysis in my face to subside, he begged me to go back to Chichen-Itza and jump in a third time in order that he might jump too. He said he wanted to find out for himself how it felt to be a Sacred Virgin, and for a long time he refused to accept my testimonial that it felt god-awful.

Nothing short of a voyage around the coast of Mayab in a crazy thirty-ton sailboat would have diverted him from the Well.

The captain of our boat had suggested we come aboard early, if we wanted choice deck space, as he was expecting a large passenger list. He discreetly did not tell us that the other passengers were to be twenty Mexican soldiers and a hundred native Indian laborers migrating to the east coast of Yucatan. The chicle companies there, after a suspension of this local industry, had gone back to work and had advertised for field hands. Here they were!

This wild mob with their women and possessions soon began to swarm down upon the little *Xpit.* Every inch of deck space became packed with half-clad, unwashed *chicleros* struggling for breathing room. Our passenger capacity had long since been reached, but still they came, the soldiers bullying the laborers, the laborers bullying their women, and the women snarling at each other.

I was all for backing out. This cargo of animals would suffocate us. Not Kit! He had come all the way from New York to have him an adventure, and this one looked promising.

So we battled our way aboard and, flaying about with Kit's mandolin, brought along as part of his impedimenta, managed to clear the deck space assigned us.

The *Xpit* was forty feet long and fifteen wide. When she sailed one hundred and twenty-six persons were aboard her. Two of them were white.

Down the east coast we headed before a good breeze, with our passengers hanging off the deck and piled in layers. The ship's cook had a contract to feed the outfit, but there was only one cooking utensil, a sort of dishpan, and one small deck stove. Into the dishpan went water and a sack of rice. The moment the kernels swelled, and while still half-raw, "dinner" was served by allowing the most pressing of the passengers to scoop out all they could with their hands. Only the fittest survived. They gorged themselves on underdone rice while the timid and weak got nothing. Once the pan was emptied, back it went on to the fire with a fresh supply. Perpetual motion all day long.

On the second day the rice gave out.

Also the water. Exposed to reckless and extravagant waste, the tank, which would have lasted a month under normal circumstances, was now emptied in forty-eight hours.

The shore offered no relief, for here it is one unbroken, uninhabited stretch of desert. Only one day more, if the wind held, to reach the next port.

The captain put out every inch of sail in an effort to make the suffering ahead as brief as possible.

Meanwhile, Kit and I, at the bow, had seized upon a piece of old canvas and stretched it between the anchor and gunwales. This cut us off from the mob-scene and offered shade. We had brought aboard enough food and water for our own use, so were not inconvenienced directly by the warfare and congestion of the menagerie. Kit played *Jingle Bells* on his mandolin. I read *Alice in Wonderland,* while one hundred and twenty people groaned for water on the other side of our defense. It wasn't that we were insensitive to their deprivations. It was only that we couldn't, like Moses, bring forth water by commanding it, and didn't see how worrying would help any.

I do not know what would have prevented the thirst aboard taking a toll of painful suffering, if one of the soldiers had not discovered that in the hatch, underneath a thin covering of general merchandise, the captain had hidden his main cargo—thirty cases of bootleg beer and ten of whisky, intended ultimately, via connecting rum-runners, for American consumption.

The news spread like wildfire. A mass assault was made upon the hatch, and presently each one of the hundred and twenty thirsty passengers was clutching a bottle he had torn from its refuge. Our negro skipper, frightened and impotent from the first, made a feeble effort to save his precious liquor. One hundred and twenty dry throats did not concern him—just so many cattle—but when his beer became involved—that roused him into action.

He may as well have tried to protect his beer from the German Army. The *chicleros* tossed him aside, fought each other over the bottles, savagely broke off the necks and annihilated beer in oceans. Thirst soon ceased to be an excuse for the debauch that took place. Our soldier "guards" led the onslaught, not retreating till they were dragged away by the succeeding waves of rum-guzzlers.

After six hours of this there wasn't a person aboard, save the captain, Kit and myself, still responsible. Even the three seamen had fallen before the flood of ambrosia.

As for the dozen native women, they seemed in no need of any defense we might have offered them. They had taken a particular fancy to the Scotch, and being as intoxicated as the men, were entirely agreeable, under violent pressure from the army, to deserting their helpless mates and having a fling at military service.

Of the five hundred bottles of beer and whisky aboard, not one remained by night. Much of their contents flowed over the deck and out the scuppers. Wallowing in alcohol and broken glass the Yucatacs lay in half-conscious heaps, oblivious to time, place and destination. Debauchery completely paralyzed the little *Xpit.* No self-respecting pig would have come aboard her.

Resigned to the loss of cargo, the distracted captain turned his attention to getting his ill-used boat into port. Kit and I were as eager to escape from the *chicleros* as the captain, and by trampling up and down drunken Indian forms half the night, did all we could to help him man the sails.

At dawn we approached a tropical island ten miles off the coast. Giant palm trees leaned out from the beach to reach the waves that flung themselves, foaming, upon the sand. The indigo of the sky was as deep as the turquoise of the sea. Close to this welcome refuge we sailed and dropped anchor before a palm-shaded little town.

Kit and I, not knowing or caring where we were, and wishing only to escape from the bleary *Xpit,* hastened to abandon the vessel with all hands and paddle ashore in a rescuing canoe.

Thus did we come to Cozumel—the land where the corals lie.

We hadn't meant to come to Cozumel at all. We'd bought passage to Puerto Barrios, four hun-

Kit at the bow of the good ship *Xpit.*

The beach at Cozum

nd where the corals lie.

The Lake is Nicaragua's glory. Volcanoes rise from its islands, waiting to act as celestial beacons along the proposed new canal.

The U. S. S. *Cleveland* which rescued Kit and me from Bluefields and transported us to Panama.

dred miles beyond. However, here we were, and if the *Xpit* was the only means of departure, here we'd rest.

Not a happy prospect! Yet it took only one look about to set us rejoicing over our fate, for no more than half a mile distant from the town we glimpsed a beach that was made in heaven, and jade surf straining to reach the shadows of the palms.

We soon learned that this splash of color called Cozumel had a most romantic past. (But we couldn't be bothered with the island's past. Only a sea-bath in that dancing spray concerned us.)

Cozumel was a holy island when the Mayas dwelt in Yucatan. Here, as to Chichen-Itza, pilgrims came in thousands. (But what of it, when the breakers were playing music on the sand and calling to one to come and forget all this dull and foolish history?)

Colossal monuments of whitest stone, pyramids, shrines, lighthouses, miraculously built by those half-fabulous Mayas, dot the island, gleam from the headlands, are lost and waiting deep in the jungle. (But who cared, when our lord, the Sun, was pouring down his blessings on the sea and charging its waters with a wild vitality?)

Where is the race that once lived like gods in Yucatan, flung their human sacrifices into the Well of Death, flowered so astonishingly, and disappeared? Here it is, found again in Cozumel—same speech, same faces, as the passed-away ones. Here Cortez landed on his way to Mexico, and built a church which has stood until this day. Here, a century after, the English pirates fought the Spanish conquerors and sank their galleons filled with gold. (But who could expect us to note all this, when we had found in the surf of Cozumel a magic fountain that cured one's sins and washed clean one's soul.)

Having found this fountain, Kit and I leaped into it and, except for an occasional meal, didn't come out of it for two weeks.

No one ever swam in such water as this—though it didn't seem like water—like champagne rather, the purest, clearest champagne, buoyant, live, laughing, sun-shot. One baptism in this elixir seduced and enslaved us. Thenceforth we couldn't keep away from it. That pale green sea became a passion and a madness that dragged us back and back for hours on end. In it we never grew cold, never tired. Out of it our only thought was to sink again into its soft and sensuous purity.

On the bottom were the coral reefs, deadly enemies to ships, though in themselves fantastically beautiful. Rainbow fish idled about the coral caves and castles—schools of red ones, pairs of yellow ones, drifting through the purple shadows, or dreaming in the sunlight where the sea was clearer than green glass.

Kit and I bought two sisal-fiber hammocks and strung them between the palms. A boy brought us food from the town, oranges and *totopostes,* roast fowl and buckets of lemonade. We swam before breakfast, and all morning and all afternoon, and half the night when the waning moon gave illumination to this land where the corals lie.

Our only departure from the beach was to visit an entrancing little land-locked bay ten acres in extent, where the coral shore fell sharply off for thirty feet and encouraged diving to the very depths. For three centuries this coral pool, deep, intimate, unbelievably clear, was a dockyard for Spanish treasure ships, and later a pirate rendezvous. On the bottom one sees no end of ancient chains, anchors, scrap-iron, broken bits of hulk. The Mayas on Cozumel swear that treasure chests are buried thick about and that the ghosts of the reckless buccaneers who buried them still haunt the place.

Here for the first time in my life I became the "compleat angler." I rigged up a string and hook and, dropping a tempting bait down through the glass, dangled it from our plank-raft before the nose of the particular fish we had nominated to be our lunch.

We could watch every move. If our victim disdained the worm we'd pursue him with it until in an exasperated effort to rid himself of the darned thing, he'd swallow it—and I'd yank him out with a cry to Kit that luncheon would soon be served.

The names and flavors of the fish were of no concern. We chose only according to their prettiness—pink for breakfast, or black with yellow stripes; and preferably plaid or polka dots for dinner. Sometimes finding a school of a million baby perch half-asleep in the depths, we'd leap into their midst and see how many we could grab with our hands or frighten to death.

Kit, already an excellent swimmer, was rapidly turning into a sea lion. The deep coral gardens where the brightest-hued sea creatures dwelt became his special hunting ground. He explored the grottoes for sunken treasure, dived from the highest rock, grew to feel as intimate with that dancing water as any inhabitant in the aquarium. I could never hope to keep up with him. While he cruised swiftly up and down our bay, I was content to splash. He called himself the *Mauretania,* me the Hoboken freight barge, and further humbled my pride by turning mahogany brown in the constant sunshine, while I blistered and suffered and courted the shade.

Kit's mandolin was not infrequently his chief garment. He felt it his duty while I cooked (in my own quaint way) the loaves and fishes, to serenade me with all four of his "pieces"—*Jingle Bells* with variations; *Don't Cry, Little Girl, Don't Cry; Long, Long Ago;* and *Listen to the Mocking Bird,* played fancy.

The music so inspired me I became a regular demon with the frying-pan.

For fourteen days this lazy life continued. We received no mail, saw no other person but the Maya boy who brought our food. Calendars were lost, cares forgotten. We had books which we never read, pen and paper we never touched. Nothing mattered but the music of the sea.

Then one day our errand boy brought news that a coastal sailboat had put into the harbor headed for Puerto Barrios, and that there probably wouldn't be another for a month. Kit and I decided to take it, chiefly because we were so loath to go—a wise time for departures.

The *Gaviotta* was just another *Xpit,* without the hundred *chicleros.* Instead she carried a hundred giant sea turtles all very much alive. The captain said that if we'd put up with his turtles, he'd put up with us.

This strange cargo proved quite a problem at such close range. The smallest turtle weighed two hundred pounds, the largest four hundred. Placed on their backs with flippers tied, their flat thick bellies completely paved the deck. We sat or promenaded on turtles, slept on turtles, ate on turtles. Everything done on that boat was done on top of turtles.

Out of the water they would remain alive only four days. One day had passed already. There must be no delay.

We sailed at midnight, slipping quietly south along the coast, past our familiar palms standing black against the stars, past our coral pool, past the southern headland—on out into the open sea, with Kit lounging on the belly of a four-hundred-pound turtle and playing *Don't Cry, Little Girl, Don't Cry.*

CHAPTER VII

THE FILIBUSTERS

Kit and I and five score turtles were landed at Puerto Barrios. The fact that the puerto is the banana capital of the world as well as the turtle center did not offer us sufficient inducement to tarry. We departed by the railroad leading west through Guatemala City to the Pacific where we could no doubt find a boat sailing somewhere else—maybe Nicaragua. It now seemed *that* was where we wanted to go.

Our train offered no dining service, and so, as we had already missed breakfast, I went foraging for portable food. Not far away I found a small shop festooned with ripe bananas (green bunches were piled mountain-high everywhere, awaiting shipment), and asked the shop-keeper for half a dozen. The price was smaller than the smallest coin I had.

Such a cheapness! A magnificent idea possessed me. At the price of one silver dollar I bought the entire bunch as it stood.

A whole bunch of bananas! It was like owning a whole elephant. It gave me a masterful and superior feeling.

Once Kit and I, with our combined efforts, had dragged our breakfast aboard the train, the problem of its disposal at once arose. The huge cluster wouldn't go on or under the seat; in the aisle it blocked passage; eating it was too heroic a measure. We finally solved the difficulty by hanging it up by a cord in the open window. There the rich yellow fruit proved highly decorative and pleasantly fragrant.

Thereupon, Kit and I charged head first into the calories; but with all our power of will and celebrated fighting spirit, we were unable to subdue more than two bananas apiece. This left us with eleven dozen.

A fat, black-eyed little girl sat across the way. We noticed that those eyes were fixed wistfully on our treasures. Kit gave her a banana and had his reward in seeing her face light up with gladness. Two small boys passed by, noticed the honeycomb swinging in the window and stopped dead in their tracks. Kit stuffed their pockets with bananas and sent them on rejoicing. Two more cherub Guatemalets, just big enough to look above the arm of our seat, appeared out of nowhere and cast loving, insinuating glances at Kit. They got theirs. The ticket collector, seeing what riches lay in our possession, exuded courtesy. He received a princely banana—so princely that before long he came back again, ostensibly to point out the scenery, but we knew what he wanted—and he got it. Then we noticed that the conductor had a friend with him who had come along to help the conductor point out the scenery. He got his banana too.

We were becoming more and more proficient at this banana benevolence. Down the aisle several seats, we caught sight of two pretty señoritas watching our philanthropies. Kit pantomimed to them that if they'd come sit in our laps we'd feed them. They giggled and looked away. Kit picked up his mandolin and offered to throw *Jingle Bells* into the bargain. Still they hesitated; so he pulled an armful of fruit and emptied it amid much hilarity into *their* laps.

This last gesture proved our downfall—or was it our triumph? Seeing that we were determined to give away bananas, every banana-hungry child on the train made a rush at us. We were stormed, stampeded, mobbed, and into every outstretched hand went a fat banana. I never saw so many children. Neither have I ever seen so many bananas. They seemed inexhaustible. The more we gave away, the more remained. It became another *Xpit* orgy, except that the beer was bananas; the drunken *chicleros,* starry-eyed children; the broken bottles, banana skins; beery breaths, a sweet aroma. And as in the case of the *Xpit,* the orgy did not subside until the last of the refreshments perished.

With all these children, each blissfully busy with his ration, pressing thick about us, Kit felt this was just the time for a mandolin concert. Having fed their bodies it would not be right to neglect their souls. So he *Jingled Belled* and *Listened to the Mocking Bird* for his enraptured (and bulging) young audience all the way into the capital.

The capital isn't much, thanks to a century of weekly earthquakes. We thought—since we had come so far and had never experienced an earthquake—the city council would be glad to arrange one for us. But they refused point blank. Not a little annoyed we took the very next train to the Pacific coast and caught a boat for Nicaragua.

The boat happened to be a large American passenger liner plying casually from California to New York via the Canal, and stopping at every seaport down the west coast. This frequently gave the passengers an opportunity for land excursions —an opportunity Kit and I always seized upon in order to enjoy the surf-bathing.

At La Libertad, in Salvador, we found a beach a mile below the docks. The beach was still in sight of the ship anchored several hundred yards off shore, yet isolated enough (so we thought) to permit us to dispense with bathing suits. As we didn't have bathing suits anyway we did not suffer much from this sacrifice.

The breakers that day were unusually violent, knocking me about so badly I soon had enough. But not Kit. He was an expert at riding the rollers and kept venturing farther and farther seaward.

During one of these long out-voyages a convent-school Saturday afternoon picnic-party consisting of half a dozen nuns and some twenty girls came very unexpectedly along the path that led abruptly from the woods and down to the water's edge. The convent building itself, we later learned, was only a few hundred yards distant, but it was so completely hidden by bluffs and trees we had not been aware of its proximity to us—or rather ours to it. In fact the beach turned out to be part of the convent's private property.

Noting the sudden and unwelcome approach of the young ladies, I retreated behind a sand dune to figure out how I'd get to our clothing waiting two hundred feet the other side of the enemy. Kit himself was so far out in the tossing sea he never saw this battalion of maidens waiting for him on the beach, nor, for that matter, did they see him, though a few of them had observed the pile of male attire and were no doubt wondering what had become of its owners.

Spying over my earthworks, I sensed approaching disaster, helpless to prevent it. Just as I expected, Kit caught a magnificent roller. I could see him flying in, head down, arms out, struggling to keep his balance on the wave—nearer and nearer, faster and faster, until with a roar the breaker flung him, breathless, blind with foam and sand, and completely nude, into the very arms of the twenty most astonished Salvadoran virgins that ever picnicked by the sea.

I did not know whether to die of shame or laughter.

From the picnickers rose shrieks of surprise and confusion. Had they not been walled away from the world lest just such disgraceful adventures as this befall them? Had they not been marshaled to this particular and private beach because it was unfrequented by men and would permit them to escape their carnal gaze? For men—were they not all barbarians, pagans and seducers?

And had they not prayed every night, along

with the petition for forgiveness of their sins, that one of these seducers be delivered into their hands?

And behold!

Now they would believe in prayer, for here was the realization of their secret dreams—a man, young and handsome enough, with sun-bleached hair, skin burned the color of oak, Nordic eyes the more arresting in their wide consternation, and all set off to best advantage in a simple little costume of salt water.

The poor maidens were torn between looking at Kit and away from him.

It is my painful duty to report that the "ats" won with an overwhelming majority.

They might have held a bacchanalian revel in honor of this gift from the sea, had not the gift, comprehending his predicament in less time than is required to tell it, taken to his heels past masses of shocked nuns, and fled whooping, pantsward, down the beach.

And then we came to Nicaragua.

I realize that much might be said about the American marine occupation of this troublesome little state; but this is only a story of Kit and myself—not of politics and economics. We were more interested in going for a swim in Lake Nicaragua than in saving the country.

To visit the lake, we left our ship and took the one short railroad through Managua, the capital. Finding this city devoid of interest, we hurried on to the shores of the greatest expanse of fresh water in the American tropics.

This lake is Nicaragua's glory. Jungle-blanketed volcanoes rise from its shores, pierce its lovely islands and tower in the clouds, waiting for the day —mark twenty years—when their volcanic fires will act as celestial beacons to guide the ships of all the world from sea to sea.

Nothing would do Kit but that we engage a sail-boat to traverse this hundred miles of water to its southern end where the San Juan River acts as a spillway into the Atlantic. Forgetting the *Xpit* and the *Gaviotta* we found an adequate craft and for two days sailed over this great inland sea, I reading sage and solemn books while Kit played *Jingle Bells* on his tin mandolin and made himself sick eating indelicate quantities of the dozen water-melons we had brought along as almost our only provisions.

Kit's colic did not improve on disembarking at San Carlos, the village near the lake's southern end. In fact after a night's rest on shore he had developed a temperature and was so miserable we gave up our idea of descending the San Juan River in a canoe as planned, and instead took a launch that was departing that day for Greytown at the river's mouth.

Aboard the launch Kit became too sick to sit upright on the one bench provided, and the roof was the only place where he could lie down. Here he tossed and sweltered as we tied up to the bank with the coming of darkness, and here until morning feebly fought the clouds of mosquitoes that attacked us.

Next day it was evident that Kit was seriously ill. I had secret fears of cholera, typhoid and all the other terrible scourges people are subject to in the tropics—and for the first time felt a real responsibility for my companion's welfare. We must get to Panama with all speed. There was no boat back to Managua for a week.

For one day more we continued down-stream, between solid banks of jungle five hundred feet apart. I observed the passing miles with more than casual interest—and so did Kit, insofar as he was able—for this river was to be the new canal—was to have been the new canal a dozen times before Panama snatched the prize away. By this river in the 1850's, Commodore Vanderbilt's company, defying the swift currents in the rapids, transported twenty-five thousand people a year on across the lake to the twelve-mile highroad joining with the Pacific. He charged three hundred dollars for a ticket from New York to San Francisco. The Panama companies had to charge six hundred dollars, since their route was a thousand miles longer, and consequently were so undersold that they finally paid Vanderbilt sixty thousand dollars *a month* not to operate his line.

Sudden collapse. The twenty-five thousand passengers a year fell to none a year. Nicaragua lapsed into her previous stagnant state. To-day, instead of the hurrying fleets of the Forty-niners, the San Juan knows only an infrequent launch carrying a few Indians and a few pigs, or perhaps a pair of American vagabonds.

At Greytown, a haunted and deserted relic of a once-booming city, the launch master and I helped Kit crawl ashore. We found there was no ship due at any time for any place—and no house fit for shelter—only swamps underfoot and countless mosquitoes overhead.

We couldn't stay here. Kit would die. We *must* go some other place; and the only means of going was on the same river launch. The town of Bluefields, with its company of marines and an army doctor, lay seventy-five miles up the coast in the opposite direction from Panama. We'd go—we'd have to go—there. The master rebelled against the risks of braving the open ocean in his diminutive river craft. But this was no time to consider hazards. I over-persuaded him, and dragged Kit back on the launch roof.

All night long the sea tumbled our little boat unmercifully. The rain drove us off the roof. Kit, burning up with fever, was too ill to note the rain or the onslaught of the seas.

At noon next day, after the most nerve-racking voyage in many moons (the *Xpit* was a happy holiday compared with this), we labored into Bluefields. I carried my companion on a stretcher to the "hotel." This lodging, run by a negro, was unspeakably dirty, with myriads of flies and mosquitoes as constant company, but there was no other.

The marine doctor came as soon as possible.

Malaria—and a particularly virulent case.

We began to pour quinine into poor helpless Kit with spoons, pills and hypodermic. He was given sixty grains a day, until the cure made him even sicker than the cause.

And as if this were not enough, ameboid dysentery—twice as dangerous as the malaria—contracted from some polluted food fed us by the wretched hotel, attacked him as well. He began to have periods of delirium and, as the days dragged past, seemed only to grow rapidly worse.

The doctor became more and more alarmed. But he had done all he knew to do.

My own helplessness was distracting. I could only stand by and watch Kit fight a losing battle.

Then the gods held a council and looked seriously into Kit's case. Here was a young man the glow of whose spirits was at its height, for whom living was vivid and beautiful, who had dreams, who had faith, who had so many adventures unfulfilled. Such a terrible mandolin player, but such a gay, spontaneous one! Prudence and reverence were not among Kit's idols, but the gods, who have become so fed up with conscientious Christians, secretly rejoice in an occasional riotous infidel like Kit. The gods decided they needed Kit, and his youth, and his eagerness. They would let him live to brighten their declining years. So they sent the U. S. Navy to the rescue.

It came in the form of the cruiser *Cleveland,* which anchored a mile off the coast. Wireless had informed me of her approach, and I determined to get Kit aboard at any cost, navy regulations notwithstanding.

Ignoring all medical threats and warnings, I pulled him on to a stretcher again, and with the help of the gods and a few marines, got him into a rowboat, hoping and praying the *Cleveland's* captain would have mercy on us.

Reaching the vessel I climbed the ladder, found the captain, explained the seriousness of the case and begged for transportation to Panama whither I knew he was headed

"Where's your sick man?"

"On a stretcher in my rowboat."

"Put him to bed in the operating room. The hospital is full. You'll have Lieutenant X's cabin and dine with me."

The good old gods! May they bless Captain Wygant and make him an admiral!

Three days later having traversed the Panama Canal aboard our battleship, we carried Kit, alive, but not much more, into the Ancon Hospital.

Six weeks passed—six anxious, fevered weeks. Every form of treatment failed. Strength ebbed but never flowed. And then one day he woke up from a long sleep and suddenly asked for his mandolin. *Jingle Bells* rang feebly on the air. It was the sign. We knew that Kit was going to get well. And at this good news, among Kit's friends, the gods, there was a great rejoicing. That I know.

CHAPTER VIII

THE S. S. RICHARD HALLIBURTON

THE governor of the Panama Canal Zone rose to greet me.

"Good morning, Governor Walker. It's kind of you to grant this interview."

"Good morning, Mr. Halliburton. Of what service may I be to-day?"

"I've come to ask a favor, sir, like almost everybody else. But at least my request is original. I want to swim the Panama Canal from the Atlantic to the Pacific."

Not a little startled, General Walker looked up:

"Swim the Canal! Why, it's fifty miles! Rather a long pull for one of your slight physique, I should say."

"You are no doubt right, Governor. I'm not a professional swimmer—not even a good swimmer. But I don't mean to do it all at once before breakfast—by slow stages rather, as many miles each day as I can, and sleep on shore."

"Do you realize the lake is twenty-five miles wide, and that when you're half-way across you'll be over twelve miles from your shore?"

"Couldn't I take a motor-boat to taxi me out and back?"

"And there are innumerable alligators. A motor-boat man would have difficulty keeping close enough to protect you."

"Then I'll take a rowboat, too. Maybe I could borrow a sharpshooter from the army."

"Perhaps. Even so, the greatest danger would be from the impurity of the water. Don't forget the thousands of ships that are passing through it. You would be exposing yourself wide open to typhoid."

"I've been inoculated."

"Well, I must say you seem determined. But I should consider it exceedingly dangerous and impossibly difficult. The sharks and barracudas are sure to get you if the alligators and diseases do not. However," he said with a gesture that dismissed the case, "there's no law against your going for a swim in the Canal. I have no authority either to permit or forbid."

"I understand that, sir. I'm willing to take the chances, with sensible protection. Where your sanction is necessary is in regard to the locks. I want to have the gates opened up, and be locked through just like a ship."

The governor stared at me. The discussion of the swim had up to this time only faintly aroused his interest, so unreasonable and so unnecessary he had considered it. But this last preposterous request of mine, by virtue of its sheer impertinence, caused him to sit up and really notice me.

Had I asked for the Canal as a present, to be packed in straw, boxed, and shipped home by express, he would not have been more surprised. He had visions of the six vast lock chambers, each of them one thousand feet long, eighty feet deep, one hundred and ten feet wide, each being filled with nine million cubic feet of water to accommodate a floating speck on the surface. He had visions of the gigantic machineries, clanking and groaning; the Titanic gates swinging ponderously open; the thousands and thousands of horsepower put into earth-shaking motion; the hugest wonder of the world stopped in its play with the leviathans of the seas and chained into the service of this thin young man standing there before the governor's desk—just because this thin young man thought it might be amusing to have the Panama Canal so serve him.

No wonder General Walker looked shocked.

"But Mr. Halliburton—that's never been done in the history of the Canal. You'd hold up traffic—and think of the terrific expense to the Government. How would you meet the lock charges?"

"Just as the other ships meet it, sir. I'd pay according to my tonnage."

"Tonnage! You!" General Walker exclaimed, looking at my one hundred and forty pounds. And he laughed as if he'd never in all his life heard anything so funny. "All right! You win! I'll send you through—on one condition, my dear fellow: that you be held strictly accountable for any damage you do the Panama Canal!"

I promptly accepted this condition. The governor called his secretary and dictated the following letter:

"Mr. Richard Halliburton,
"Hotel Tivoli,
"Ancon, Canal Zone.

"Sir: With reference to our personal conversation of to-day, you are informed that there is no objection on the part of the Canal authorities to your projected swim from Colon to Panama.

"In this connection you are advised to take a course of antityphoid vaccination. You are also informed that alligators have been observed frequently in Gaillard Cut.

"You are authorized to have a rowboat con-

taining a rifleman accompany you. You are also authorized to swim through the locks.

"It is understood that any expenses in connection with this expedition will be borne by yourself, and that the Panama Canal will not be held responsible for any damages sustained.

"Respectfully,

"M. L. Walker, Governor."

I floated from the office with my head in the clouds, feeling that I had just been favored with a most colossal courtesy.

To swim the Panama Canal had been in my mind for months. From the very first time I had thought of it the idea of the adventure had bitten deep into my fancy. But always accompanying it was the thought that this was a task hopelessly beyond my strength. I might dream without end and resolve uncompromisingly, but lungs and legs would not obey beyond a certain point. I had once vowed by all the gods that nothing would stop me from swimming from Scylla to Charybdis, and, not half-way across, rebellious limbs faltered, failed and had to be rescued. Now, in the case of the Panama Canal, mind might triumph over matter to some extent, but not when matter was fifty miles of water, and mind supported only by arms that had not swum half a mile in three years.* [True, I'd spent two weeks on the beach at Cozumel, but there Kit did most of the swimming.] Now I was only in such condition as a month of languid travel in Central America might permit.

Further to discourage me, every Zone dweller I met en route to Panama had the most harrowing tales to tell of the barracudas. The harbor of Panama City was terrorized, according to their reports, by these villainous fish; and as for the alligators in Gatun Lake, they were big as dragons and as deadly dangerous. In short, any attempt to swim the Canal would be suicide a dozen times.

A lot of this I discounted as the usual fables attached to the unexplored. I'd heard suicide too often.

Even so, disregarding the dangers, there was no exaggeration about the fifty miles. Obviously, the Panama Canal swim was a dream that could never come to pass.

This was my resigned attitude when the *U. S. S. Cleveland* entered Colon Bay, on the Atlantic side, and began its passage through the Canal en route to Panama City and the Pacific naval base. But

*Editor's note—The author had swum the Hellespont three years previously, the first person to do so since Lord Byron. The feat has since become a popular pastime.

resigned or not, of all the million or more people who have passed through the Canal, not one ever counted the miles so meticulously as I, or ever noted the water, its currents, its color, its temperature, so intently, or ever watched so apprehensively for logs on the shore to move, or ever surveyed, memorized, drank in the gorgeous pageant of turquoise and emerald. Perhaps, maybe, with the guide buoys to rest on, with such bewildering, breath-taking beauty to disguise the miles—with no plan other than to swim as far each day as the mood dictated—and with a promise to myself of no self-scorn if I abandoned the enterprise before it was well begun—perhaps it might be within the realm of reason after all.

This hope and this desire swelled to a high pitch as the *Cleveland* entered the Gatun locks, and began to be lifted so silently, so swiftly up the Gargantuan steps.

The whole Canal that followed was one long astonishment. I had not dreamed it was so beautiful. I'd expected a man-made thing which Nature, scarred and mutilated, brooded over with silent rebelliousness.

How different it proved to be! The years since 1914, when the first ship passed through, have glossed over every wound with luxurious vegetation. The entire Zone is a garden that looks as if it might have been a garden always.

All through the fifty miles of this grand parade I kept my eyes glued to the scenery. The whole day passed—nine hours—before we anchored off Balboa docks (the Pacific terminal in the American Zone, built right beside Panama City), and saw the South Sea, Balboa's ocean, stretching out into the distance. It had been the shortest nine hours I'd ever spent aboard a ship. But suppose I'd been swimming in the cruiser's wake, with only arms and legs, and no huge, tireless turbines, to propel me, no previous pioneer—so far as I knew—to test the alligators, to experiment with the sharks, to blast the trail and prove it humanly possible! Nine hours for a battleship—nine days for a swimmer—nine weeks for *this* swimmer. . . .

"Oh forget it, forget it," common sense insisted with some exasperation as I disembarked from the *Cleveland.* "It's too hopelessly far. You can't swim fifty miles and you know it, and even if you could the Canal authorities wouldn't let you. Let's go to Kelly's Ritz, find a Panamanian damsel and dance till to-morrow morning. That's something you *can* do."

But at Kelly's Ritz I heard about Wendell Green.

In 1915—and likewise to-day—Wendell Green was an American resident in the Canal Zone, employed in the Government postal service. From boyhood he had been an ardent swimmer, and even before the Canal was entirely completed he conceived the idea that it might be swum. However, he had to be hard at work six days in the week, with only one day, Sunday, in which he could pursue such a plan. Very well then, he'd swim on Sundays. Likewise he would avoid the barracudas in Colon harbor by beginning the swim where the actual channel starts to cut across the isthmus. Not being afflicted with my own impertinent disposition he did not ask to have the lock gates opened for him, but was content to climb around them and swim the length of each chamber when a respite from ships permitted.

On the sixth Sunday he reached Balboa, having swum about forty-five miles in all, or about eight and a half miles each swimming day. He encountered few alligators, since in 1915 the Canal was so new that they had not been enticed into it from the upper reaches of the Chagres River by the refuse from the countless ships which now feeds them so bountifully.

And yet, however little the circumstances of his swim would resemble those I should encounter, here was an unexpected and a vast encouragement.

Immediately I sought and found this all important gentleman. Besides authenticating the details of his feat he gave me the benefit of his hard-earned experience with tides and currents, and advised me—in case I got authority from the governor to undertake this stunt—to begin on the Atlantic side.

So, everything was secured now except the permission to swim—and the ability. The first might, by some fluke, be obtained. If only the second could likewise be bestowed upon me by the authorities!

But what was the use after all, of bothering the governor for permission to fly to Mars? Even if he gave it to me, I still couldn't fly. For the first time in my life I grew angry at my ancestors who had bequeathed me such an inadequate frame. *Why* couldn't I weigh two hundred pounds and have a barrel chest like Green? Why couldn't I be a floater, blubber-bound to keep out the cold? Why hadn't I taken swimming more seriously? Why couldn't I enjoy the most beautiful aquatic adventure the world offered? Because I was too weak, too thin, too afraid.

May as well give up. I'd go and tackle Ancon Hill, rising just behind the city. This was five hundred feet high. No doubt my legs and lungs would stand for that.

I reached the top to find the view enchanting. I could see for miles around—the blue Pacific—the jungle—the Spanish city—the traffic of ships, ships, ships, specks on the horizon, steaming past the islands in the outer bay, crowding into the harbor from a hundred nations and a thousand ports, waiting to climb the magic steps and descend upon the other Ocean. Inland they sailed up the channel toward the Miraflores locks—battleships, tankers, tramps, huge long liners, sailboats, tugboats, freight boats, every flag, every color, the endless pageant steaming up the blue fiord through the sunshine on toward the most romantic voyage granted the ships of the sea.

One did not need to be an ardent lover of ships to be stirred by this royal procession. One did not need to know the blood-and-gold-drenched past of the setting there below, need not know the fabulous history of this world-famous isthmus, of the battles, the pirates, the plunder, of Columbus and Balboa, that have steeped Panama with drama, to be awed by the majesty and significance of the view from Ancon Hill.

This picture dug into me. It would haunt me the rest of my life unless I accepted its challenge.

No matter what happened in the future, no adventure could ever be so beautiful as the one that here offered itself. Were I to conquer Everest, or take wing to the moon, I should feel profitless and dissatisfied, for on the Himalayan summit or the other planet's surface, I should never escape the relentless recollection that I *hadn't* swum the Panama Canal. I would forget the mountain and the moon, but never the swim from sea to sea. It is the adventures we have that pass; the adventures we can not have, remain.

Damn the barracudas! If it took me a week for every mile, I was going to swim!

CHAPTER IX

THE MAGIC STAIRS

BEFORE night the report of the governor's unique order was in the local newspapers. It seemed to strike the American colony's sense of humor. Immediately I was showered with courtesies. The commander-in-chief of the American Army in Panama loaned me the sharpshootingest sergeant on the isthmus; the Associated Press and the United Press sent dispatches to America; a dozen reporters escorted me from Panama via the railroad to Colon to cover the event—and I hadn't swum a hundred yards consecutively in three years, used only an antiquated side-stroke obsolete in 1885—didn't even have a bathing suit. Swell Canal challenger I was!

I had visions of the newspaper headlines next day: "Canal challenger swims hundred feet. Sinks exhausted. Drowns," and of the ridicule I'd be subject to now that the U. P. and the A. P. had broadcast a lot of bombastic defiance I was supposed to have hurled at the Canal. (I'd urged the

Courtesy Panama-Pacific Steamship Co.

The approach to the Gatun locks. Gatun Lake lies beyond. The intersecting water course is a remnant of the French canal. It was against the current at this point that the S. S. *Richard Halliburton* made such slow progress.

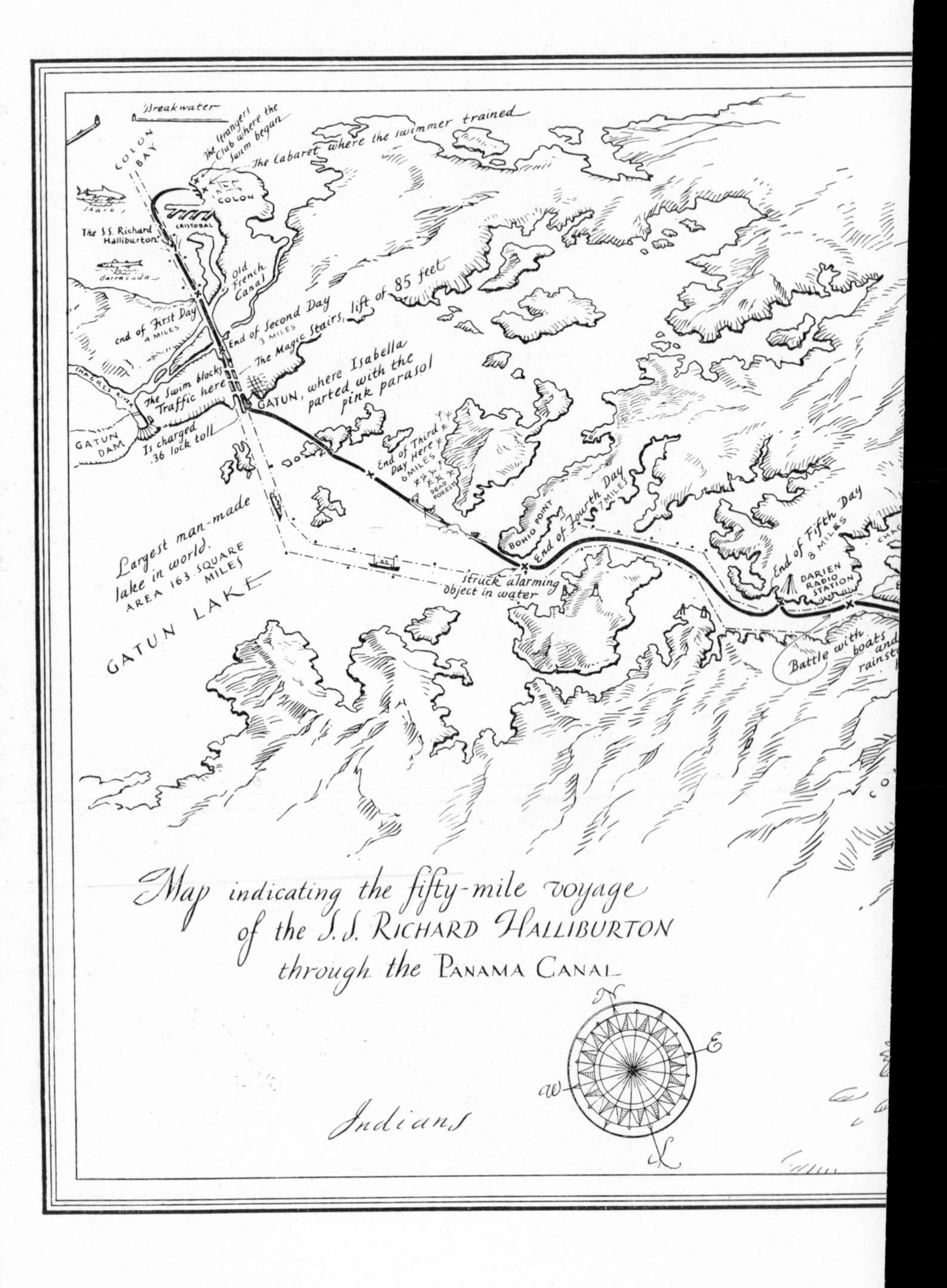

Map indicating the fifty-mile voyage of the S.S. Richard Halliburton through the Panama Canal

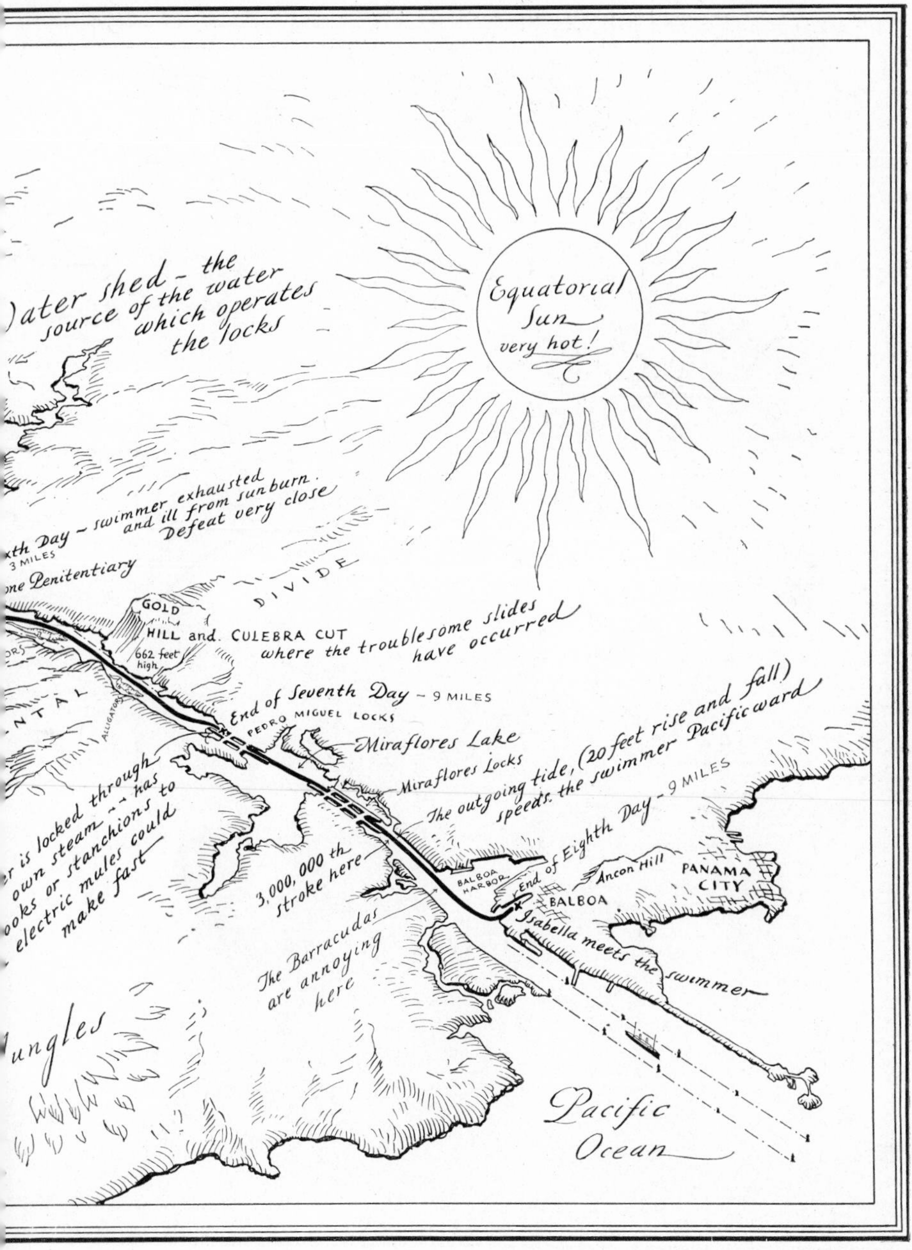

)ater shed - the
source of the water
which operates
the locks

Equatorial
Sun
very hot!

xth Day - swimmer exhausted
and ill from sunburn.
Defeat very close
3 MILES

me Penitentiary

DIVIDE

GOLD
HILL and. CULEBRA CUT
where the troublesome slides
have occurred

662 feet
high

NTAL

ALLIGATOR

End of Seventh Day - 9 MILES

PEDRO MIGUEL LOCKS

Miraflores Lake

Miraflores Locks

The outgoing tide, (20 feet rise and fall)
speeds the swimmer Pacificward

er is locked through
own steam - has
ooks or stanchions to
electric mules could
make fast

3,000,000 th
stroke here

End of Eighth Day - 9 MILES

BALBOA
HARBOR

Ancon Hill

PANAMA
CITY

BALBOA

Isabella meets the swimmer

The Barracudas
are annoying
here

Jungles

Pacific
Ocean

The American children in Panama were particularly interested in the Canal swim.

Sergeant Thomas Wright, the swimmer's faithful escort.

The S. S. *Richard Halliburton* takes two mermaids in tow. Panama is famous for its swimming children.

reporters to wait until I had swum it, and then say so if they wished. But no! The take-off was the best part of the story—especially if I *would* drown the first few yards.) The only hope I saw lay in water-wings, or some pitying water god's charitable assistance. The first would be too absurd. The second unlikely, as the water gods had probably been eaten by the alligators.

To postpone the debacle as long as possible I suggested to my companions that we should first have a *morituri te salutamus* party. So instead of disturbing Colon harbor as per schedule with my drowning gurgles we all went to the American Cabaret in the afternoon and didn't depart till next morning.

Even if it was my own, I've never been to a better party, though I had nothing to do with making it so except pay the bill. Army and navy pay day supplied the zip. The place was a madhouse of soldiers and sailors, all flush with money, singing, dancing, rioting. On such a night as this the damsels were not lacking. There must have been a hundred there. The dance floor was a writhing mob, the music loud, unceasing.

At midnight the show began—one *artiste* after another skipped hither and yon, quivering before this table of gobs, undulating past the army, breaking the hearts of a dozen marines. The entertainers' skill as dancers, or charm as singers, had nothing to do with the amount of applause accorded them. It was entirely a matter of flesh apparent. The fewer the clothes the more acclaim, and I might say that as the hours and the houris passed, the acclaim got louder and louder, until the final number—well, if people *will* go to such places . . .

I must admit that our own group was not altogether shy about taking part in this quaint merry-making. We were almost the only civilians in the place and felt it a matter of honor not to dance with any less abandon than the navy.

I found myself sometime between midnight and morning left alone at our table—there weren't enough dance partners to go round. But the music was too intoxicating. I mustn't waste a note of it, for on the morrow, was I not to die?

Way off in the corner I saw a girl all alone, like myself. I walked over to her, past the crowded tables that intervened. She was incredibly young, unmistakably Latin, and undeniably pretty, but with an inconspicuous costume and quiet manner that left her almost invisible among her gaudy, gold-digging sisters.

"What's your name, Señorita?" I said, sitting

down opposite her. This was no place for a girl who couldn't speak English.

"Isabella," she replied in such a soft Spanish voice I liked her instantly.

"Isabella! You little wag! How did you know I was Columbus?"

I thought that was *very* funny—everything was funny by this time—but she looked completely blank. And properly, since he's "Cristobal Colon" in Panama.

"What's a wag?" she asked. "Is it nice?"

"Is it nice! Why, my dear Isabella, it's the nicest thing in the world. A wag is beautiful, gentle, virtuous. It's the Russian word for sunshine and the Greek word for Aphrodite." But her English was sailor-taught and did not include such words as virtue and Aphrodite. She still looked uncomprehending. "Well, when a man calls you a wag, he likes you—he's crazy about you, see?"

"I see," she said, all smiles. "And you like me?"

"*Mucho—mucho*—Isabella. Come dance with Cristobal Colon."

And how she could dance! The navy had done well by her there. She didn't weigh a hundred pounds and simply floated around.

"Why you so sad?" she asked, when the music stopped.

"Oh—am I?" I wanted to say that places where people go resolutely and grimly to amuse themselves were quite the saddest places in the world, but knew she would neither understand nor agree. "Well, it's because I may drown to-morrow and don't feel especially gay."

"Drown . . . ?"

"Sure—you know—like this—water—*agua*—glug"—and I pantomimed a person dying of strangulation.

"Why? Who makes you?" she asked, somewhat perturbed.

"Nobody makes me. *I* make me. I've got to swim—like this—swim—the Panama Canal."

"The Canal! But the barracudas!"

"Poohpooh. I'm not afraid—not afraid of the barracudas. It's *me* I'm afraid of, afraid I can't swim one mile, much less fifty."

"But *why?*"

How could I tell her why? I didn't know myself—the difficulty of it—the novelty of it—the drama of it—the appeal of a thing so powerful and so beautiful—the sport—the urge—the dream—the great adventure that would not pass. I couldn't say it all intelligibly in English, much less Spanish. So I pantomimed wheels around my head and said "cuckoo," and she understood.

Six o'clock had struck when my journalist guests insisted it was time I get busy and give them something to write about other than Panamanian cabarets. In fact they were so cold-blooded as to suggest I do some swimming.

"Must tell Isabella good-by," I insisted. "Isabella, my little wag, will you meet Cristobal Colon here to-morrow night—I mean to-night—at half past eight? My first voyage isn't going to be very long. If you will see me again, maybe I won't drown."

She understood—at least she understood "here" and "half past eight"—and "wag."

Then, fortified by her promise, in the early morning light I ran across the street, which faced the harbor, followed by the equally joyous squad of reporters. In the Strangers' Club built over the water, I left my clothes somewhere or other, dived off from the veranda and swam four miles without stopping across Colon Bay. Since Columbus discovered it in 1502 this bay had probably never known another swimmer in all the four hundred years of its dramatic history.

This unexpected and precipitous take-off had found the rowboat that was to accompany me entirely unprepared. There was much confusion. The crew, roused by the reporters, collected themselves and rushed about gathering oars, rifles, water bottles, my clothes, jumped into the boat and came hurrying after the departing swimmer.

Such a departure was very sensible. All the top-heavy preparations, all the worry over barracudas and sharks, over sinking and the humiliation of failure, were swept aside. I had no time for contemplation, no sense of danger. All that faded before the exhilaration of the cold salt water, before the joy of being on my way. I just swam with never a thought as to whether I was able to or not.

As for sharks and barracudas, we did not see a single one. Even so, the rowboat never wandered more than six feet away. In it, taut, sharp-eyed, rifle ready, eager for trouble, sat Sergeant Thomas Wright, six feet eight inches tall, two hundred pounds of tough physique, the finest shot, the faithfullest escort that ever graced the American Army. No man in Panama had as many sharpshooting medals as he. They would have covered him from head to foot. Small wonder the barracudas kept out of sight.

With such a guard, such a moral and physical support, I felt not unlike a small boy championed by a traffic cop. I was ready to defy sharks, barracudas, alligators, locks, lake—anything, with this cool eye, this grim fidelity, this deadly rifle, at my service. And yet because I was city-bred, had a college degree, spoke English grammatically, had a letter from the governor, this young giant treated me with the self-effacing deference with which he might have treated General Walker.

At the oars of my rowboat sat Quentin, a grinning Jamaica negro, who after ten years of service in the lighthouse department, knew every inch of the Canal. No man in Panama could have been so proud as Quentin when the authorities commissioned him to escort me.

It was ten o'clock by the time we had reached the entrance to the Canal proper where Mr. Green had begun his Sunday swims. The exhilaration of the first assault by now had worn off, and the reaction left me utterly spent. I'd not even had breakfast. So, noting the nearest buoy, I climbed aboard the *Daisy*, was rowed back to Colon, found a room at the hotel and slept till half past eight when I had to meet Queen Isabella at the American Cabaret.

She was there.

"*Ah-h-h, Señor Cristobal, buenas noches!* You swim?"

"*Si.* I swim. But I'm not much of a fish, Isabella," I said, sinking painfully into a cabaret chair.

"You dance with me?"

"Dance! Isabella, I'm so sore I can't even move."

However, dancing might limber my aching muscles. So I hobbled to the dance floor, feeling very much like one of the tin soldiers in the toy-shop ballet whose joints creak when at the magic hour he first comes to life. But, as in the same ballet, the stiffness gradually departed before the radiance of the mechanical French doll, until at midnight—that moment when the cuckoo clock warns the rioting toys that the hour of enchantment has gone—Isabella and I were having a whirl.

Next morning my troubles began in earnest. Once more deposited by the *Daisy* at the buoy marked the day before, I struck out up the channel toward the Gatun locks clearly visible three miles inland. Fresh and rested though I was, all efforts at progress were of no avail. No matter how hard I struggled, the trees and the buoys refused to slide past. It seemed I was dragging iron anchors behind me.

The explanation was simple enough. Every few minutes a ship steamed by, Gatun bound, and every time such a ship was either lifted from or lowered into the first chamber, the gates were opened and out rushed nine million cubic feet of water down the five-hundred-foot channel helter-skelter out into the Atlantic. And I was trying to swim not only up-stream but up-hill, for no sooner had the discharge from one lockage swept past but that another rushed after it.

In desperation we tried clinging to the shore line where the current was somewhat less severe. This was tempting the alligators beyond all reason, but I had to take the chance. Sometimes the palmettos hung overhead. Sometimes I bumped my knees on unexpected shallow spots. Dense jungles hid the shore. Herons and cranes rose from the muddy banks and flapped away at our approach. Parrots of a hundred hues screeched overhead. Swimming, resting, clinging to branches, I struggled inland through the tropical scenery, gaining scarcely half a mile an hour, cursing back at the passengers and crew that waved from the decks of ships sailing gallantly past, since I knew that each ship, soon after it saluted me so amiably, would send from the emptying lock chamber another mountain of water against which I must swim.

All morning and half the afternoon went by. We reached the old French canal, scarcely a hundred feet wide, at the junction where it intersects the present channel. What a ghostly relic of failure and despair that old canal presents! This short, stagnant, stretch of water is all the evidence left of the heroic but futile attempt to defy heaven and hell and join the oceans in the face of appalling ravages of yellow fever and malaria.

At length, late that afternoon, I reached the lowest gate of Gatun locks, having spent seven hours in advancing three miles.

And I was so exhausted that not even dancing could have revived the sun-scorched, cut, bruised, utterly discouraged wreck that fell into bed that night at Colon. In two days I had done only seven miles. I had forty-three more to go—and one more day like this, and the *S. S. Richard Halliburton* would have to retire even as the French.

But what miracles sleep can work! Next morning we went back to the battle-field ready to charge the Gatun locks and gain the fair haven of Gatun Lake.

Armed with my omnipotent letter from the governor, I knocked on the colossal outer gates and demanded entrance. The gate-keeper looked down from the control house and would have shooed me away with a rock, if I had not waved my imperial order.

"What nonsense is this?" he asked, seeing I insisted on standing by my rights.

And when he read my letter he could not decide which was the more insane, me or the governor.

"Do you realize what you're asking?" he said. He led me into the vast and awesome control room. "Do you see all this machinery?" It looked to me as if all the engines in the world had been collected in this place. It made me dizzy to try to comprehend the power it represented, and the silent, gleaming magic with which the greatest ship on earth, once this terrible power spoke with its deep-rumbling voice, was lifted like thistledown from the mud of the Atlantic channel into the fairy seas and fairy isles beyond the magician's shining castle.

"Do you see all this?" the magician repeated. "Look out the window there." The majestically beautiful thirty-thousand-ton *California,* the hugest passenger ship ever built in America, was descending the magic stairs. "It takes all this"—he swept his hand across the ocean of engines, down toward the *California* and the three one-thousand-foot chambers—"to lock you through. It will take nine million cubic feet of water three times displaced to raise you into the lake. It will take just as much horse-power as it takes to lower the *California.* And most important of all, it will take twice as long. For three hours you will hold up ship traffic in the Gatun locks. Do you think you are worth it?"

Did I think I was worth it! Was a microscopic earthworm justified in assaulting the gates of heaven and loudly demanding that they swing ajar?

Did I think I was worth it!

"Y-yes, sir!"

There was nothing else for the superintendent to do but acquiesce. The governor had commanded.

"Very well. But I have this to say, young man. You certainly have your nerve."

Even so, the lights were beginning to twinkle in his eyes.

"One other thing," he added, "before you start blocking the Canal. Don't think the locks are free toll. The governor doesn't say anything about waiving charges."

"Quite right, sir. Governor Walker and I agreed I was to pay like all other ships—according to my tonnage. I'm the *S. S. Richard Halliburton,* registered in Memphis, Tennessee. Length, five feet ten inches; beam, one foot; tonnage, one hundred and forty pounds—that's one-thirteenth of one ton."

"One-thirteenth of one ton, eh." He got down his tables. "You're the smallest ship in the history

I dived off from the veranda of the Strangers' Club and swam four miles without stopping, across Colon Harbor.

This vast thousand-foot lock chamber, and two more like it, were filled and emptied in order that an infinitesimal speck upon its surface might climb the magic stairs.

For the first time in the history of the Panama Canal, the locks were operated for a single individual.

Courtesy Paramount News and Associated Press

When the gate-jaws of the Miraflores lock were no more than fifteen feet apart, I plunged in from the *Daisy* and was catapulted out to sea.

of the Panama Canal." And then after a bit of calculation: "You owe me thirty-six cents."

Meanwhile several hundred people had lined the edges of the locks, for the newspapers had announced that this unique event would take place, and the curious had flocked, many from Colon, to see the first swimmer locked through.

Pushing past these spectators I rejoined the sergeant and Quentin who had been waiting in the rowboat before the haughty gates.

We gave the signal. Those Titanic steel jaws, each leaf seventy feet high, seventy feet wide and seven feet thick, weighing eight hundred thousand pounds each, peeped apart, and slowly swung wide to admit me.

I dived from the rowboat and swam into the over-towering chamber, with the *Daisy* not a foot away. I looked up and back and saw the monstrous doors silently swing closed, imprisoning me at the bottom of this sunken thousand-foot lake. It was a long thousand feet to swim. I should have liked to have one of the electric "mules" that tow ships through tow me, but I had no hooks or stanchions on which the hawsers could make fast.

As I moved along, great numbers of fish, sucked into the lock system from Gatun Lake, splashed all about me, frantic with alarm over the violent adventure of being swirled so unexpectedly from fresh water into salt. Innumerable hell-divers attracted by the hysterical fish scurried over the surface of the water glutting themselves on the unwary perch. Small alligators, water snakes, tarpons, every kind of life that inhabits the tropical lake, caught in the descending flood were now jumping and swimming about me.

Reaching the second set of gates, holding back the water in the lock above, we found everything ready for the magic elevator. Once more the magician in the tower raised his wand, and opened not the gates but the doors of the three great conduits, each the size of a Hudson River tube, which allows the water to flow in underneath from the upper lock into the lower. Gravity is the chief engine. When the levels of the two locks become the same, the gates open again and the ship glides on.

The inflow is very violent and caused such whirlpools and suctions that I was forced to hold on to the *Daisy* as the submarine geysers boiled up and lifted, lifted me.

It was a most dramatic experience, to look down the vast chamber and realize what was happening: this entire rock-walled lake, and two more like it, being filled and emptied that this infinitesimal speck upon its surface might climb the magic stairs! What sensation could approach that of feeling one's self carried up by these superhuman forces just as if one were the biggest battleship on earth, cruising forth to fight the battles of the nation, or a great liner laden with a thousand passengers.

For fifteen minutes the water surface rose. Then as before the steel jaws folded back and I found myself half-way along what was now a single chamber two thousand feet in length.

Once more I sideswiped on; and as before, the gates closed behind me. And again I was raised another thirty feet. Three times this process was repeated until I'd reached the level of the lake and swum out upon its calm blue waters.

Here, the first thing I encountered was the exasperated glances of the captains on the line of ships who had been killing time as best they could until the *S. S. Richard Halliburton* paddled out of their way and permitted traffic through the locks to resume its normal flow.

There was one glance however that was kindly, sympathetic—even proud for me. It came from a girl half-hidden by a parasol, one of the people who had lined the locks and watched me struggle through. This girl had followed me on out to the end of the breakwater that jutted into the lake, and when I swam around it, seeking the dock at the lakeside town of Gatun, she shouted down:

"*Buenos días, Señor Cristobal.* I am here."

This greeting came at a very opportune time. Of the gallery of five hundred or more people scarcely one had any sentiment for me other than ridicule. They had gathered expecting a sensational swimmer to rip across the waters, to give an exhibition of perfect form that would shame the sea lions.

And instead of a sea lion they had seen an amateur, with no swimming form whatsoever, sideswipe his way into the Olympian locks. The gallery had been let down, cheated. I was an impostor and a fraud. They all marched home indignant.

All—but Isabella.

She seemed to understand, understand that I was a land animal doing my utmost to be a dolphin, and she appreciated the difficulties I was having.

"Isabella," I said, crawling up beside her and hiding under her parasol to escape the scorching sun, "I'm a disgrace to the Panama Canal."

"Disgrace——?"

"Sure. Rotten—bum—punk."

"Ah no! Not punk. Not very good—not very bad. You reach Panama by and by."

"And when I do will you be there to meet me? I probably won't arrive till next year."

"Si."

"And we'll go to Kelly's Ritz and dance?"

"Si, si!"

"Then I'm on my way, my little wag." And I stood up to dive off.

"Momentito, Señor Cristobal. Mucho sol," she said, pointing to my shoulders and face scarlet from the sunburn that had begun the day before to torment me. *"Aqui*—have my parasol."

I accepted it laughingly and gave it for safe keeping to Sergeant Wright, who, as I plunged in for the twenty-four-mile grind across the lake, raised Isabella's pink sunshade above his pine-tree frame and settled back into the boat to watch for crocodiles.

CHAPTER X

ONLY FORTY MILES TO GO

A GLANCE at the map will show that the channel across the lake makes a fifty-degree bend. Quentin suggested we might save a mile by not following the ship's route along the two sides of the broad triangle, but swimming across the base of it.

And so for two days we carved a channel of our own, skirting the islands, getting farther and farther from communications and headquarters, into ever wilder and ever stranger waters. Across the lake, glimpses of the never-ending stream of ships, following the buoy-lined course, could be seen beyond the intervening isles. Near-by the forests of gaunt, dead trees raised their skinny arms to heaven, remonstrating against the slow strangulaton. They brought to mind the fact that this inland sea over which we moved covered what was not long ago dense jungles, valleys where the streams tumbled over the rocks, meadows where the cattle grazed, villages, farms, roads, the trail across which once tramped the Spanish conquerors and once flowed the incalculable riches of Peru—all buried now eighty feet beneath the flood, with only green islets that once were the green hills, and only stark skeletons where the jungle giants had stood.

But how fascinating was this ghostly forest. Not all the trees were barren. Many were festooned with moss and trailing water plants, ferns, flowering vines, clusters of orchids. Floating islands dotted the expanse, and masses of water hyacinths, the scourge of the Canal, had to be warily swum round.

Animating this tangle of life and death were innumerable birds. Cormorants by the thousand roosted in the dead branches. Pelicans were everywhere, white herons, kingfishers, gulls, squawking parrots. Manatees have been seen swimming where I swam. And here we entered alligator country. But these brutes were apparently terrified by the sergeant's medals and dived out of sight at our approach.

With this endless, changing spectacle, the miles did not seem long. There were times, however, when the land receded and left wide bays of deep and open water across which it was a mechanical process without relief, requiring scores, hundreds, thousands of strokes to propel me to the next landmark. Then too, the cold gradually penetrating my unblubbered frame would become very bitter. During these long and tedious hours I seemed to have no thought, no feeling, no realization of what I was doing or why. I was kept going by a half-conscious dynamo of will-power that had been turned on and drove my arms and legs through their revolutions.

Thus we crawled across the blue sheen of Gatun Lake, never quite too engrossed with the struggle to be aware of the painted beauty of the deep-hued waters, of the riot of flowers on the islands' shores, of the castled clouds against the tropical sky, of the blue and emerald fairyland that stretched on and on into the summer afternoons.

At sunset of the second day in the lake we reached Bohio Point where, having crossed the base of the triangle described by the bend in the ship's channel, we once more struck the great highway. I had swum eight hours that day, but was determined to make the point before quitting for the night. When still a thousand feet from it, something very hard and very heavy crashed against my side. I let out a wild yelp. The sergeant leaped to his feet and in a flash I was yanked out of the water into the boat. We saw nothing. But Quentin believed it was an awkward alligator we had bumped into by accident, or one that had nosed too close out of curiosity.

Needless to say, we decided I'd swum enough that day. We hitched on to a passing motor-launch, and beneath the rising moon sped across the twelve miles of lake back to Gatun. Quentin was very talkative. He regaled us with harrowing tales of saurian ravages—how only the week before a half-grown boy, in broad day, had been dragged off a floating log and devoured; how a canoe containing three Indians had been overturned up the Chagres River, and how all three were heard to scream with agony and seen to disappear amid a pool of blood. Pretty stories!

Next morning, still alarmed over the adventure of the afternoon before, the sergeant gave me an army belt to which was buckled a sheath containing a murderous knife. This weapon worn in the water did not increase my speed any, but it gave me a very welcome feeling of security. For himself he brought along a six-inch dagger. His idea was that if a cayman seized me the rifle would be useless, since in the mix-up he'd probably shoot me and not the alligator, but with the knives we might by slashing at the brute's eyes persuade him to retreat. This was all theory, mind you. It has rarely, if ever, been practised.

Back at Bohio Point the long stretch up the ship channel lay before us. All morning the procession sailed past. The crews and the passengers lined the rails, for the newspapers had printed daily bulletins regarding the progress of our stunt and every ship was on the lookout. When they came abreast, each ship saluted me with a loud blast from the whistle, and the crews, particularly the American, hallooed and waved until I almost felt I was doing something difficult instead of loitering along on this private little excursion in my absurd sideswiping fashion, and being much more concerned with the sights and the colors, the ships, the passing pageantry, than I was with getting any place.

When again night overtook us we had progressed too far from Gatun to consider returning, and so took advantage of the hospitality of the near-by radio station, run by the Navy Department. The wife of one of the officers there was called upon in a nursing capacity. The sunburn from which I had been suffering since the first day's swim had steadily grown worse until now my entire back was one great blister. And this had become infected.

That night I had a high fever, with the pain from the burn so intense that sleep was out of the question. It looked as if my expedition was going to be wrecked by this totally unexpected enemy—not exhaustion, not alligators, not inability to swim the fifty miles, but the actinic ray of the tropical sun.

This ray seemed to penetrate the water and attack me even though I was completely submerged. My shaven head and my face I had thought to protect with oil, but supposed the water would protect the rest of me. It was a disastrous supposition, as my swollen, blistered flesh revealed at the radio station.

Next morning as I couldn't sleep anyway, we started off before dawn, plastered in petroleum from head to foot. Even so, every stroke was torment. Speed, already reduced by my belt and alligator knife, was now cut in half. And then, in keeping with the superstition that troubles come not singly, a sudden and violent rainstorm broke upon us accompanied by high winds and a fog so dense we could not see thirty feet. This happened just as the first rush of ships, coming from either end of the Canal, met and began to pass each other in this narrow channel.

The first tempestuous gust had driven the *Daisy* away from me. A ship loomed out of the mist not a hundred feet ahead bearing straight down on top of us. I swam desperately to one side—the wrong side. Quentin shouted to me to turn about. I couldn't. The freighter was upon us. At the last second it saw the rowboat and, to avoid a collision, veered violently *toward me.*

Desperately I struggled to escape, and succeeded by only a very few feet. I felt the churn of the propeller as the monster scraped past.

Completely exhausted by this last encounter with

the ship and the storm, I pulled over to the bank and crawled ashore. Any more swimming that day was out of the question. We marked the spot and rowed on into Gamboa, at the mouth of the Chagres, only a mile away. Here, in the home of a Canal official, all that afternoon and night I nursed along my sunburn.

Next morning, arrayed in a black shirt, smeared from top to toe with oil and wearing water goggles, I returned to the spot where the storm had struck us, swam on back past the river mouth and entered the eight-mile-long Culebra Cut which led Pacific-ward.

At lunch time that day we were off the Zone penitentiary and decided to call upon the warden and beg a meal.

"You're just in time," he said. "The men are marching into the dining room right now. Help yourself to a seat."

So the sergeant and I marched in too and, asking one of the convicts at the end of the long bench to move over, sat down with the ninety prisoners. Our visit completely stopped the flow of penitential soup—this gigantic soldier body-guarding a wild-looking, sun-scarified, lard-smeared, shaven-headed, begoggled apparition.

The warden announced during the meal that I was not Number Ninety-one, but an amateur swimmer negotiating the Canal. Whereupon the gentleman at my left rudely suggested that I'd come to the wrong asylum.

That afternoon the alligators began in earnest. The Chagres River brings them down by the dozen into the Canal from the interior, and consequently they are notoriously thick for a few miles in either direction from the river's mouth.

The first victim of the sergeant's deadly rifle was encountered a few hundred yards beyond the prison. The brute, all of eight feet long, was dozing on the mud bank. So noiselessly had we approached that he had not noticed the boat, nor we him, until less than a hundred yards divided us. Without warning, a sudden bark came from the army rifle. I looked to the shore and saw an alligator writhing in death agony, his white belly flashing in the sun as he thrashed into the water. A trickle of blood, flowing from a submerged source, rose to the surface, moving down-stream with the current.

As Gold Hill loomed in sight the battle grew in violence. Within one mile the sergeant had hit three enemies. Always they writhed, always they lashed their great tails in their dying moments, but always, even though their brains were drilled and death upon them, they managed somehow to reach the water and deprive us of any trophies.

And then came Gold Hill itself, and we forgot the alligators. The sensation of swimming beneath that soaring six-hundred-foot cliff which had been torn asunder by human hands was as awesome as the journey through the locks themselves. One is appalled at the very sight of this great void where once a mountain stood. Here, even more than with the locks, one has the feeling that this is the work of gods, not men.

I crawled ashore at the base of the hill, put on my boots and climbed to the summit. The *Daisy* seemed only a speck on the ribbon below. The toy ships streamed past. At our feet lay the Pacific locks, seen in miniature from the heights above —Panama City ten miles away—and, at last, the great South Sea.

That night when I swam up to the Pedro Miguel breakwater we had to steer by the harbor lights. I was well ready to quit, for I had put nine miles behind us that day.

Next morning, the eighth morning, the last morning of the swim, a good part of the white population of Panama City seemed to be on hand. The single Pedro Miguel lock swept me through in record time. In the one-mile-wide Miraflores Lake that separates the two Pacific-lock systems the wind was behind me and I simply galloped across. By now too, I had accustomed my muscles

And then came Culebra Cut. The sensation of swimming beneath that soaring six-hundred-foot cliff was as awesome as the journey through the locks.

Courtesy Panama-Pacific Steamship Co.

The point in the main channel where I was overtaken by the storm and almost run over in the confusion of ship traffic.

The S. S. *Richard Halliburton* docks at Balboa after the fifty-mile voyage, fifteen pounds lighter than at the beginning.

and lungs to the labor of swimming, and was able to make twice the speed with twice the endurance I had enjoyed at first. Several of my friends from the marine flying forces wheeled about overhead in their seaplanes, glided up to greet me, and asked if I didn't want a tow. It was a particularly brilliant summer day, and the sunshine, and the deep blue lake, the passing ships, the seaplanes, the crowds of brightly-dressed people, gave the whole scene a carnival aspect.

The Miraflores locks are even more stupendous than those at Gatun. The gates here are eighty-five feet high and doubly strong to resist the tremendous Pacific tides.

When the water in the last chamber had been lowered to sea level, and these last and greatest gates of all began to swing wide, I plunged in from the *Daisy* and, when the jaws were no more than fifteen feet apart, was catapulted through them by the rush of the swirling water, for the tide was going full speed out to sea.

The last six miles were easiest of all. We raced down-hill and into the harbor of Balboa, until I had only a quarter of a mile more to go. I could look ashore and see the docks crowded with people —and beyond to Ancon Hill, where I'd resolved to take the plunge. Now it was all over, almost. I'd done it, in my blundering way, almost—quarter of a mile more and there'd be no more cold, no more sunburn, no more weary arms. I was very happy. I was a little proud. . . .

And then came the fall.

There was a wild splash in the water ten feet ahead, a wild yell from the sergeant, and I was dragged into the boat with such violence I thought the *Daisy* had run over me. Barracudas! Two of them at once, "big as elephants," had leaped out of the water square ahead of us with a m-m-m-m-lunch! look in their eyes. I never saw them, for they had departed as suddenly as they appeared. But the agitated looks on the faces of Quentin and the sergeant were eloquent enough.

What was I to do! Forty-nine and three-quarters miles I had swum—only a few hundred yards more to go—several thousand people watching from the docks—and at the very gates to the goal I had struggled for and prayed for during the eight interminable days, I crawl in a rowboat and row home!

On the other hand—those horrible teeth, those jaws that maimed for life. . . .

It was a miserable dilemma.

So I compromised. I went back into the water but swam *beneath* the revolving oar, almost touching the boat's side. The sergeant in a cold perspiration from anxiety, stood up and lashed the water ahead and behind with—in desperate need —our pink parasol, letting forth with each lash a shout that must have driven even the barracudas in terror out to sea.

And thus did this yelling, ocean-thrashing, parasol-wielding, oar-hugging, barracuda-fleeing outfit sideswipe across the line.

A hundred arms reached down to pull me ashore. On one of them were Isabella's bracelets.

And that night we all went to Kelly's Ritz and took along the sergeant and the little wag. We ordered all the champagne in Panama, and we danced and we sang, and we laughed and we lived, for to-morrow we were *not* going to swim the Panama Canal, we were not going to drown. We were going to climb back up to Ancon Hill, to seek new challenges, to find more new adventures that would not pass. Already the Panama Canal was fading fast; already the peaks of Darien were dreaming in the distance, and must be climbed; the treasure of the Inca kings was hidden in Peru, waiting to be found; and in the West the Hesperides were beckoning. These things seemed all important now, all beautiful, for

It is the things we have, that go;
The things we can not have, remain.

SONNET ON FIRST LOOKING INTO CHAPMAN'S HOMER

Much have I travell'd in the realms of gold,
And many goodly states and kingdoms seen;
Round many western islands have I been
Which bards in fealty to Apollo hold.
Oft of one wide expanse had I been told
That deep-brow'd Homer ruled as his demesne,
Yet did I never breathe its pure serene
Till I heard Chapman speak out loud and bold:
Then felt I like some watcher of the skies
When a new planet swims into his ken;
Or like stout Cortez when with eagle eyes
He stared at the Pacific—and all his men
Look'd at each other with a wild surmise—
Silent, upon a peak in Darien.

JOHN KEATS.

CHAPTER XI

UPON A PEAK IN DARIEN

It is unfortunate that in the one great poem which mentions the discovery of the Pacific Ocean, Keats made the mistake of naming Cortez as the discoverer instead of Vasco Nuñez de Balboa who alone deserves the full measure of credit.

This event is almost as important to history as Columbus' first voyage to the New World. It took place in September, 1513, twenty years after the great admiral landed on San Salvador. In that month Balboa, at the head of one hundred and ninety Spanish adventurers, set out to march across the Isthmus of Panama. He was seeking the empire of the Incas which the Panama Indians had told him was fabulously rich in gold.

To reach it Balboa had learned that he must first march inland from the Atlantic shores through what is now the province of Darien, until he came to another great ocean. Then in ships he must sail many suns along the coast.

The other ocean—so the Indians said—lay to the south, only fifty miles away.

Fifty miles! A two, at most three, days' journey. So it would seem. But it took Balboa's expedition twenty-three days of relentless struggle to cross the Isthmus of Panama.

When one sees the country through which the Spaniards had to cut their way, it seems remarkable that they ever crossed at all. Then, as now, this part of the isthmus was one endless tangle of jungle. And the march was undertaken when the rainy season was upon the land, the swamps overflowing, the rivers turned to floods.

Through this pathless wilderness the expedition plowed its way. Hostile Indians contested every step. Porters fell by the wayside in scores. The weight of the steel armor became ever more unendurable. The one hundred and ninety Spaniards were soon cut to less than half that number.

But for Balboa there could be no retreat. Ahead lay the mysterious ocean, an ocean no white man had ever seen, and, with the discovery of it, immortality—and the treasure realms beyond. He had staked his very life on this one throw. By all the saints, he was going to look upon the Southern Sea!

And at length on the twentieth day of marching the guides led the little army up the slopes of a densely forested mountain range. As the weary

Spaniards neared the top—only sixty-seven remained—the Indians told Balboa that from the summit of this mountain he could see his long-sought goal.

Breathlessly he hurried ahead—reached the crest—and behold!—sparkling in the summer sun, blue as indigo, lay El Mar del Sur, the greatest ocean in the world.

Speechless with wonder, Balboa beckoned to his followers. They came and stood by his side. With eagle eyes the indomitable leader

> "*. . . stared at the Pacific—and all his men*
> *Look'd at each other with a wild surmise—*
> *Silent, upon a peak in Darien.*"

This happened on the twenty-fifth of September, 1513. It was my own good fortune on a twenty-fifth of September to climb the peak in Darien in quest of the very same prospect that had brought Balboa his great moment.

To-day the province of Darien, though within one hundred miles of the Panama Canal, is wilder and more desolate than it was four hundred years ago. The Indians there are not one-tenth as numerous as in Balboa's day. One who seeks the peak must be prepared for all the hardships Balboa endured. And there is no promise of a Land of Gold to spur one on.

Even so I was not discouraged. Ever since first reading Keats' sonnet I had wanted to stand upon the peak and rediscover the Southern Sea. All the more reason to go if the region were primeval, if Balboa's mountain were still inviolate.

To assist in my investigations I called upon the foremost historian in Panama. He assured me the great discoverer first saw the Pacific from the summit of Mount Piri, a five-thousand-foot mountain and the highest for miles around, situated squarely in the middle of the isthmus.

My destination was then settled.

Once I had recovered from my Canal swim, a small steamer took me from Panama City down the coast to San Miguel Bay. From here I hired an Indian boatman to transport me in a dugout forty miles up the Tuira River to the village of El Real in sight of which Mount Piri stood, fifteen miles away.

In El Real nobody had ever heard about Balboa or ever climbed Piri. But I did find one grizzled old negro who thought he knew the best way to the top, and under his guidance I plunged into the wilderness.

The first day, having progressed five miles along a trail, we came at sunset upon an Indian hut which offered shelter for the night. The Indian family living there, a father, mother and two grown sons, appeared as untouched by the outside world as were their ancestors when Balboa passed that way. Except for a gee-string each, they were entirely nude. For beds they used only cane benches built a foot above the cane floor. All about the hut the forest stretched dense and dripping, waiting with hungry, evil eyes for the family to relax its eternal vigilance that it might pounce upon the tiny clearing and devour every trace of human habitation.

When night came we had no light other than the open fire. Once that had died our primeval little hut was left to dream in the jungle darkness.

I had been asleep on one of the cane benches for two hours—under a mosquito netting I'd brought along, you may be sure—when a most alarming adventure befell me. I was suddenly and startlingly awakened by something heavy and yet soft crawling over my knees.

All I could think of was rattlesnakes. In the blackness I lay like ice, not daring to move, for I was trapped on my bench by the netting.

This four pounds of clutching, terrifying, live thing from out of the jungle depths had crept up to my chest, though my heart was pounding hard enough to knock the intruder off had he not stuck his claws into my shirt.

Claws? Then it wasn't a rattlesnake.

Perhaps it was a vampire bat preparing to plunge its teeth into my throat.

I could stand the suspense no longer. Taut with fright I moved my trembling fingers toward this dreadful visitation.

I touched something furry. Then it wasn't a bat. It had a long tail—it had stiff little ears. As my fingers moved cautiously over the body it began to purr furiously.

Some sort of a cat!—though certainly not a domestic cat. It was too solid, too strong, too bold. In any case the animal was friendly, for a hard, scraping tongue began to lick my fingers; a warm body snuggled down beside me.

There, whatever it was, it seemed to be satisfied, and as the rain outside had brought a chill to the air I was quite willing to allow the purring hot-water bottle to rest close by. So with this strange and unseen bedfellow I tucked in the disturbed mosquito netting to keep out any more unannounced visitors, and slept, befriended and comforted, till morning.

At dawn my furry comrade disturbed me again by walking once more up and down my chest. I awoke to look straight into the face of a baby ocelot.

Ocelots are the commonest variety of jungle cat found in Panama. They most resemble the leopard, without growing as large or having such a royal coat of spots. The mother of my little playmate, I found, had been killed a few weeks before by the Indians in whose hut I was residing, and the baby captured to be brought up as a pet. His apartment was a box among the rafters. From there, driven out by the unusual coolness of the night, he had come to me seeking warmth and protection, and had made his first appearance in the somewhat startling manner I have related.

After our midnight rapprochement the Thomas cat and I became inseparable friends, and the next day when the two Indian brothers, who were to act as porters, and Sam and I started for Piri, I did not have the heart to leave him behind. So I put a cord about his neck and carried him with me in the tracks of Balboa.

The summit of the peak was still ten miles away, and there was not the faintest suggestion of a trail. We had to hack one of our own. Each of my three companions carried a heavy machete—a three-pound kitchen knife used everywhere in Latin America—and with these weapons tunneled through seas of vines, roots and underbrush. I brought up the rear, carrying the rifle and the cat.

It was a beautiful jungle—for one day at least—filled with flowers and color, bright parrots and noble trees. True, it poured rain interminably, and we had to plunge through water waist-deep in crossing the flooded streams.

By the first night I figured we had chopped our way four miles. It was necessary to stop well before dark and build a camp. Beneath a shelter of palmetto leaves we cooked our supper and rested comfortably though the rain poured down in torrents. As before, Tommy curled up under my chin and purred himself to sleep.

Next morning we struggled on up the mountain, sympathizing more and more with Balboa and his armor-laden men. The red bugs had assaulted me in legions until I was on fire from head to foot . . . but suppose on top of these itching insects I had been wearing a coat of mail. . . .

All during the second day of our march the slope grew steeper, progress slower, and Tommy, riding on my shoulder, ever heavier. For his own part, the cat seemed to be enjoying the adventure thoroughly—and indeed why not, since he never had to walk a step and was kept supplied with nice green parrots felled by my rifle.

There was little sleep the second night. The sand flies and mosquitoes had bitten me in a thou-

Tommy, the baby ocelot, that adopted me in Darien and with me climbed Balboa's peak to rediscover the Pacific.

Photograph by Lieutenant Hayne Boyden

The view of the Pacific from the summit of the Peak in Darien. This was the picture that opened before Balboa's eyes on the morning of September 25th, 1513, when he first beheld the "South Sea."

sand places. All night long I tossed in torment. But so had Balboa—though that thought gave me small relief.

To-morrow, however, would compensate for everything—to-morrow was the twenty-fifth of September. We were very near the top, and at ten o'clock I would behold the Southern Sea.

As ten o'clock approached we neared the summit, up the ridge facing El Real, along which Balboa must likewise have climbed. I could picture him hurrying ahead of his companions, reaching the eminence, and staring, with eagle eyes, spellbound, at the great ocean. I, too, hurried on and reached the summit of the sacred peak in Darien. Here Balboa, at ten o'clock September twenty-fifth, more than four hundred years ago, stood alone. Here he made his great discovery. . . . A gap in the trees opened to the south. With pounding pulse I turned to gaze at the Mar del Sur—the Southern Sea—the illimitable Pacific. . . .

Nowhere was it to be seen!

CHAPTER XII

EL MAR DEL SUR

I STARED a second time. That ocean *had* to be there! It *must* be there!

But it wasn't, only endless leagues of smoky jungle—jungle, to the utmost horizon. I might have been in the heart of darkest Africa. Nor was it the weather. At the moment the sun was shining brightly. Nor were my eyes to blame. There simply wasn't any Pacific!

It is recorded Balboa sank on his knees before the wonder of the landscape before him. I sank down on a fallen tree, weak from the reaction that now followed the intoxication of the idea that had lured me to the summit of this crazy mountain.

For the first time in three days I looked myself over. The thorns had ripped the sleeves out of my clothes, and my bare arms were a mass of scratches and insect bites. The diet of bananas and parrots now found me ill and faint. I'd not enjoyed one dry garment in thirty-six hours. The only thing about me intact was Tommy. He squirmed down from my shoulder, stretched and yawned, as much as to say he'd never seen such an idiot as myself, splashing around in this wet jungle so far from home when there were perfectly good parrakeets right at the front door. As I sat on the tree trunk cursing Balboa and all the demented historians who had sent me off on this preposterous expedition, Tommy looked at me rather dolefully. And no wonder—it had begun to rain again!

But rain or no rain, red bugs or no red bugs, I was going to have me my peak in Darien. Obviously Balboa never climbed Mount Piri, history books to the contrary, for it is forty miles from the ocean and thirty from his logical line of march. He had blazed a trail straight across the isthmus to San Miguel Bay. It was into the waters of this bay that he waded—authentic history states that much—to claim the new ocean for the King of Spain. He himself named the bay San Miguel. A range of hills some thousand feet high slopes inland from its shores. From the top of *this* range the Pacific was revealed to him. Nothing could have been more evident had I stopped to consider it.

So back down the river I went, still guided by Sam and still accompanied by the cat which I had secured from the Indians in exchange for a shirt with the buttons off and two cans of baked beans.

Reaching the bay again I found the radio station operated by the United States Navy. With this as my headquarters I took a canoe to the inland shores up from which rises Balboa's ridge, and once more engaged in a battle with the jungle. All of another day and night, still carrying my mascot, Sam and I hacked our way across the savannas that spread between the ridge and the water, and on up the slopes.

It was again at ten o'clock in the morning when we approached the top. Dense foliage hid everything. I climbed a tree—with some difficulty, as I wanted Tommy to share the great moment and insisted on lugging him along—pushed aside a branch, and there was my South Sea at last.

Imagination was turned loose as I rested in my treetop and looked, perhaps the first visitor since Balboa stood near-by, out over the same seascape that he had seen. As if in compensation for his sacrifices, Providence, realizing there was no denying him his ocean, led him to it at a spot that for concentrated lyrical beauty has few rivals from Alaska to Cape Horn. All his physical wretchedness must have gone away as this glorious sight burst upon his eyes—blue, blue jungles, and the green waters studded with a hundred island jewels. He saw the colors in the bay, the tropic shores, the palms along the line of foam, the painted sky, the battlemented clouds upon the horizon of a great calm sea. It was this beauty and this majesty that silenced the conquistador. In that first enchanted moment he forgot it *was* discovery.

Back at the radio station, I found that Lieutenant Hayne Boyden, of the United States Marine Corps Aviation Force, had flown down the hundred miles from Panama City in his seaplane to take me back.

We climbed aboard, the lieutenant and the Thomas cat and I. Then, Balboa's spirit looking from his peak beheld a miracle that must have made him stare more eagle-eyed than he had ever stared on earth. He saw this gigantic, gleaming bird that had appeared, like the magic thing it was, out of the heavens, rush with a roar across the waters of the bay, take flight, wheel higher and higher, and sail straight for the summit of his ridge.

From within the seaplane Tommy and I glanced down upon the familiar scene. There was the peak below, there the waters of the bay into which the discoverer waded in the name of his king; beyond, the Southern Sea that led on to the Land of Gold.

The thought came to me that the nations given birth by Balboa's discovery have grown rich and powerful; that ten thousand ships sail upon the waters he added to the map, and yet to this man who through his own magnificent courage gave the world so much, there is, in all the lands of both the Americas, not one monument.

With this fact in mind I looked back at the ridge top as our plane swept out across the great ocean, and pictured a spot, on the backbone of the immortal hill, cleared of jungle, and standing there in heroic size hewn from eternal stone, the indomitable figure of Vasco Nuñez de Balboa, staring at the Pacific with eagle eyes, surrounded by his men looking at each other with a wild surmise—silent, upon a peak in Darien.*

* It may interest readers to know that Tommy, the ocelot, is now in the Bronx Zoo. I have paid him several visits, but our relations are not what they were. He has reached his full growth and no longer remembers me.

CHAPTER XIII

INCA GOLD

SEVENTEEN years have passed since the discovery of the Pacific. It is now 1530. But the Land of Gold is still inviolate, for though the new-found Ocean has become a familiar field for Spanish navigators, no Spanish captain has yet reached the empire Balboa set out to subdue.

Balboa himself has been beheaded—as a reward for his contributions to the Spanish realm. His first lieutenant has taken his place as leader in the conquest of Peru.

This lieutenant had been one of those to make the first desperate crossing of the Isthmus of Panama. His name followed Balboa's own on the list of Spaniards present at the great moment on the peak in Darien. His name was Francisco Pizarro.

Fate directed that this extraordinary man should seize the torch from the discoverer's dying hands and carry on the explorations which the executed leader had begun so magnificently. But seventeen years of defeat had to be endured before Pizarro actually landed on the shores of the Land of Gold.

There he found that the tidings of Peru which he had heard had not exaggerated the country's riches. Indeed, he soon saw that this land, densely populated by a highly civilized race of Indians called the Incas, was unbelievably rich in gold.

The Incas themselves had small appreciation of the yellow metal. In their country it was so commonplace and so bountiful that they splashed it about with lavish extravagance. As they worshiped the Sun, gold was particularly adaptable to their religious uses, and as a symbol of the Sun God, gleamed from temple wall and altar. In the temple gardens the flowers and the trees were gold flowers and gold trees. Gold—gold—gold—it was beautiful—it gladdened the eye—it warmed the heart—but that it was worth sailing five thousand miles across the sea for, worth fighting for and dying for, never entered the benighted Incas' heads.

But to the Spaniards it was a crime against both heaven and earth that such oceans of treasure should remain in the hands of infidel Indians. And to correct this situation, Pizarro, with his army of one hundred and sixty-five adventurers, assaulted a well-armed nation of eleven million people. That the conquest succeeded is one of history's military miracles.

Scarcely had the Spaniards landed on the shores

of Peru, when the Inca King, Atahualpa, was enticed into the Spanish camp on some treacherous pretext of hospitality and, after the slaughter of his helpless retinue, made prisoner.

It was soon evident to the Inca what had inspired Pizarro's invasion—the seizure of this shining worthless stuff the local interior decorators used to brighten up the temples. "If that is what you want," he exclaimed, "I'll fill this very room with it if you will give me back my liberty."

A roomful of gold! Such an order would take all the gold in the universe—but no more than Atahualpa had at his command.

For days the treasure poured in. The golden flood climbed swiftly up the walls, yet not swiftly enough for the gold-crazed Spaniards. And so to speed things along a bit they strangled Atahualpa.

This murder by no means profited them; in fact it had quite the opposite effect. The news of the king's death spread across Peru, and the hundred laden llama trains still en route to the fatal room were halted—since there was no longer a king to ransom—and their precious burdens hidden away in caves, in the forests, in the mountains, from the on-marching Spaniards. Likewise the temple vessels, the golden gardens, the incalculable treasures that had not gone to rescue Atahualpa, were carried off into the impenetrable Andean cañons, and buried, abandoned, destroyed—anything to deprive the Spanish demons of the fruits of their conquest.

Exactly what happened to all this untold treasure has ever been a mystery. For centuries people have searched for it—several expeditions are searching for it now—up and down the vast heights and depths of the Andes. Enough has been found to keep the fires of hope and faith burning bright.

And it was my own good fortune, after centuries of resolute treasure hunters had failed, after men had spent their lives and met their deaths in vain pursuit of this fabled gold, to stumble upon, to blunder into, to find by a miraculous twist of luck—in a remote cañon—in Peru . . .

But let me tell the story from the first.

Having returned to Panama City from the peak in Darien, I reëquipped myself, and with Balboa dead, took up the pursuit of Pizarro. Sailing from Panama City as he had sailed, I drifted on along the west coast of South America, past Colombia and Equador, to the land of the ancient Incas.

Very shortly I found myself deep into the country, climbing over the Andes and down into one of the steaming, densely-forested Amazonian cañons which legend has sprinkled with the buried treasure. This particular cañon I was following had once been an Inca stronghold and is marked even to-day with relics of their civilization. It was along its depths that I made the great discovery.

This particular day had followed a week of endless rain. Now, with the return of the sunshine, myriads of jungle creatures—Sun worshipers even as the early Peruvians—sang and hummed and flew and crawled wherever the warmth and the light broke through the steaming forest.

The heat of the morning had made me very thirsty. To find a water supply well above the contaminations of the valley floor, I left the trail and plunged upward through the overhanging jungle alongside a tiny stream that tumbled down the slope. The source was not far away. I stooped to drink.

But as I did, a quick metallic glint, finding its way through the trees, caught my eye. The glitter made me hesitate, look twice, leave the spring behind and push through the underbrush toward the curious gleaming. It multiplied from one to a thousand gleams as I approached a sun-flooded glade from which the strange light came. One unobstructed glance from the edge of the wood, and what I saw made my pulse turn somersault.

The entire surface of the glade was buried under a glittering canopy of copper gold that quivered in the sunlight—gold, gold, tons of it, yards of it, a billion dollars' worth of it, all spread across this secret depository in the woods. Had I found the hidden Inca treasure that treasure seekers for four centuries had sacrificed their lives to find—the gold from the temples and the palaces which the Incas spirited away when Pizarro came? For four hundred years the world had wondered where these riches, once seen in such fabulous abundance, had all vanished to . . . and here by accident, in this ancient valley, a hundred yards from a path trod every day, I had blundered on them, melted down to coin form, and poured in one vast sheet across the cañon side.

Strange the gold should still be burnished after so many years of rain and sun. Strange the way it throbbed and trembled, quick with life, fresh, glowing, electric. I rubbed my eyes. Perhaps I was bewitched.

No, my eyes saw clear, saw gold, such as Balboa or Pizarro never hoped to see. Aladdin and his famous lamp never had as much; I was as rich as Atahualpa. I broke into the glade. I would fill my pockets, my hands; swim in it, dance in it, be drunk from it. Into the sea of gold I plunged. . . .

Magic! The treasure, each countless coin, came suddenly to life, leaped from the earth in a blinding cloud, blotted out the scene, hid the sun, rose and fell and buried me in flame.

And then I knew. I had not found the Inca gold at all. I had found the butterflies.

CHAPTER XIV

HOW TO MEET A PRESIDENT

THE President of Peru and I fell upon our hands and knees, and all but bumped our heads together. We were looking for my collar-button.

He laughed merrily—and then I did. And now we're friends for life.

It happened this way:

My very first day in Lima [I had come straight to Lima from Panama; the discovery of the Inca gold happened later.] I called on Mr. Alexander Moore, the American Minister. I hadn't intended to call—not until I got dressed up in my one dark suit. But Mr. Moore caught me, yellow corduroy trousers, blue sweater, and with my new beard in some disarray, asking the porter at what time that afternoon the ambassador received callers.

"Looking for me?" he asked abruptly, stepping out of his Rolls-Royce that had rolled up to the door.

"N-no, sir—yes, sir!"

"No—yes! What do you mean?"

"I mean I was asking your porter what time you might receive me this afternoon—so I could come back properly dressed up."

"You are funny-looking. Trying to grow a beard?" he said, pushing me into his office and into a chair.

I had thought my beard was already very elegant, and felt piqued that he questioned its tangibility.

"It's only three weeks old," I apologized. "One more week and I'll look like the Smith Brothers."

"Do you always wear crazy clothes like that?"

"Not always. My wardrobe does include a dark and very dignified suit. But it's being polished up at present for a formal call on you this afternoon. I must admit, though, I haven't a silk hat like yours to go with it. In fact I haven't any hat at all."

"Then you'd better come along with me," Mr. Moore said, standing up again. "I'm going to a Peruvian tailor for a fitting. You evidently need to meet him."

He dismissed the imperial chariot, and together we strolled down the street to the shop.

As the tailor pinned and chalked my amiable companion's new blue serge suit (brought, I suspect, as a diplomatic gesture to Peru), he chatted away at a great rate.

"By the way, what brought you to Lima?" he asked. "—Entomology—archeology—or mineralogy?"

"None of 'em. It was claustrophobia."

"*What's* that?"

"Not very sure myself. I think it means an abnormal fear of being compressed by a lot of people. At least that's why I came to South America—the 'empty continent.' But I came to Lima to meet you."

"Hum! What else?" he asked, putting on his vest.

"The president. He's the one South American I'm most eager to know."

"He's the one South American best worth your knowing. Few of us in the United States realize what a commanding dictator Augusto Leguia is. He has the iron will of Pizarro himself, and more cunning, and better statesmanship. Don't think I'm just using big words. I think he is the most romantic figure among the rulers of the world to-day—and he weighs only ninety-seven pounds."

We had walked back to the legation again, Mr. Moore singing the president's praises. At the front door, as I prepared to say good-by, the ambassador turned to me in his abrupt manner.

"You say you're a writer? What have *you* written?"

I mentioned the name of a book or two.

"Oh, I've read those," he exclaimed. "They were perfectly terrible. You must come to dinner to-night—half past eight. No! Come to lunch right now, and dinner too. We'll plan for you to meet the president."

Thus it was I found myself, bearded and corduroyed, in boots and sweater, lunching in state with the American Minister one hour after I'd had the exceedingly good fortune to make that genial gentleman's acquaintance.

Next morning the 'phone rang early: "Hello—Halliburton? This is Moore. Come to the legation at once. I'll take you out to the flying field. A new airplane mail line is being inaugurated and President Leguia will be on hand. You can meet him there."

I threw on the dark suit and galloped to the legation. The royal Rolls took us out to the new plane that awaited the president's arrival. Presently, surrounded by police, the diminutive dictator of Peru, almost lost in his own motor, was driven up. An immaculate little figure emerged—sharp black eyes, gray mustache, distinguished, poised, instantly arresting, dressed with the utmost care. Immediately Mr. Moore, pulling me through the dense crowd, joined him.

After a few words of greeting, the ambassador pushed me forward.

"Mr. President, this is a friend of mine, Mr. Richard Halliburton. He is eager to make your acquaintance."

Leguia extended his hand. "I am happy to meet you," he said in perfect English. "I read of your Panama Canal swim in the Lima papers. Perhaps you would come to my office to-morrow morning at half past eleven and tell me all about it."

I almost fell over dead.

CHAPTER XV

AND THE PRESIDENT SAID TO ME . . .

NEXT morning, an hour before my appointment, I began to get ready. Leguia's own attire I knew would be flawless. I would have to press and polish heroically with my limited wardrobe if I were to feel other than slovenly in his presence. The stiff-bosomed shirt was dragged out—a starched collar—my sedate black tie. In dressing, the back collar-button slipped out and disappeared somewhere in my clothing. With a new one in, I finished dressing, gave my beard a final stroke, and set out for Pizarro's gray, grim palace, in the innermost sanctuary of which I was to find the little dynamo that vitalizes and dominates Peru.

Although I had no document to verify the president's invitation, I was armed with a weapon which promised to plow through any officious guards that blocked my progress.

The evening before a press photographer had brought me a group picture he had taken the moment Mr. Moore was introducing me to Leguia.

President Leguia of Peru (with Ambassador Alexander Moore beside him), invites me to come to his office in Pizarro's palace for a visit.

Augusto Leguia, one of the most romantic figures among the rulers of the world to-day.

The figures were unmistakable; and I held the photograph in readiness.

At the very first entrance the guards demanded credentials. I waved my argument before their eyes and indicated that this person in the picture talking to the president was *me.*

All the credentials in the world could have been no more eloquent to the guards. I was salaamed through halls and corridors (along which, four hundred years before, assassins had rushed to murder Pizarro) until stopped by a second line of defense. Once more I waved my photograph. Once more I was sped forward until Leguia's own secretary, properly awed by the picture, sat me down in the waiting room.

My turn came. I entered.

Leguia advanced to meet me. He had been seeing streams of people for three hours before my arrival; he would continue to see them for hours after my departure, but each person is made to feel that he is the Shah of Persia whom it is an honor to receive. At least that's the way Leguia made me feel. Nor is he insincere. It is simply that he concentrates on one person at a time the whole force of his overwhelming personality. This partly explains his dazzling success as president. He needs only to greet one to gain for himself a new champion. He doesn't shoot political enemies. He merely charms them into submission.

This was the great little man who now came forward.

"I apologize for keeping you waiting," he said. "Do sit down."

"It is very generous of you to see me," I began. "Ambassador Moore offered to come along, but I told him I was not afraid to face you alone."

"Am I so fearsome?" he laughed. "Surely after braving the crocodiles in the Panama Canal you shouldn't be afraid of me. I do congratulate you, —can't imagine a more romantic adventure. How did you get through the locks?"

I told him everything I could think of about the escapade, and he listened with such interest and amusement that a quarter of an hour passed before it occurred to me how I was squandering the president's terrifically valuable time.

"Good Lord!" I exclaimed, looking at the clock, "I've wasted fifteen minutes talking about myself, and haven't asked one of the hundred questions I wanted to—and there are three or four generals waiting outside."

"Oh, that's all right," he said, offering me a cigarette. "I wanted you to tell me about your swim. And it's such a relief not having you ask for a concession, or bring me a grievance. What were some of your questions?"

"Tell me—what was the most important day in your career?"

He thought a minute. "The *No Firmo* Day, I suppose."

He saw I was waiting for an explanation.

"At least that was the most *exciting* day in my career. It happened the first year I was president.*

"At that time Peru was owned body and soul by a few powerful families, and these families resented and feared the democratic changes I was introducing. And they went about removing me in typical Latin-America fashion.

"A great mob of insurgents, led by the son and brother of the preceding president, broke into the courtyard of the palace here"—he made a gesture out the window—"and without warning began to shoot down all my guards. A secretary rushed in with excited eyes, crying, 'They've come to kill you—they've come to kill you.' So I put on my hat and coat and walked out to investigate the terrible commotion. At once I saw that the trouble was tragically serious. My guards lay dead

* Leguia was president from 1908 to 1912, and again from 1919 to the present time.

and dying all about the palace. People were firing and running and shouting.

"When the assassins saw me they made a rush all at once—led by ex-President Pardo's son. I was almost smothered by their numbers. They kicked and struck me—tore my clothes, dragged me down the marble steps where Pizarro was slain, and out into the street.

"This shouting, drunken mob led me to my own house, where it was hoped that the sight of my family and fear for their safety would induce me to sign the abdication document they were trying to force on me. But I had no intention of submitting.

"So they led me next to the Inquisition Plaza and continued to threaten and maltreat me.

"My only possible policy was to spar for time in the hope my own soldiers would organize and come to the rescue. I thought of every argument I could to delay the execution. A big drunken negro was standing over me with a paving stone in his hands, raised ready to bash my brains in—and he would have, too, had I not been so self-possessed.

"Half an hour of argument had passed. Pardo feeling his own resolution slipping fast forced the abdication document into my hands and ordered me to sign it or be shot on the spot.

" 'But I must read such an important paper before signing,' I said. So I took as long as possible to read it—being almost suffocated meanwhile by the hundreds of yelling rebels surging all about me —and found that in their haste to prepare it my captors had put in November twenty-ninth instead of May twenty-ninth.

" 'See here,' I said, 'I can not sign this paper dated next November when it's only May. It would be a grave error.'

"Getting more and more exasperated Pardo snatched the paper from my hand and began to erase the date.

"Just then I heard shots in the distance, and in a moment more a company of my own cavalry charged across the plaza firing into the mob. How the bullets whizzed! It was worse than the war with Chili. The negro with the paving stone fell dead on top of me, and several of his companions on top of him.

"Dead bodies and blood were strewn all over the place, and the whole plaza was a mass of stampeding people. My captors fled, but not before they had killed the officer in charge of my cavalry.

"I had a dreadful time dragging myself out from beneath the pile of corpses, and when I did, my soldiers thought I was just another escaping rebel and began to fire again. But I called out: 'I am the president! I am the president!' They recognized me then. They brought me a cavalry horse, and we rode through the streets back here to my palace. The people were cheering everywhere, and I knew I was *still* president."

The date of this dramatic revolution, May twenty-ninth, has become a national holiday in Peru. It is called the *No Firmo* Day, the "I-will-not-sign Day." All the banks and schools close in honor of the little Inca who set his country such a splendid example of high courage and staunch character.

"I suppose you're not afraid of assassination any more," I said, accepting another of his cigarettes.

"No, not any more," he laughed. "I've been assassinated so often—on the street, in my house, in my office—I've become used to it."

As I sat before him the hands of the clock were flying fast. But I was unconscious of time. For a solid hour I continued to ask questions and he to talk—about the Peruvian Indians, about the ancient Incas and their amazing civilization, of Cuzco, of Pizarro, of his own sons and daughters.

The clock struck two. I started up. I'd come at half past twelve. All apologies, I prepared to excuse myself.

"Before you go," he said, "haven't you a picture to show me?" He saw two photographs lying on the table.

"Yes, sir. One of them was taken at the airport yesterday. It's of you and me," I said, smiling, "—and Ambassador Moore. You see my Spanish is still in its infancy, and as I had only an oral invitation to call on you I feared I'd have trouble getting by the lines of defense. So I brought the photograph of *us* along and waved it before the eyes of everybody who dared question my right to get in. They seemed terribly awe-inspired. Worked much better than a passport."

He seemed eager to see the omnipotent picture, and smiled over my effective use of it.

"But you've another," he said.

"That one's just of you."

"Where did you get *this?*"

"I bought it."

"What a waste of money. But at least I can inscribe it."

So he got out the white ink and gave the picture a flourishing autograph. I thanked him, and stood up to make my departure—and as I did so, my brass collar-button, that had disappeared mysteriously while I was dressing that morning, bounced down my trouser leg and rolled across the presidential carpet. He stooped to recover it, and I in my desperate haste to get there first and spare him such an indignity, all but bumped my head against his. I probably turned scarlet. The president only laughed heartily and held up the impudent, disrespectful bit of brass.

All charm, all courtliness, all courage and honor, Leguia bade me good-by, and I strode down Pizarro's bloody steps rejoicing with Peru that her destiny rests in the hands of this twentieth-century *conquistadore.*

CHAPTER XVI

LIMA NIGHTS

FROM coast to coast, from pole to pole, the beauty and the wit of Lima's ladies have been sung. After several days of investigation at the capital of Peru into the cause of so much singing, I had about decided in my unkind heart that the Limeñas' reputation was founded more on chivalry than on fact—when I met Manuella, and reversed my decision on the spot.

It was not for any startling perfection of her features that I loved my Manuella. Her nose was a trifle Louis Seize. Nor was it for a youthful sprightliness. She admitted twenty-five. Certainly my interest was not aroused by her figure, since her figure had considerable embonpoint. But I'm ready any time to fight a duel with anybody who claims that she is not the most beautiful señorita in South America. After all, a large nose is generally a sign of strong and generous character. As for age, I'd reached the time myself when very young and very pretty-faced *jeunes filles* had ceased to attract me. And as for the figure, who can deny that the buxom models are vastly superior to all other makes? They are invariably jolly; their laughter frequent and infectious; their health inexpensive; their dispositions like unto the angels; their bosoms motherly, comforting, all encompassing. Ever since knowing Manuella, in my nightly prayers I've never failed to ask God please to bless the fat girls.

I became acquainted with her at a party given at the Lima Country Club. A friend, seeing me standing all alone, asked if I would not like to meet one of the grandest girls in Peru.

"She knows all about history," he said. "She's been places. Speaks English better than you do. She's becoming quite famous as a raconteur . . . really terribly intelligent."

"Then maybe I'm the wrong one to meet her. Terribly intelligent women scare me to death."

"This girl won't," he assured me.

Tremblingly I submitted. He led me up to Manuella and we were introduced.

Her appearance was instantly arresting—handsome black eyes, jet hair and pink healthy skin that seemed out of place in olive-cheeked Lima. Vivacity and abundant good humor shone from her face. No wonder she was somewhat overweight; such a merry nature could not be otherwise.

Our friend, making some quip about my struggling beard, sent her into tinkling, unrestrained laughter that infected everybody in her company. Her English was splendid, and with reason, since I learned that her mother was of that nationality, and that she had been reared from childhood equally at home in the language of either of her parents. But she was jealous of her Lima heritage, and though her gown was straight from Paris, her hair done in the smartest French mode, though continental culture dominated her completely, Lima was her home and her heaven.

The moment we met I liked everything about this buxom, handsome lady.

I told her she looked like the Mona Lisa, only lovelier.

She told me that with my chin beard I looked like John the Baptist, only funnier.

Seated on a sofa away from the crowd we were fast getting acquainted.

"Manuella"—it never occurred to me to call her anything else from the very first—"you're the answer to all my prayers. I've been in this town over a week trying to make friends with you Lima girls, but all the others insist on speaking Spanish and I'm so dumb I can't understand unless they say things out of my phrase book like 'Good morning, Señor, how are you?' or 'I have a red pencil,' or count up to one hundred, so I've not made much headway.

"And now *you* come along—just when I was giving up hope. I want you to rescue all the romantic dreams I had about this place—before I came. As it is, these dreams are fast being shot to pieces. I'd expected to find sixteenth century relics, Moorish balconies and medieval churches, and all I've been able to find are bank buildings and garages."

"You see very badly," she said, defending her city. "Lima overflows with ancient things."

"—And I had visions of Spanish gentlemen with guitars serenading their ladies at every street corner, and conversing only through the barred windows with dark-eyed damsels in shawls and mantillas—and look at this," I said, indicating the guests dancing about us, all dressed in the severest Parisian or Bond Street manner, "—I'll bet there's not a mantilla or Spanish shawl left in all Lima—much less a barred window."

"I have a mantilla," exclaimed Manuella, refusing to allow her home town to appear as prosaic as I was trying to paint it, "—several in fact—and a barred window, too!"

"Well, see here! I've a guitar. (I didn't have,

but I'd seen one in a shop window.) Let me come to call on you and bring it along. All I can play is *Jolly Farmer,* but it will look well in the picture."

"I'd love to hear you play *Jolly Farmer,*" she laughed. "If you *will* come and serenade me I'll sit behind the window and wear all the shawls and mantillas in the house."

"Could I come to-morrow night?"

"*Bueno.* To-morrow night."

She gave me her address, and I agreed to be there with the guitar, *a las ocho.*

As the hour for my date with Manuella approached, the problem of what costume best fitted my guitar, bought only that afternoon, confronted me. If I dressed up the way I'd seen Spaniards dress when they were "playing bear"* in the movies, I'd be arrested in black-garmented Lima before I could get out of the hotel. But if Manuella was going to greet me in shawls and mantillas, it would not do to appear myself in my Sears-Roebuck creations.

So I got out the yellow corduroy trousers, yellow flannel shirt and blue sweater. This, with my freshly clipped hair and John-the-Baptist beard,

* The South American custom of courting through a barred window called in Spanish *haciendo el oso,* "playing bear," has practically died out with the emancipation of Latin women.

could hardly be called a Spanish get-up—but it certainly wasn't Grand Rapids.

The lift boy stared at me as I entered his elevator.

"Don't stop at the lobby," I said. "Take me all the way down."

There was a tradesman's entrance leading into the street from the basement by which I could escape without passing the desk. I dived into a taxicab and was whisked down the boulevard through the motor traffic and out to the suburban address Manuella had given me. It was a large and elaborate modern house set back in a walled garden. The butler came out as I rang the bell on the garden gate and informed me that Señorita Manuella would receive me on the terrace at the side of the house.

It was impossible to miss her. Brilliant electric light streamed out through an enormous barred window on to the terrace, and there behind the bars sat the Lady, all dressed up in about six shawls and mantillas.

I had planned my entrance very carefully, just as I'd seen it done in the movies. I was going to slip very quietly up to the rendezvous, lean languidly against the bars, and lure my inamorata to her starlit window with the soft strains of *Jolly*

Farmer. Then I'd recite something from *Romeo and Juliet* in amorous tones, as she sat and toyed with a rose.

And instead here was this glare of electric light, the Lady already waiting for me, and inside the room a radio loud-speaker blaring forth its usual raucous din.

When Manuella saw me and my costume there was a cascade of laughter.

"I'll bet you rented the guitar," she said by way of greeting.

"You're so unromantic, Señorita. You don't know how to 'play bear' at all. For the Lord's sake turn the light off—and that blasted radio. I can't compete with such screeching."

She obeyed, but just before the light went out she asked me if I'd rather have Luckies or Camels —or Spearmint! "Papa always keeps Spearmint for our American guests."

I took the chewing gum—anything to quiet her so I could play *Jolly Farmer.*

I thought it sounded elegant in the quiet starlit garden, but the only response I got was another peal of laughter.

"If you'll stop laughing long enough I'll sing, too," I offered.

That sent her off into fresh gales.

"Very well then, I won't sing. *You* sing."

"No, no. I'm no singer."

"But I heard that you tell the most beautiful stories. Do you know the one about the negro woman in the graveyard?"

"Oh, not *that* kind. All I know are history stories. Stories about Lima."

"Then tell me a history story about a Lima girl named Manuella."

"I'm afraid she lived too recently to be interesting. But I know a nice one about a girl named Benedicta."

"Very well. I hope this story has something about love in it."

"Lots—and about hate too. You promise to listen very attentively?"

"I promise."

And so she told me:

In the year 1675 Lima was already a great city, the greatest city in the New World. The viceroy held his court here, and had become as powerful on this continent as the king was in Spain—and richer, for Lima sat on top the gold mines of Peru. The social life was in keeping. Dukes and marquises, great artists and rich merchants, courtly women, the princes of the church, lived and moved

Assisted by my beard and my guitar, I "play bear" with Manuella through the bars of a sixteenth century window in Lima.

The strains of *Jolly Farmer* entice Manuella out into the patio, where she shows me how a guitar really should be played.

in Lima while New York was still being scalped by Indians.

One of the gayest and most beautiful of the court ladies was a girl named Benedicta Ramos. Many men were in love with her. She loved only one—Aquilino del Leuro. He was an officer in the viceroy's guard, and a very fine caballero, too. But he had a fickle heart, for in time—a short time —he abandoned the girl who loved him too well. In shame she was exiled from court and forced to work for her own living. Repeatedly she tried to renew their old association, to rekindle his former ardor for her, but without the smallest success. At the height of Benedicta's grief over his infidelity he married a rich heiress.

Benedicta was now truly without honor or position. Her life became more and more secluded. But even though she was very sad and very poor, her beauty was no less arresting. It still called upon her the attention of every passing man, particularly the attention of Fortunato Dulces, a young soldier who lived near-by. Whenever they passed he spoke gentle and pleading words to her. But her heart was lead. She noticed no one.

Then one night when Fortunato was strolling along the river bank Benedicta walked up to him and, even before he managed to speak a word, greeted him cordially. He escorted her to her door and was in ecstasy when she invited him into her own apartment.

They had been talking for some time and Fortunato was almost sure of winning the girl, when a knock was heard. With great excitement Benedicta told her guest that they would be in danger if he were seen with her, and that he must go into the back room and neither stir nor speak.

He obeyed reluctantly, uneasy and puzzled.

Benedicta's sudden change of attitude toward her neighbor must be explained. On that very same afternoon she had met her former lover and had been inspired to avenge herself. So she begged him, in memory of his past devotion, to come to see her one more time that they might enjoy one last night of love before parting for ever. And Aquilino, willing to give this troublesome affair a pleasant ending, agreed.

But Benedicta in her heart knew her purposes were not so amiable. The entertainment she planned for Aquilino demanded an accomplice, and to gain one she had encouraged Fortunato with her sudden coquetry.

The two former lovers met. There were no recriminations. By no gesture did she reveal that

Aquilino's disloyalty had ruined her life, or that she was unforgiving. With caresses and wine she played her game until she had managed to drop a drug into her lover's glass.

In a few moments he was asleep. Then she bound and gagged him and waited until he should awaken. At midnight the poor man opened his eyes to find Benedicta standing before him, his own poniard in her hands, her eyes hard and blazing.

In calm and calculated words she denounced her lover for the villainy of his conduct. His pleading eyes stirred no pity in her breast. She gripped the dagger with both hands and plunged it through his heart.

During these terrible moments Fortunato was standing behind the intervening wall. He could hear everything. When Benedicta, with crimson fingers, opened the door, he stared at her and shook with horror.

She assured him his own life was not in danger; told him the dead man had been her lover whom she had justly executed for his betrayal, and that if Fortunato desired her love, he would have to assist her dispose of the corpse. The street was empty; the night dark; the river flowed in front of the house. It would be very easy.

And that woman with the devil's heart kissed the

ardent young soldier passionately on the mouth, fascinating him completely and giving courage to his poor soul.

It was a perfect night for crime. Heavy clouds hid the stars. When the door of Benedicta's house opened two persons came out of it. One was Fortunato, who carried on his shoulders the dead body of Aquilino placed in a bag; the other was Benedicta.

"Are you listening, Señor?"

"Manuella! Of course I'm listening. Don't stop there."

Manuella continued:

As Benedicta walked behind Fortunato in the darkness she *sewed* his coat firmly to the bag containing the corpse.

The two shadows arrived at a place on the riverside where they knew the water was very deep. Fortunato leaned forward and pitched the body from his shoulder. He was dragged helplessly into the river by the corpse and drowned.

On her death-bed twenty years after, Benedicta confessed her crime.

Next day it became clearly evident to me that if I were further to impress Manuella I must develop my musical talents. *Jolly Farmer* had already ceased to thrill her, so I took my guitar back to the music store and asked the manager to suggest a new piece that would prove irresistible to a Lima girl fifteen pounds overweight.

Without hesitation he suggested *Oh! You beautiful doll, You great, big, beautiful doll!* This was a bit out of date, but too appropriate to resist. So the manager played it over slowly—with feeling—several times on his piano and I blundered along in accompaniment till I could play *Beautiful Doll* by ear.

That evening, all flush with my new piece, I hurried back to Manuella's, climbed the garden wall this time, and reached the barred window. It was open as before, but dark. I unslung my guitar and with ravishing notes and nightingale song called to my lady:

"Oh! You beautiful doll *(plink, plink!)*,
You great, big, beautiful doll *(plink, plink!)!*
Let me put my arms about you,
I could never live without you;
Oh! You beautiful doll!
You great, big, beautiful doll *(plink, plink!)!*
If you ever leave me how my heart will ache,
I want to hug you but I fear you'd break;
Oh, oh, oh, oh, oh, Oh! you beautiful doll
(Plink!)!"

From the floor above, out into the night, down

into the garden, rippled a waterfall of laughter. Manuella had heard the Apollonian strains and was soon back at the bars, half-hidden as before in all her Spanish shawls.

"Buenas noches, Señor Chopin."

"Greeting, Señorita. I'm back again. You spoiled me last night. I've become like Caliph Shahryar in the *Arabian Nights.* If you don't tell me another good story every evening, I'll behead you."

"I'll tell you a new story, if you'll play me new music. Is that a bargain?"

I saw myself spending all my days in the music store, taking a laborious lesson from the pianist and learning new lullabies on my guitar to play for Manuella. But this was worth the effort if it would prolong these Lima nights.

"All right. That's a bargain; and you'll have to reward me right now for *Beautiful Doll.*"

"Very well. I'll tell you a story about the beautiful dolls."

"I suppose you mean the women."

She did mean the women, and this was her story:

Three hundred years ago, on a February day, there existed in Lima the greatest state of alarm the city had felt in a generation. The agitation was against Spain itself, and so violent had it become that every one thought the Castilian yoke was about to be severed. A great throng of excited people had collected in the plaza, and most of the throng were women.

Everybody talked at once; noble ladies to their sisters of the lower classes, or even of free life. Ready to keep this mob in control, a company of lancers could be seen in the courtyard of the Government House with their horses saddled expecting battle any moment in defense of the royal authority. It was clear that the Government foresaw a dark situation.

And it is small wonder that there was a rebellion in the air. The day before, a fleet of ships coming from Spain had anchored in Callao harbor bringing the royal mail. In this mail was a decree from the throne affecting all the colonies of Spain. It was this decree that caused the uproar, for every woman said: "We will separate from Spain rather than accept it! We will guard our liberties against such tyranny! It is better to die than obey!"

And no wonder the city was so excited. The King of Spain had commanded that no woman, no matter what her rank, wear the farthingale, because King Philip—a narrow-minded old crank—thought it immoral and sinful. He also forbade women to wear sloped doublets. Every woman in

Lima wore a farthingale in even more exaggerated form than the ones worn in Madrid, and as for doublets the Lima ladies disregarded openly the sermons of the priest against them.

The king didn't approve of pretty shoes, either. The decree abolished *high heels*—said they, too, were immoral—and that there must be no ornaments or stones on them. Shoes must be plain and hide the ankle.

And then on top of that, as if it weren't enough, the king ordered that all the *tapadas* must go. He declared that if any woman wore a *tapada* she would be fined one hundred pesos and imprisoned.

The moment——

"Now hold on, Manuella," I interrupted. "You're getting out of my bounds. I know what a farthingale is; I've a slight notion about sloped doublets, but when it comes to *tapadas*—you've got me there."

Manuella had to stop and explain. A *tapada* was a Turkish veil which covered the head and shoulders, and was drawn across the face so as to leave only the right eye visible. Every woman wore one, rich and poor, high and low, each looking exactly like the other. Disguised this way they went everywhere, to mass, to balls, to every public place. And under every manta lurked a devil of

Photograph by Dubreuil, Lima

Three ladies of Lima dressed in the farthingale style which the Spanish king tried unsuccessfully to suppress.

Photograph by Dubreuil, Lima

The king of Spain also commanded that the tapada, the Turkish veil worn by all the Limeñas during colonial times, must go. It was this restriction that caused the famous mutiny of the Lima women.

mischief. The greatest joy of the seventeenth century Limeñas was to gossip about the pranks and adventures they enjoyed hidden under these veils.

And now the king had stepped in and threatened the viceroy with loss of office unless he abolished the *tapada* and all the other immoral garments. The decree from Madrid had been published. The women were defiant. The city was in an uproar.

But not even kings can control women's fashions. Everybody was against the law. The leaders among the rebellious women vowed that on the feast of Corpus every woman in town would appear wearing her *tapada,* decree or no decree—and farthingales as well, and hoops and sloped doublets and high heels with jeweled buckles that did *not* hide their ankles.

They did it too. By night almost every woman in Lima had been arrested. The viceroy was just as determined as the women. He put the city under martial law. He was resolved to obey the king's orders—until he learned that his own wife and daughters were among the imprisoned lawbreakers.

In despair the poor man retired to Callao. It was soon found the Government could not imprison half the population of Lima all at once—especially the women half. There was no one left to cook, no one to keep house, to care for the children—sweethearts, wives, daughters, all in gaol.

Very soon the men joined the rebellion, and the women were released, still defiant, still wearing their beautiful high heels and their adored *tapadas*. The viceroy had to surrender. The decrees were burned. All the church bells rang. Once more crowds of people thronged the streets, but joyous crowds this time. *Tapadas* were everywhere. The women of Lima had triumphed over the mightiest king in Christendom and put him properly in his place.

"Then I suppose that, womanlike, just as soon as they didn't *have* to abolish them, the style changed and *tapadas* became as obsolete as bustles are now," I suggested.

"Exactly."

"Well, I'm glad they changed, Manuella. It was a dumb custom—the Lima girls hiding their faces and their knees with veils and farthingales. I think the King of Spain was right! If he were in power to-day he'd probably insist on the Limeñas hiding their ears. . . . Have you ears, Manuella?"

"Of course I have ears, Señor! Both!"

"Don't believe it! Show me!" I pleaded, reaching through the bars.

"Most certainly not," she laughed, drawing away.

"Then tell me another story, and come on out on the terrace and tell me."

"Think I'd best stay right where I am," she replied with a smile. "This window-seat is very comfortable."

"Well, this window-*sill* isn't," I said, looking around for a terrace chair. "It's going to leave its mark on me for a week."

I found a garden bench and dragged it up to the bars, reseating myself.

"Now, let's have a story that's louder and funnier — and give me some of your papa's Spearmint . . . you're quite sure you won't come over?"

"I'm quite sure. . . . You say you want a story that's loud and funny. . . . Let me think. . . . I believe the Bellringer and the Heretic Mayor will fill that case."

"Very well. . . . Once upon a time . . ."

Once upon a time there was a heretic mayor of Lima named Don Diego de Esquivel. Though an unbeliever in the Holy Catholic Church, he was otherwise, to all appearances, a model mayor. He had a reputation for austere morals, and a detached attitude toward all women.

But that was just his reputation and his pose by day. At night things were different.

It must be explained that during early colonial days all the churches were required to ring their bells whenever the mayor or the archbishop or the viceroy passed. Mayor Esquivel took a special pride in this homage paid him, and on every Sunday afternoon would drive about the city in his coach, never forgetting to ride deliberately before the churches.

But one afternoon the bells in the San Augustine chapel failed to ring. The mayor was piqued at this discourtesy and blamed the Superior of the Augustine friars for it. Inquiries revealed that the bellman, one Jorge Escoiquiz by name, had not rung his bells because he thought it improper to pay homage to a mayor who was a heretic.

Such an explanation was not acceptable. Jorge was sternly reprimanded and threatened with more severe punishment if he were ever again so disrespectful.

One week later, late at night, all the city was suddenly awakened by wild alarums coming from the bell tower of the San Augustine Church. People came rushing out from their houses, fearing that an Indian uprising or a conflagration was upon them.

Instead they found their supposedly austere,

woman-proof mayor, slightly the worse for wine, carousing down the street in the company of several not too virtuous ladies. Jorge had obeyed his orders—to ring the bells whenever the mayor passed—and made the poor man the object of ridicule and jest for every tongue in town.

CHAPTER XVII

THE END OF PIZARRO

BEFORE leaving Manuella's that night I had promised to return again the next night with new music. And so the music problem had to be faced once more. I thought of all the unplayed songs I knew: *Going Back to Nassau Hall, Dixie, Jesus Loves Me.* But none of these seemed to fit our game of "bear."

Then I had an inspiration. I remembered Cyrano de Bergerac, and how he doubled for Christian in the balcony scene with Roxane, speaking the love words while Christian did the gestures . . . and I asked the shop manager if he knew of an expert guitar player I could engage for an hour. He had to look no further than his own assistant who agreed, for a price, to help me. It was my plan that he should wreck Manuella's heart completely on the following night with his seductive strains, while I got the credit.

"But don't play too well," I said. "Hit lots of wrong notes. Remember I'm only an amateur.

The girl we're serenading is going to be suspicious anyway."

He promised to play as clumsily as he could . . . and at eight o'clock we climbed over the garden wall together.

Fortunately it was a dark night with a mist in the air. And no light came from Manuella's bars.

I pushed the artist up near to the window, and stood directly in front of him. "Remember," I whispered, "when she comes, make mistakes—don't use too many fingers."

Unslinging my guitar, he began to thrum the strings and with soft and singing tones sent real music drifting into Manuella's house. This was Andalusia playing, with the unmistakable, distinctive, tango-time rhythm that enters into all popular music played by Spanish people.

Some one had come to the window—I could see Manuella's dark shadow there.

For the moment the musician acted his part, stumbling over a few sour notes, and then off he sailed on silver wings, drawing forth music I did not know, songs I'd never heard—all muted, and harmonious with the geranium garden and the night and the breeze. He forgot to play flat notes. I forgot to remind him. Manuella sat motionless behind the window, lost and listening.

But I mustn't overdo it. After ten minutes of this concert I took the guitar away from my minstrel, gave him a significant punch and moved closer to the bars.

"Señorita——"

"*Qué hermoso, señor!* You learn all that to-day?" she asked, only half-holding back her laughter.

"I felt you were due much music to-night for all your stories," I replied, knowing perfectly well she hadn't swallowed my clumsy deceit.

"Why didn't you play this way last night?"

"I wanted to keep something back as a surprise."

"Well, don't stop. I like you when you play like that."

"Then not another note," I said, leaping at this chance to escape and flinging the guitar decisively into a wicker chair. "I refuse to bribe you into liking me. I'm far ahead already. You'll have to give me the entire history of Peru to even up. But I'll be merciful. If you'll tell me just one more story I'll take you down to the plaza and buy you a red balloon."

"Thanks, I have a balloon," she laughed. "But there is one place you really *can* take me—to the Cathedral. There's a special service to-night. It won't be too late if we arrive before nine."

"At your service, Señorita—but the story first."

"What story shall it be?"

"Let's have more bloodshed. You're specially good at murdering people."

"Would you like to hear the biggest murder story in Peruvian history?"

"Grand! How many were killed?"

I soon learned.

Ten years after the death of Atahualpa, the last Inca emperor, for whose ransom a room was filled with gold, Francisco Pizarro ruled supreme in the conquered empire. Ten million Incas had been subdued and enslaved. The city of Lima had been founded and had become the center of government in the New World. Here in his vast palace, Pizarro—the ex-swineherd who could neither read nor write—lived with his glittering court.

To attain this royal position Pizarro had ridden ruthlessly through every obstacle, sacrificing friend and foe alike. Not only had he had to overcome desperate Inca armies, but civil wars in his own ranks as well.

Each rebellion had been successfully suppressed, yet each suppression had gained for the conqueror a fresh company of enemies.

Of these the most vindictive were the Knights of the Cape. Their leader was Almagro's own son—

Almagro who had been Pizarro's chief confederate in the invasion of Peru until the conqueror executed him for being too strong a rival.

Now the son had sworn vengeance and with eleven of his dethroned companions had come to Lima to carry out their bloody plans.

In Lima the Knights were forced to live in the utmost simplicity, for the failure of their former rebellion had deprived them of all source of income. Their clothes were almost in rags, and there was only one cape among them. Since fashion insisted that no gentleman could walk in the streets without wearing a cape, they had to take turns in departing from their rendezvous, for while one was wearing the garment the other eleven had to stay at home. That's how they had come to be known as *Los Caballeros de la Capa.*

But their poverty only inflamed their bitterness against Pizarro. Their whole thought was given over to conspiracy upon his life, and they swore to cut his grave clothes from the famous cape.

Gossip began to spread throughout the city that these partizans of Almagro planned to kill the marqués, and he was warned. Pizarro paid no heed. He had lived too long in constant danger to bother over one more threat—and anyway, with the sword by his side which had slaughtered whole phalanxes of enemies, he had no small confidence in his ability to take care of himself.

However, he did go so far as to request the mayor to make inquiry. The mayor was careless about his secret-service duties and allowed the news to reach the conspirators that their murder plot was detected. In fear of their lives they resolved to strike boldly and at once, for if they let things go, they believed the marqués would kill them all.

They seized their swords and rushed across the plaza shouting, "Death to the tyrant!"

Pizarro was just finishing his noonday meal, along with no less than fifteen guests, when a page came rushing in and crying: "*Los Caballeros de la Capa* are coming to kill my lord!"

The upheaval was enormous. All the governor's guests fled through the window into the garden, leaving him supported only by his two pages. The attack came so suddenly he had no time to don his cuirass. The guards were unable to stop the assassins at the gate. The two young pages rushed to defend their master. The three of them stood at the threshold to meet the onslaught. Pizarro had passed his sixty-fourth year, but he fought like the grand old lion he was.

"Traitors," he cried out, "—assaulting my house like robbers!" And he wielded his terrible sword with such skill and power that for a moment he held back the entire band.

But the assassins were many. There was only one Pizarro. The pressure of the onslaught had borne down the two faithful pages. Enraged at such defiance one of the Knights of the Cape seized a fellow conspirator and bodily flung him at the roaring old man. Pizarro stabbed the human missile to death, but before he could regain his guard, Martin de Bilboa plunged a sword into his neck. He fell—and the pack was upon him.

The conqueror of Peru pronounced only one word, *Jesus*. As he lay on the floor dying, he painted a cross on the flagstone with his finger and his own blood. As he touched this sign with his lips, one of the murderers seized a heavy porcelain flower vase, crashed it upon the head of the prostrate conqueror—and Don Francisco Pizarro breathed his last.

I did not speak for a moment when Manuella had finished her tale, so vivid was the bloody picture before my eyes. On returning to the twentieth century I asked if it were known where Pizarro was buried.

"Yes," she said. "His mummified body you may see in a glass coffin in a side chapel of the Cathedral—where you promised to take me to-night."

It was late when we reached the Cathedral. A few moments more and it would be closing. But there being some special service that evening a number of worshipers still moved about in its vast sixteenth-century depths. Like two ants we passed beneath the colossal portal. The music of the distant organ swelled and ebbed from the half-lit choir. Manuella pointed to one of the side chapels. "He is there," she said. "Wait for me"—and she was lost in the shadows.

The glass coffin of Francisco Pizarro lay close at hand, built into the inside front wall of the Cathedral itself. I walked up to the candle-illuminated case and looked intently at the well-preserved figure within. Even the centuries seem unable to conquer that iron body. The mummy, haughty of mien, arrogant, indomitable, still commands the attention of every one who comes into its presence. Unconsciously I saluted the grizzled tyrant, and wished for him that all along his immortal way he might have a new battle every morning, new traitors to execute, new empires to cast down, and the clash of steel and martial glory for his daily bread. Lying in one of the hugest churches in Christendom, it is to be supposed that God has blessed this heroic old villain and forgiven him his countless sins. But if God has withheld this beneficence, who is God that the Marqués Don Francisco Pizarro, the conqueror of Peru, should care!

The Cathedral was closing. Manuella had rejoined me. Together we stood on the broad stone steps as the great doors boomed behind us, and in the starlight looked out across the ancient city of Lima—Lima the proud old noblewoman who, seeing the forces of a new and hostile civilization about to overwhelm her, still clutches to her withered breast the faded remnant of the power and the glory that once was the Empire of Spain.

CHAPTER XVIII

THE PLACE WHERE THE SUN IS TIED

IN THE land of the Incas, at the time of the Spanish Conquest, there stood in the imperial city of Cuzco two buildings that were the wonders of the Inca World. One was the great Temple of the Sun; the other, the convent where the Sun virgins lived.

Like the vestals of ancient Rome and the Rain God's brides in Mayab, these Sun virgins of ancient Peru were, next to the emperor himself, the most sacred personages of the empire, and their cult the holiest of institutions. In honor of the Sun, many of the particularly beautiful and high-born young Inca maids were collected in the Cuzco convent where they were trained in temple duties and consecrated to the lifelong service of the great god.

Into this university of beauty and virginity, the conquistadors burst in 1531. Cuzco and its fabulous treasures lay helpless before the invincible

Spaniards—its fabulous treasures of the gold mines and its virginal treasures of the flesh.

Soon glutted with gold, the conquerors, seeking new diversions, battled their way into the sacred convent, each mail-clad soldier seizing for himself one of the inviolate maids.

But by no means all of the vestals suffered this fate. One hundred of them managed to escape, flee together over the crest of the Andes above Cuzco and disappear down one of the great tropical cañons that descend the eastern slope of the mountains and lead on to Brazil.

For four hundred years the fate of these refugees remained an unsolved mystery. Then, in 1911, by an archeological accident, they were found—found in a secret city at a place in the mountain fastnesses where the Sun is tied.

I first read of this romantic discovery back in 1913. In that year, in the April number, the *National Geographic Magazine* presented to its readers Dr. Hiram Bingham's report of a newly-discovered Inca city in Peru—a magic, fantastic city, poised upon a pinnacle of rock and surrounded by cañons half a mile deep. By some twist of fate it had got lost in the Andean wilderness four hundred years ago along with its sacred

Photograph by Chambi, Cuzco

Here in the high Andes was the ancient capital of Manchu Picchu, hidden away from the invading Spaniards, and found again but yesterday, almost as intact as the day it was built, mysterious and dramatic and beautiful.

Photograph by Chambi, Cuzco

Perhaps like the angel architects of Cambodia, the people who built Manchu Picchu understood the magic arts, causing monstrous stones to drop, already squared, from the granite cliffs, and take wing across the cañons to the temple walls. Otherwise the labor required appalls the imagination.

virgins and remained totally concealed from the world till the American expedition blundered upon it.

No one could have been more intrigued by the discovery than I. My schoolboy eyes simply bulged over the gorgeous pictures of the city's architectural marvels and spectacular setting, over the history of its rise and its glory, its four centuries of oblivion and its final rescue. Here was an ancient capital, hidden away from the invading Spaniards, and found again but yesterday almost as intact as the day it was built, mysterious and dramatic and beautiful.

And to add a final glamour was the story of the lost Inca vestals who had inhabited it.

Lord! To think that such wonders and such romances could still be discovered in this all-discovered age; that the sweep of modern civilization which had made commonplace every remotest corner of the earth could have overlooked for so long this supreme source of archeological treasure. To think that in 1911, even as in 1511, there could still be new worlds to conquer!

It did not make the story less dramatic for me that the New World, in this case, had been for a long, long time unutterably dead.

Dead, but imperishable.

No sooner had I laid eyes on the first published photographs of Manchu Picchu and read the extraordinary history of its exiled virgins, than I placed this lost Inca city high on my list of sacred shrines. Manchu Picchu went down in my golden book along with Popocatepetl and the Matterhorn, Ilium and Angkor, the Acropolis and the Hellespont, Lhasa, Persia, Timbuktu—the magic places that must be visited before I could feel that I had seen enough of the wonders of the world to quench my wanderlust and rest content with my farmhouse, my cat and my slippers.

And now that I had left Lima behind, and traveled south three hundred miles along the Peruvian coast, and five hundred miles inland to Cuzco, Manchu Picchu could not be far away.

Cuzco lies in the high Andes, near the summit of the continental divide. To reach Manchu Picchu one must surmount the fourteen-thousand-foot crest and descend into the tropical Urubamba cañon that winds into the Amazon.*

Cuzco is one of the great sights of the New World, but I knew I had a yet greater sight ahead of me. So I did not tarry, but climbed to the climax of the divide, looking back at the Pacific slope deserts, and forward into the jungles.

*It was in the Urubamba cañon near the base of the Manchu Picchu cliffs that I found the "Inca Gold."

For sixty miles I followed the Urubamba gorge, marveling at the two-thousand-foot precipices and the twenty-thousand-foot glacier-crowned peaks that imprisoned me beside the hysterical river which alone has been able to cut its way through this forbidding granite world.

It was down this same cañon that the hundred vestals fled in 1531. They were not fleeing blindly. Some seven hundred years before, the early Peruvians had built Manchu Picchu, a fortified citadel, on a crag-top above the cañon. Some five hundred years later the mountain city had been abandoned by its king in favor of Cuzco. The original capital was forgotten by all but the religious authorities who for two centuries secretly kept it in a state of repair as an invulnerable retreat in case the Sun God failed them and such a refuge were necessary.

Such a refuge had become necessary—very necessary. And now, under the guidance of a priest, the hundred terrified maidens from the Cuzco temples were climbing the two-thousand-foot cañon wall to hide themselves away from the rapacious white demons, and to remain hidden, along with their secret city, for four hundred years.

Down this same Urubamba cañon Doctor Bingham's expedition moved in 1911. Never was an explorer more unsuspicious of what lay ahead of him, for not the faintest whisper of the ancient capital had found its way into any of the records and histories of Peru that flowed forth from Cuzco, only sixty miles away. No maps included it; no explorers knew of it. Peru was colonized and civilized, the treasure-mine of Europe, the home of luxury, science and culture, for one hundred and fifty years before North America began to emerge from a savage wilderness. And yet this wonderful city, so near a center of government, with its four hundred hewn-stone houses, temples, palaces, eluded for four centuries even the Indians who passed and repassed a thousand times along the cañon at its base.

Manchu Picchu was still sleeping when Doctor Bingham, alert for hidden treasures, learned from a native that "some old terraces" could be seen on top a neighboring and particularly steep ridge across the valley.

Anticipating nothing of importance, Doctor Bingham nevertheless made the laborious climb and had the good fortune to burst upon the largest surviving Inca city (except Cuzco)—a city unknown, untouched, undesecrated by four centuries of Spanish fanaticism and lust for destruction. And there, when the four centuries of jungle growth had been removed, in their burial caves were found the skeletons of the hundred long-lost virgins of the Sun.

And now at last, late one afternoon, I too had reached the point in the Urubamba gorge, two thousand feet above which the secret city was waiting in the clouds.

A rattle-trap bridge leaping from boulder to boulder led me across the torrent. Then up through the moss-draped jungle that hung above the frothing river I followed the zig-zag path, up the terrific precipice, stumbling over roots, clutching at vines. A thousand feet of this and the vegetation thinned. I could look ahead now and see the gabled end of a stone house or two, another thousand feet above—and in my enthusiasm I hurried on as fast as my lungs would let me.

As on a number of previous occasions, I was approaching a scene anticipated for years. In this same mood I had hurried to meet Mount Olympus, and the snowy poem of Popo, and the summit of Gibraltar. In every case realization had surpassed expectation. I had waited twenty years to see the mound of earth that once was Troy. It had been well worth the wait. In Angkor I had expected magic—and magic was revealed.

Now came the Sun virgins' refuge of Manchu Picchu! Was *it* going to disappoint? Anxiously I raced on up the cliff. I came to the first great stone stairs near the summit—up them two at a time. Here was an Inca building—then another and another—dozens—hundreds—gleaming, sun-flooded, flawless granite, rising tier on tier toward the climax of the ridge. I was too eager to see everything at once to stop and examine anything. On up through the dazzling maze—across the sacred plaza—past the granite temple—up the winding granite stairs to the sun-dial on the tip-top of the peak—on to the sun-dial—to the edge of the appalling chasm that fell sheer two thousand feet below—the edge from which I could see the copper sun sinking into the glaciers of a far-off cloud-capped world, and hear the voice of the tempestuous Urubamba thundering at the feet of these breakneck precipices.

A rainstorm was at that moment surging across the amphitheater of forested peaks that rose to the heavens on the opposite side, blackening the pinnacles with angry mist from the Amazon, as it struggled to climb the barriers and look, even as I, upon this fabulous city. The thunder of the battle broke and bellowed down the cañon. The lightning struck at the tops of the mountain fortresses.

The rain swept triumphantly through a shaggy eastern pass.

But in the west the Sun God of the Incas blazed away not one beam less brightly for the tempest in the east, pouring his fire against the glittering granite walls of the temples below me. Then, just before the close of day, seeing the infinitesimal speck standing speechless with wonder on top his holy altar, and knowing full well he found in me a faithful worshiper, he opened wide his treasure-chest of glories, and reaching for his one supremest prize, flung before my eyes a bewildering double rainbow across the face of the cloud-and-mountain combat, and then sank in a frenzy of color into the western snows.

No, Manchu Picchu did not disappoint me.

CHAPTER XIX

VIRGIN GHOSTS

It was twilight when I climbed down from the sun-dial. Back at the little plaza about which the city is clustered, for the first time I began to notice the details of the surrounding buildings. On one side was the chief temple, built of irregular, dissimilar, many-joined stones of gigantic size, and molded together with such incredible nicety that after supporting four centuries of jungle growth, they have emerged brilliantly white, magically undisturbed.

One block in the temple wall is fourteen feet long and eight feet high. How the builders of this granite aerie ever moved such weights up to the pinnacles of these crags, which an unburdened climber ascends only with difficulty, is a profound mystery. Perhaps like the angel-architects of Cambodia, the Incas who built Manchu Picchu understood the magic arts, causing monstrous stones to drop, already squared, from the granite cliffs, and take wing across the cañons to the temple walls. Otherwise the labor, the patience, the years, required for the builders, with only stone hammers for tools, and only their own muscles for machinery, appall the imagination.

In the starlight, with nothing but the far-off rumble of the Urubamba to break the stillness, I spread my supply of bread and bananas on the temple altar—a block of granite that must have weighed a hundred tons. Water came from a tiny spring near-by. My elaborate dinner over, I set out to explore the city where the virgins of the Sun had lived and died.

To go anywhere in Manchu Picchu one must climb either up-stairs or down—and the steps are as imperishable and as ingeniously cut as the houses. By these stairs, with no other illumination than the stars, I wandered alone about the dim and ghostly city, trying to picture in my mind's eye the hundred last inhabitants, who, doomed to lifelong exile, cut off from the world, denied the company and the love of men, moved along these very streets. Here were the burial caves, where, with all the honor deserving their rank, they had been interred. There, above, were rows and tiers of private dwellings made of the purest unstained granite, in which they had lived.

A few hundred yards farther on I came to the great military wall, stretching from precipice to precipice across the spur along the summit of which Manchu Picchu is built. Beyond the wall I found the stone terraces where the ancient inhabitants tilled the tiny fields that climbed dizzily and with complete abandon up and down the surrounding cliffs. The limitations of the field-supply soon made it evident that the city in its prime could never have sheltered a large population—probably no more than nine thousand people.

But that does not make Manchu Picchu any the less extraordinary. Remember it is an eagle's nest eight thousand feet above the Amazon forests and two thousand above the waters of the cañons that all but surround it. The founders were seeking security, not expansion. They looked the length and breadth of the Andes and picked out the most aerial spot of all where there was yet room enough to hold up a building. No wonder it remained secret from the Spanish conquerors. No wonder the Sun virgins chose it as their refuge.

Yes, Manchu Picchu, compared to Cuzco, or Chichen-Itza in Yucatan, or Memphis on the Nile, or Athens, or Carthage, is small, but oh, how much grander in general effect than any one of these! The other ancient capitals in all their original glory could never have overwhelmed one as do the ruins of this audacious, pinnacled little Inca city in Peru.

Retracing my steps to the sacred plaza I seized my duffel-bag and dragged it back up to the *Inti-huatana* (*inti* is the Inca word for sun, *huatana,* roped), "the place where the sun is tied"—the great stone dial at the very apex of the city where I had stood earlier in the afternoon and seen the sunset.

The *Intihuatana* was a romantic, rather than a restful, couch on which to spend the night. Three feet in diameter, with a square hub a foot high in the center, the ancient clock had a very strong resemblance to an execution block. I tried curling myself around the hub and holding on with my arms lest I roll off and drop half a mile into the *exceedingly* cold water of the Urubamba.

Sleep was out of the question, so I lay listening to the ceaseless rumble that came clearly from the black abyss below me, increasing and fading in the volume of its music as the wind-organist pressed the pedals, now *dolce,* now *sotto voce,* now *fortissimo.*

I turned to the stars. The Southern Cross shone clear. The Dipper rested on the mountaintops.

Sirius and Orion fought a duel across the spangled dome to decide which was the champion lighthouse of the skies. And all the poetry I knew about the stars came crowding into my mind as I lay on my world-weary duffel-bag and looked up into the universe. . . .

"Bright Star! would I were steadfast as thou art—
Not in lone splendor hung aloft the night,
And watching, with eternal lids apart,
Like Nature's patient, sleepless Eremite,
The moving waters at their priestlike task
Of pure ablution round earth's human shores,
Or gazing on the new soft-fallen mask
Of snow upon the mountains and the moors. . . ."

I sighed that I must enjoy these meadows of the night all by myself, and this music, these stones, these heights and depths, this union of earth and sky. Here I was, surrounded by enchantment, and I had no one to share it with, no one to show it to. How futile to possess such an extravagance of beauty—alone. How could I rejoice in it and appreciate it, without companionship?

And yet I may not have been unaccompanied after all. There are ghosts in Manchu Picchu, ghosts of the hundred virgins of the Sun—some young ghosts, some middle-aged ghosts, some very old ghosts, but all very virginal ghosts. How was I to know that they were not at that moment sit-

Photograph by Chambi, Cuzco

At the summit of the ridge along which Manchu Picchu is built, I found this stone sundial called in the Inca language the *Intihuatana,* "the place where the sun is tied."

Manchu Picchu, with four hundred hewn-stone houses, temples, palaces, is the largest existi Inca city except Cuzco. Yet so steep are the surrounding cliffs that it remained hidden fr the world till 1911. In that year American archeologists came by accident upon its sleepi stones which for four centuries had eluded even the Indians who passed and repassed alo the cañon at its base. The early Peruvians, looking for the most spectacular setting in Andes for their city, chose this unrivaled spot. Towering, snow-clad mountains imprison The Urubamba River roars unceasingly far below. One climbs laboriously from the ca floor, and comes suddenly upon the miraculous buildings—dozens—hundreds—gleaming, s flooded, flawless granite, rising tier on tier toward the climax of the ridge. One climbs up through the dazzling maze—across the sacred plaza—past the granite temple—up winding granite stairs to the sundial on the tip-top of the ridge—to the edge of the appall

Photograph and copyright by Richard Halliburton

m that falls sheer two thousand feet below—the edge from which one can see the glaciers far-off cloud-capped world and hear the voice of the tempestuous Urubamba thundering e feet of these breakneck precipices.

t was to this secret city that one hundred Sun Virgins fled when Pizarro came to Cuzco, ve out their lives, lost from the world, in this granite eagle's nest.

'he photograph shows less than half of the buildings, the others being behind the point of . At the height of its glory Manchu Picchu contained no more than nine thousand ɔitants. Yet, comparatively small though it is, no other ancient capital in the history of world ever had the overwhelming majesty of this audacious, pinnacled, little Inca city eru.

Photograph by Chambi, Cuzco

Sleep was out of the question, so I lay listening to the endless rumble that came clearly from the black abyss below me, increasing and fading in the volume of its music as the wind-organist pressed the pedals, now *dolce*, now *sotto voce*, now *fortissimo*.

ting by my side, still lonely and disconsolate, still yearning for the temples of Cuzco?

The thought came to me that this refugee community of virgins must have been at the same time a curious as well as tragic one. Never descending from their retreat, scrupulously guarding themselves from all contact with the outer world lest the secret of their existence reach the ears of Pizarro's ravagers, these high-born and beautiful maidens, governing themselves, complete within themselves, raising their own food, repairing their own shelters, without a single man, perhaps, to work for them, to guard them, to love them, lived out their chaste and barren lives. There were no cradles to rock, no children to sing to sleep, no sons to take pride in, no daughters to keep them company. Having known only chastity and seclusion all their lives, I wondered if they continued to be happy with this tiny sphere, this altogether feminine society? Did they continue with undiminished fervor to conduct Sun worship in the temples of their refuge as they had conducted it in Cuzco? Were they content to be married to the Sun?

Or were they human after all? Did they darkly, vaguely, feel an indefinable hunger, a loneliness which all the company of their sisters could not satisfy? When the twilight brought the purple haze to the topless barriers across the cañon and the scarlet faded from the western snows, did they look out over the unfathomable depths that were their prison walls and with a touch of anguish realize that their loveliness had been given them to no end but this? Did they stop, a little wistfully, at the fountain, when their water jars were filled, and gaze into the water mirror, back into their own dark eyes, and wish in their secret souls that their lord, the Sun God, who gave them his heat and his light, would look more deeply into their hearts and know that what they wanted more than these things was his love? I wondered if at least *one* maid, less pious than the rest, sometimes climbed up, alone, when the moon was bright, to the sun-dial where I lay dreaming, and wished she had not been in such a beastly hurry to get away from the atrocities of Pizarro's lusty conquerors.

But Pizarro and his conquerors, by some strange mystery, never learned of the mountain trail that led to Cythera. The seasons and the years drag past. The virgins of the Sun live on in Manchu Picchu unaware that storm after storm is devastating Cuzco; that their temples have been hurled down, that their people have been slaughtered and enslaved, that their Sun God is in exile—that

Pizarro himself has been long since in his grave. The time comes when the beauty of these virgin prisoners, that raised them to the Sun God's service, has faded and left them safe from Spanish ravagers. But the habit of fear is too deep-fixed. In exile they grow old, still chaste, still childless, still lonely. One by one death overtakes these consecrated women. The burial caves receive them one by one as the ever-decreasing living entomb the ever-increasing dead. In time only a few are left alive, very aged, very weary, forgotten by the world, forgetting it. These also pass, until but two remain. Then one buries the other—and one lives on amid the desolate, miraculous granite walls, the empty temples, the barren terraces, with only virgin shades for company. Already the ruthless, ravenous jungle is creeping up; already the grass grows deep upon the stair-stepped streets, and the bamboo waves above the temple doors. The city's roofs of thatch have fallen in; the serpents sun themselves upon the granite dial, since no one ever comes to count the hours. Alone, in the midst of all this ruin, the old, old woman, the last of the sacred virgins of the Sun, sits, listening to the far-away rumble of the river, and waiting—for the darkness.

CHAPTER XX

ALEXANDER SELKIRK'S EMPIRE

A GENERATION after the death of Pizarro, a city called Valparaiso—the Vale of Paradise—had been founded by the Spanish pioneers on the coast of Chile two thousand miles below Callao, the port for Lima. In the year 1570, voyaging between these two ports, a Spanish navigator named Juan Fernandez, venturing four hundred miles out into the Pacific to escape the contrary currents along the coast, bumped into an island, at the same latitude as Valparaiso—an island that no human being had ever seen before.

It was a most astonishing island, twelve miles long by three wide, and covered with grim volcanic crags that rose three thousand feet above the sea. The navigator had difficulty landing for the shoreline was buttressed with an all but continuous wall of cliffs five hundred to a thousand feet high against which the Pacific hurled itself with interminable rage. Only one small bay and stretch of sand were to be found, and there Juan Fernandez landed, to name the island after himself and take possession for the King of Spain.

On examining his new discovery he came upon numerous springs of fresh water, groves of sandalwood, thousands of seals, and giant lobsters that swarmed ashore in such countless myriads that they formed a solid carpet on the beach.

The report of this island and its rich resources soon spread abroad, and for the next two centuries it was the rendezvous and provisioning station for all the wild and warlike ships that roamed the South Pacific in those piratical days.

In the year 1704 a British ship stopped by for wood and water. A quarrel had taken place aboard her between the captain and his sailing master. The latter vowed he'd rather be put ashore on this forbidding and uninhabited island than continue with the ship. The captain was obliging, set his disgruntled officer down upon the land, and sailed away to England.

The officer's name was Alexander Selkirk.

For four years and four months Selkirk lived alone in a shallow cave by the sea, snaring wild goats, from the skins of which he made his clothes, and dining on lobster which he killed when they crawled ashore. Every day to watch for a ship he climbed to a notch in the mountain ridge above his abode from which point he could command a view of the entire circumference of his domain.

One thousand five hundred and eighty days he kept his vigil before a sail appeared at last. He built a fire to attract attention, and was thus liberated by another British vessel.

In 1711 Selkirk reached England where the tales of his solitary life on Juan Fernandez found considerable audience.

Among this audience was Daniel Defoe to whom Selkirk's adventures suggested the fictitious story of Robinson Crusoe. In 1719 Defoe's book was published, but in it he embellishes the original facts to such an extent that they are scarcely recognizable. Likewise with great care and in unmistakable terms he places Crusoe not on the Pacific island at all but on the island of Tobago in the West Indies.

Yet even though the Robinson Crusoe, so dear to our boyhood, never came within four thousand miles of Juan Fernandez, I had a desire to go there, and go there I did.

From Manchu Picchu it was a long journey. I returned to Cuzco, crossed Lake Titicaca and sojourned for a while in La Paz, the capital of

Bolivia, held there by the astonishing twenty-two-thousand-foot range of snowy Andes that soar for one hundred unbroken miles of whiteness beyond the city.

A railroad journey carried me on across the deserts of Bolivia and down to the Chile coast where I booked passage for Valparaiso.

From this port, now and then, a little sailboat braves the Pacific and struggles outward four hundred miles to Juan Fernandez. My voyage aboard her was a most seasickening adventure. For four days and nights I traveled on a wave-lashed deck, breathing the odors of ancient lobster, and soaring and sinking over the mountainous rollers. The island, when it came in sight, seemed very beautiful, if only because it was solid ground.

For a month I dwelt upon and roamed about Selkirk's empire. I explored the crags, hunted the goats, caught the lobsters, used his cave for my headquarters, and climbed almost every afternoon to his lookout in the notch to watch the sun go down in glory across the sea.

On the face of a small cliff near-by I found the famous bronze tablet set up there, a century and a half after Selkirk's rescue, by a group of his admiring countrymen, who, like himself, were followers of the sea. The inscription reads:

IN MEMORY OF

ALEXANDER SELKIRK,

MARINER,

A NATIVE OF LARGO, IN THE COUNTY OF FIFE, SCOTLAND.

WHO LIVED ON THIS ISLAND IN COM PLETE SOLITUDE, FOR FOUR YEARS AND FOUR MONTHS.

HE WAS LANDED FROM THE CINQUE PORTS GALLEY, 96 TONS, 16 GUNS, A.D. 1704, AND WAS TAKEN OFF IN THE DUKE, PRIVATEER, 12TH FEB, 1709.

HE DIED LIEUTENANT OF H.M.S. WEY MOUTH, A.D. 1723, AGED 47 YEARS.

THIS TABLET IS ERECTED
NEAR SELKIRK'S LOOKOUT, BY
COMMODORE POWELL AND THE
OFFICERS OF H.M.S. TOPAZE, A.D. 1868.

One could scarcely have found a more perfect picture than the prospect seen from the notch, with this wild, black-visaged island pitching and tumbling down about one, and the unbroken blue, stretching for a hundred miles on every side. If Selkirk had a sense of beauty his daily vigil must never have grown old. Or did beauty become hateful and monotonous when seen in such constant loneliness? Did Selkirk exclaim with the poet—

> *"I am monarch of all I survey,*
> *My right there is none to dispute;*
> *From the center all round to the sea,*
> *I'm lord of the fowl and the brute!*
> *O Solitude! where are the charms*
> *That sages have seen in thy face?*
> *Better dwell in the midst of alarms,*
> *Than reign in this horrible place."*

Four years and four months, and not a sail.

And weeks and weeks, in present times, and not a ship.

But Juan Fernandez has not always been thus isolated. In the 1840's it was a port of call for all the Forty-niner packets, California bound. American whalers—seven hundred or more a year —Darwin and his *Beagle,* Richard Dana sailing "Two Years Before the Mast," Captain Palmer and his *Annawan,* all visited the island in its days of prosperity.

But who was Captain Palmer? The others are familiar.

A most amazing story!

In 1831 the island (there are two islands ninety miles apart, but only the larger one nearer the mainland concerns us) had been for some years a penal colony for Chilean convicts. Dungeons (still very much in evidence) were dug in the hillside and the prisoners quartered there.

But a revolt had taken place, the guards had been overpowered, and three hundred liberated convicts of both sexes held possession of the settlement.

Unaware of this situation one Captain Palmer, sailing a clipper ship out of Nantucket, put into the Juan Fernandez Bay for fresh water, and went unsuspectingly ashore. Instantly he was pounced upon by the convicts who prepared to murder him in order that they might take his ship and escape.

But the captain was a Mason, and when the rebel ringleader who was also a Mason (it's the story, anyway) saw Palmer's insignia, he begged the insurrectionists to reconsider and realize that if they killed the ship's captain they'd have difficulty sailing the ship.

So Palmer was released under oath to steer to the nearest point on the mainland.

Cumberland Bay and the island of Juan Fernandez, three hundred and ninety miles west of the mainland of Chile, where Alexander Selkirk, from 1704, lived alone for four years and four months,

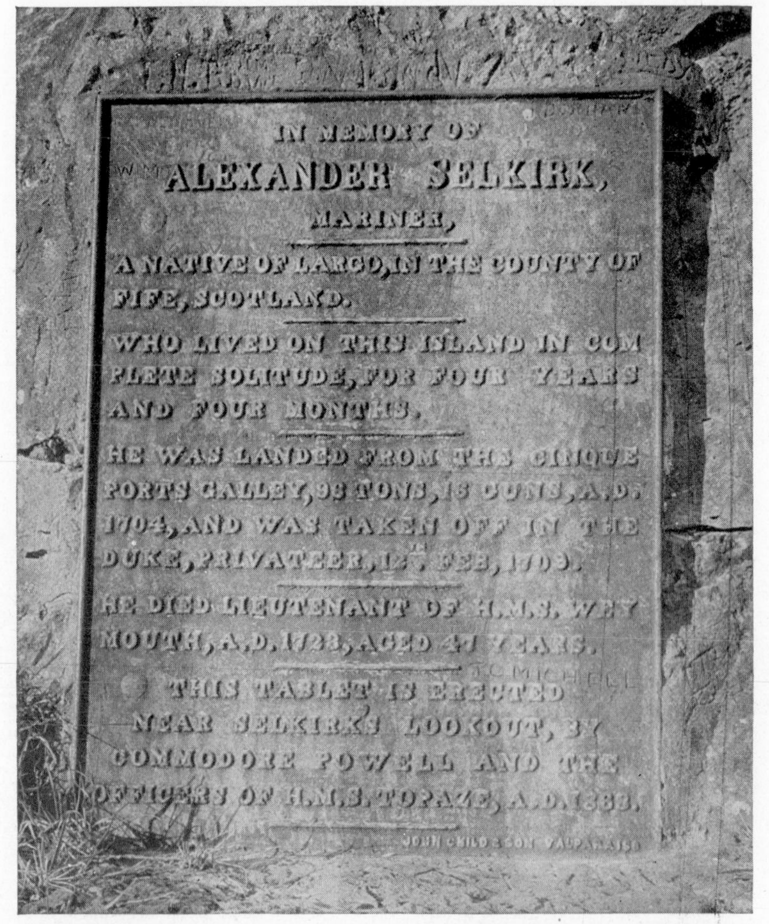

Courtesy National Geographic Magazine

The bronze tablet commemorating Selkirk's residence on Juan Fernandez.

Then three hundred yelling convicts clambered aboard. Among them were a score or so of women. These the captain absolutely refused to admit on his ship for the very good reason that *Mrs.* Palmer was secreted in the spare cabin which would naturally have been commandeered by the lady prisoners. So the poor women were driven back to shore, screaming and protesting, and the *Annawan* sailed off to Chile with her extraordinary cargo.

Meanwhile Mrs. Palmer, the only woman among these three hundred cutthroats, remained hidden. For ten days she had no food, her distracted husband not daring to approach and reveal her hiding-place.

But land at last was reached, and the convicts, wild with joy, rushed ashore. Palmer told them it was Peru. In fact it was a spot only thirty miles from Valparaiso and not three from a camp of Chilean soldiers who promptly rearrested the escaping wretches.

Before I forget it, let me add that Mrs. Palmer was liberated—and lived.

Having been on Juan Fernandez four weeks I began to agree with Selkirk about the over-valuation of solitude, so, taking a tip from the convicts I commandeered a fishing boat and ordered the captain to put me ashore at Valparaiso. There, with better luck than they had, I was not arrested, but escaped successfully over the trans-Andean railroad into Argentina and the celebrated City of Good Airs.

CHAPTER XXI

MONKEY BUSINESS

Of all the girls that I have ever met, there is one who stands forth boldly in my heart. This girl cheers me and delights me when all else fails. To her I always go, whenever—just before meals—I feel depressed. A smile from her is like a burst of sunshine in my dark forest; to hear her sing makes me happy for the day. Her name is Trudis, and she's six years old.

Oftentimes Trudis is my hostess for Sunday tea. On one such occasion I was relating to her my activities of that afternoon:

"Trudis," I said, "I have just come from the biggest church in New York. It's called the Cathedral of Saint John the Divine. And I heard the most wonderful music. It was played on an organ."

"Oh!" she exclaimed, her face suddenly bright, her eyes dancing, "—*Tell* me about the monkey!"

The monkey! Who ever heard of an organ without a monkey! It would be like Christmas without the Christmas trees, like the fairies without their wings, like the spring without the daffodils, like the world without Trudises. It would simply be impossible.

That is why, when I bought Niño, a Paraguayan monkey, from an Italian organ-grinder in the city of Buenos Aires, I bought the organ as well.

To become the owner of such an outfit was quite the last thing in my mind when, on strolling down a suburban boulevard, I heard the strains of automatic joy pouring forth from a hurdy-gurdy up a side street. All the urchins for blocks seemed to be running in that direction and drew me, no less curious, to the spot.

There I found a swarthy Neapolitan, red bandanna, earrings, black mustache, and all the rest, cranking out *La Paloma* at the top of his hand-organ's lungs; and there was Niño, dressed in his red coat and hat, begging for pennies with a technique that was utterly irresistible.

As I pushed my way through the circle of enraptured children, Niño caught sight of my white collar. Ah, here was big game—a rich American with pesos, not pennies. The monk came straight to me, climbed up my arm and began systematically to explore my pocket treasure realms. And what's more he did find a silver peso.

Had it been a hundred-dollar gold piece, I think I would have let him keep it. The boldness and confidence, the roguish impudence, with which he conducted his systematic search made a peso seem small payment for the amusement he afforded.

Never in all my adventures with monkeys had I seen one with such amiability. When I stroked his neck he curled up on my arm and purred like a kitten. He climbed to my shoulder, and when I gave him a nut, he skilfully shelled and ate it with his small and fragile fingers.

Before our acquaintance was five minutes old, a desire to own him myself took possession of me. Reason railed against such a crazy idea. There was nothing in the world I was less in need of than a monkey. But then it isn't often the things we need that we want. Also I was the guest of Argentine friends at the Plaza Hotel who would be scandalized at the introduction of so plebeian an animal into their elegant ménage. All true—but still I wanted him.

Thus was I struggling with temptation when the hand-organ broke forth in heaven-rending strains of *Valencia* and set Niño to dancing with ecstatic abandon. The spectacle overcame my last resistance. I surrendered unconditionally.

"Señor, how much will you take for your monkey?"

"I can not sell him. I love him," Antonio replied in Spanish, sensing the economic fact that resistance would boost the price. But he added: "How much will you give?"

I hadn't the slightest idea of monkey values. "Fifty pesos"—twenty dollars—I said recklessly.

The Italian grinned with ill-concealed delight. "*Bueno!* He's yours."

I handed him a fifty-peso bank note.

He handed me the most affectionate but most rascally monkey in Argentina.

The circle of children, consumed with curiosity, crowded close.

They made me remember Trudis and her famous remark and ask myself what good the monkey was, now that I had him, without the hand-organ. This way he was only half-complete.

So I bought the hand-organ too—and all three of its tunes—*Valencia, La Paloma* and the *Marseillaise.*

Then, feeling I was already lost beyond all hope, I bought the Italian's red bandanna, earrings, hat.

Suddenly and utterly bereft of his property and of a good part of his clothes as well, he thought it diplomatic to depart with his pesos before I came to my senses.

Thus did I find myself, surrounded by swarms of children, in the middle of Buenos Aires, clutching a dilapidated music-box and a ragamuffin monkey—when a moment before I had been at peace with the world.

Now that I had become a hurdy-gurdy man, I must do something about it. I tried turning the hand-crank. It worked, and forth came the tin-pan strains of *Valencia* no less fortissimo than for the Italian. At the very first note Niño went into his rhapsodic dance, leaped upon a newly arrived spectator, reached into his pockets, extracted a penny and deposited it in my hand. The monkey's allegiance to Antonio was not, apparently, very binding. Whoever held the end of his chain, played *Valencia* and provided the peanuts and the protection—that was his country.

Niño had probably never been in the Plaza Hotel before. Even so his behavior there was no worse than that of some of the other guests. Without the knowledge of my hosts I tied him to a post in the basement and fed him fruit salad.

Next morning, resolved to take the organ-grinding profession quite seriously, I put on my corduroy pants, an old sweater and the bandanna and sneaked down to Niño's apartment. He refused to speak to me. Growling and whimpering he ran to the end of his leash and scorned every attempt I made at a rapprochement. There was no mistaking the nature of his grievances: I had completely forsaken him all night—here in this dark and dreadful basement. Even Antonio gave him more consideration. He ate from Antonio's table, slept on his bed, was never left alone. But *I* was a brutal, an inhuman master.

I tried to explain, to apologize. Niño would have none of it.

"Don't you speak to me," he growled. "Don't come near me. You don't love me—I'm going to run away."

But I continued to beg his pardon in my most cajoling tones until slowly and rebelliously he turned about and on his stomach crawled into my outstretched hands. Still quarreling violently, still denouncing my heartlessness, he climbed on to my shoulder where I scratched his head, stroked his neck, fed him breakfast and besought him to take me back. After half an apple and a banana his anger began to cool, his quarreling tones to change to purrs. Presently his arms went about my neck.

"Niño," I said, "am I forgiven?"

"I suppose so," he sighed.

"Shall we go out and entertain the Argentine-lets?"

In answer he hopped down and tugged at his chain, as much as to say: "All right. I'm ready. But don't forget the hand-organ. We're not much good without it."

With the monkey and the hurdy-gurdy under my arm, I escaped unseen out the back door. San Martin Park lay close by. I made a break for it and sought refuge amid the friendly trees.

Niño, however, saw no need for all this shyness. It was time to go to work, to earn our daily bread, to sing and dance for our supper. He began to quarrel at me again impatiently.

Shamed by his own courage, I touched the organ crank. Out leaped the stirring *Marseillaise*—and from every side the children poured down upon me. It was a radiant spring morning; the sun flooded the garden, and a good part of Buenos Aires' childhood seemed to be present at this playground. Here they came, small ones and big ones, slim ones and fat ones, toddling babies, little girls with their dolls, little boys with their dogs, all laughing and dancing to my tune.

Niño—every inch a showman—did not fail to take advantage of such an audience. I released him from his chain, and he was free to climb on to the shoulders of his "public." Some of the very littlest ones were afraid of these advances, but most of them, sensing his harmlessness, crowded up to shake his hand and offer peanuts. Niño's fairy-like black paws went exploring into every baby's pocket, and there were few pockets from which he did not extract at least one grubby penny. If the baby wept, the penny was returned.

One urchin offered him a bottle of soda-water. Nothing he loved more! He sat on his haunches and, lifting the bottle with both hands to his mouth, drank vast quantities of strawberry pop. Down on top of this went candy and peanuts. Never have I seen a monkey so destructive of peanuts. It soon became obvious that food was Niño's great weakness. He had no sense of proportion. No matter what or how much food he was given, he would eat every particle of it and cry for more. I would have died before night had I eaten one half of the indigestible combinations Niño seemed to thrive upon.

It was only natural that all this loud, tin music and shrieking mobs of children would sooner or later attract the police. Presently the park guard pushed through the circle and brusquely ordered me to get my objectionable monkey and self out of the exclusive confines of the San Martin gardens.

However much I may have resented the unreasonableness of the guard's walking orders, I had no other choice than to obey. But if I must depart, I'd keep my children with me as long as possible.

Up went the hurdy-gurdy. Carrying it by the neck-strap I moved across the park, grinding out *Valencia* with a vengeance:

Valencia—in my dreams it always seems I hear you softly call to me—
Valencia—where the or-ange trees for ever scent the breeze beside the sea—
Valencia—in my arms I held your charms beneath the blossoms high above—
You loved me; in Valencia long ago we found our Paradise of love, tra, la, la, la——

Niño hopped gayly behind me, and behind Niño danced my train:

All the little boys and girls,
With rosy cheeks and dark brown curls,
Tripping and skipping, came merrily after
The wonderful music with shouting and laughter——

—after the wonderful music, and the pied organ-grinder of Buenos Aires.

There was no cave in a near-by hill into which

to lead my flock. Anyway, I had no reason to steal the children in payment for having rid Buenos Aires of rats. When we came to the far end of the garden I gave my followers a few final flourishes from the *Marseillaise,* bade them good-by and with Niño on my shoulder strolled along the Avenida Santa Fé.

Within the first two blocks we came to a small private hospital, built close upon the sidewalk. This was a place that probably needed a little cheering up. Down went the organ—forth came *La Paloma* with anything but dovelike softness—up went a score of hospital windows for three stories above—and out leaned a number of hospital inmates. One look at our gay troupe, one moment of Niño's antics, and all hospital aches and pains were forgotten. Everybody was laughing, some were singing to my music—*Valencia*—*La Paloma*—*Marseillaise*—*Valencia*—*La Paloma*—*Marseillaise*—and, as always, from everywhere the children came running.

A little hospital boy leaning out from his bed by the window threw down a penny. Niño leaped upon it. I held up my beret cap with the best imitation I could register of that ingratiating smile which always accompanies the Italian hand-organist's plea for alms. It worked something grand.

Several more coins fell down on top of us. Niño was almost beside himself trying to keep up with them.

The next stop was a hotel. We parked before the front door, hoping to repeat the hospital triumph on a larger scale. Again street crowds gathered around us instantly, but no beneficence flowed from the hotel. Perhaps I wasn't playing loud enough, so I brought more pressure to bear on *Valencia* until the music could have been heard three blocks. At last—a porter came out of his den, but with nothing more than a curt proposition that if I'd go away, and quickly, he'd give me a peso.

Somewhat hurt by this lack of appreciation for my art, I accepted the bribe and wandered on down Santa Fé Street, taking a stand at every corner or beneath every house that looked fertile, and remaining there till the police drove me on.

Having observed the no more than mild interest caused in North America by the appearance of a hurdy-gurdy man, I was not prepared for the happy riots my own show invariably excited in Buenos Aires. Had I been told of the extent to which the average citizen of this city was demoralized by a dancing monkey I should not have credited it. The children, naturally, were the most enraptured. But they had to fight to hold their vantage points against the pressure of their elders. Old gentlemen stopped to watch the monkey and laughed like the children when Niño explored their pockets for pesos. Automobiles drew up to the curb, and the occupants stood on the seats to get a good view. If a trolley car passed, the first person to observe the monkey would cry out: *Monito! Monito!*—A monkey! A monkey!—and all the passengers would flock to our side and lean out the window, whistling at the little red-dressed performer and exclaiming over his monkey-shines. Shop-keepers ran to the sidewalk; business stopped when Niño climbed on top my head and beat his hands together and sang out his chirrup-chirrup song.

This gentleness and simplicity of the Buenos Aireans impressed me more than all the capital's grand rococo buildings and fancy boulevards. None of your self-conscious Anglo-Saxon reserve about *these* people They've come from Italy—one third of them—and from Spain and Portugal. They have warmer hearts than ours, more spontaneity. They were not the least ashamed to stop and watch a monkey dancing to *Valencia,* or to sing loud and lustily when the tin organ pealed forth the *Marseillaise*—nor did they pinch their

Niño and I concertized before the national Capitol building of Argentina, and, as always, attracted a crowd of children.

The pied organ-grinder of Buenos Aires.

pennies when, the performance over, Niño held out his mercenary paw.

But it wasn't altogether their Latin temperaments that explained such responsiveness. It was partly Niño and his own winsomeness. He had the most extraordinary way of melting people. A hard-boiled truck-driver would climb down from his truck, a grin all over his face, get on his knees, take Niño in his arms and talk Spanish baby-talk to the smiling *monito.* Niño was a pal of everybody's, and he knew it. Utterly without evil in his own heart, he never suspected design in the hearts of others. To him the world was all goodness, all generosity, and he met it with complete and loving trust. In his presence the young and the old, the high and the low, were reduced as if by magic to one common denominator—a tender and a happy child.

If my early career as a monkey-man in Buenos Aires was incredibly successful, the explanation may have been partly my lack of competition in an unexploited field. Any predecessors I may have had were furtive and retiring, plying their trade only in the remote and shady suburbs. But I, not knowing any better, marched brazenly down the Avenida de Mayo, the ultra-fashionable avenue of Buenos Aires, performed before Cartier's, collected from guests at the Ritz, played *La Paloma* for the edification of the Grand Central Station.

At the end of the Avenida, blocking out the sky with its colossal dome stands the national Capitol building of Argentina. Its majestic marble steps looked to me like an ideal stage for Niño's dancing. But the moment I struck up *Valencia,* about ten narrow-minded gendarmes, appearing from amid the marble columns, came swooping down and catapulted us violently off the steps.

With a terrified screech the poor monk leaped to my shoulder and, clinging to my neck with his trembling arms, urged me to push at full speed through the usual mob of curious spectators and flee down a side street.

We soon found an obscure wine shop and dived into it for refuge and refreshment. Over a large bottle of beer we counted our pesos—ten pesos, eleven pesos, twelve pesos, twelve pesos and sixty centimes—over five dollars we had earned that day. I was so intent over the gold count I did not notice that Niño's head was deep in my beer mug. The little fellow, after four hours of ceaseless activity, was desperately thirsty. By the time he had his fill of beer, he was disgracefully tight.

So novel and so entertaining had my excursion into the realm of monkey business turned out to be, that I decided not to retire after just one day's minstrelsy, but to carry on as long as it amused me. This ridiculous pastime was proving a bit of comic relief to the boredom of life, and I was determined to enjoy every imprudent adventure it offered before returning to sobriety.

So on the second morning, still keeping our nefarious doings from my Plaza Hotel hosts, Niño and I went to work again.

This time we sought the water-front and concertized along the Avenida Leandro Alem. This, to me, is Buenos Aires' most colorful street. It is given over almost exclusively to seamen and seamen's needs. Every other shop is a slop chest with everything on earth for sale at bargain prices. Alternating with the shops are beer parlors and cabarets. At night the street is hideous with the bedlam of a hundred tin pianos and a score of café bands. The moral tone of the avenida fell so low recently that the city declared the cafés out of bounds for idle ladies. This would have been a death blow to the cabarets dependent on a seaman clientele had the managers not hit upon an ingenious means of getting around it. They enrolled all the idle ladies in a large orchestra only two or three members of which could play a note. The other members, sometimes as many as thirty, sat at the edge of the balcony in very scanty and very short clothes, sawing away at violins with dead strings and blowing into brass instruments that were totally mute. Thus they were not idle ladies. They were, to all appearances, *artistes.*

But these dummy orchestras foregather only at night. During the day my hand-organ had no competition. Niño and I went from café to café grinding out our repertoire and passing the hat, rarely failing to extract a few pennies from the beer-drinking seamen. The Scandinavians all thought I was Swedish, and were surprised that I couldn't understand one word of their speech. The Italians never heard of a monkey-man who wasn't Italian, and greeted me as one of themselves—with no more success. American seemed to be the last thing in the world they suspected me of being. In fact, unless contested, I shall henceforth claim to be the only American hurdy-gurdy man in history.

On the third morning, Niño's and my partnership business met a great disaster and all but perished.

It happened in the San Martin Park, to which, despite our ejection of two days before, I had recklessly returned.

I wanted to see again my flock of children.

But the very first person I encountered was my bitter enemy, the park guard. He rushed at me with a battery of abuses. I was a vagrant and a bum. Hadn't he warned me once before he'd have me locked up if I came near his park again? He seized me by the arm and started to drag us to the sidewalk. Niño was squealing in alarm at the end of his leash. The guard reached down to seize him too, meaning to fling him bodily across the street. In the struggle Niño bit the officer's hand, receiving in return a vicious kick in the ribs. I didn't mind being battered myself, but objected to having the little animal thus assaulted. I seized the single table leg which supported the organ and which had been broken loose in the mêlée, and with it gave the guard a beautiful crack over the head.

Instantly he blew his riot whistle. Two other police came running to his aid. My crimes were excitedly explained, and I was led over to a near-by police telephone where the patrol wagon was summoned. In another moment it came rushing up. I was shoved into it, the organ and the monkey after me—and off we rolled to jail.

CHAPTER XXII

MY TRAVELING CIRCUS

EXCEPT for Niño's suffering I was not especially alarmed over my predicament. It struck me as being altogether ludicrous—three agitated police and a clanging patrol car rushing a wandering minstrel and his monkey to the Bastille. I'd never ridden in a patrol wagon before and found it very exciting having all the traffic stopped to let my vehicle charge past at full speed. This was next best to riding on a fire engine.

In the suburban police station, small opportunity was given me to defend myself. I had struck an officer of the law with a club. I didn't have a musician's license. I was a tramp and a nuisance. Cell number one for me! They'd tie Niño in the courtyard.

Niño and I really didn't need to submit to this incarceration. My host at the Plaza Hotel was as influential as need be in Argentina to get my case dismissed instantly, for there, as in a sister North American republic, justice has its bosses.

But frankly, I was curious about Argentine jails. It would be a new adventure—for one night. To-morrow I should merely mention the name of my patron and walk out. So I faced the music not without a sense of amusement.

My cell was a surprise and not at all like prison cells I'd been in before. In fact, it was the only cell in the station, and roomy enough to accommodate two dozen inmates. There was no furniture except a concrete bench. The barred iron door was the only opening. Through this door I soon began to hear Niño quarreling in the courtyard and wrestling with his chain. Already I was regretting that I had been so agreeable over my arrest. It wasn't going to be much fun after all.

The fun lasted till six o'clock the next afternoon. Not till that hour did I have a chance to explain things to the commandant.

All apologies, he telephoned the Plaza Hotel to verify my claims to royal patronage.

"Have you a guest named Halliburton?" I heard him ask.

"Yes—off and on. Why?"

"I'm the captain of the X Police Station. He's in jail here!"

"So! *That's* where he's been. Tell him I'll be right over."

Deliverance soon came. Before the bewildered eyes of our rescuers I thrust my liberated circus into the motor-car and sank on to the cushions. Niño, weak from hunger and exposure, clutched my neck with his companionable arms.

We were at large again.

One would have thought that after such an adventure I should have been ready to retire from the monkey business. And so I was—in Buenos Aires. But the provinces! What fresh interests might they not offer! The children there would dance with more abandon than in the city, more truly appreciate the qualities of my monkey. Anyway, I wanted to move on to Rio de Janiero, and so decided to journey overland—overland via the Paraná River and the great Iguassú Falls and the wilds of western Brazil. Nobody in Buenos Aires had ever been known to take this trip. Then all the more reason to go—and just to make it doubly original I resolved to make my way on the earnings of my circus.

Baggage on such an expedition would be disastrous. I sent what little I had on ahead by ship and used the half-hollow organ for a traveling bag. It held my razor, soap, toothbrush, cigarettes and library nicely.

My first destination would be Posadas, forty-eight hours to the north, where, en route to Iguassú, one leaves the rails for boat transportation.

I deliberately chose a local train since it stopped at every station. At each stop I'd get off and shatter the peace of the springtime pampa with heavy-pedal strains of the *Marseillaise.* Baggage-men, idlers, children, new passengers, came flocking up with shouts of *monito, monito,* and always paid and paid for the unexpected and transient entertainment. With each fresh contribution to the treasury I'd buy another ticket from the conductor and ride away as far as the generosity of the last station group permitted.

For two days and nights this concert tour continued. As we approached Posadas the towns grew smaller and smaller, and the box office receipts fell off to such an extent that I should not have been able to make even third class ends meet had the conductor not been so taken with Niño that he let us ride the last few miles for half-fare.

In Posadas I made seven dollars in two days more and bought a deck passage on a river steamer bound up the Paraná. The few passengers were soon parted from all their pennies, and as there were almost no stops along the utterly undistinguished river I had nothing to do but peruse the books I had tucked away inside the organ box.

Niño seemed just as willing to relax from toil. Somebody gave him a broken mirror that kept him entertained for hours. Another less innocent friend learned he liked beer, and the poor monkey never drew a sober breath the rest of the voyage.

It was midnight when, after two days aboard, we came to our point of disembarkation. Upon the river's jungle bank we found a Ford truck waiting for cargo and bummed a ride over several miles of moonlit jungle road. Halting at a clearing, the driver showed me a path which he said would lead to what I had come to see.

Niño and I followed the path, conscious of a strange, far-off rumbling in the air.

Then, abruptly, we came to the edge of a terrific mile-wide chasm—and stood appalled before what seemed at the moment to be all the beauty in the world transformed into mist and moonlight, floating out from some miraculous source among the stars and falling and fading into bottomless mysteries. . . .

I was in the presence of the Iguassú, the greatest waterfall on earth.

At first the realness of the picture did not register. I felt as if I'd been enchanted and allowed

Photograph by Ewing Galloway

The Iguassú River deploys itself into a thousand channels, and then when every water drop is ready, with one mighty charge, along a front ten thousand feet in length, it hurls itself, cheering, over the brink, in superb two-hundred-foot cataracts of foam.

On the Copacabana Beach in Rio de Janeiro, Niño and I attracted innumerable children with our music, but they were usually in bathing suits and innocent of pennies.

a glimpse of the dream-realm of the Titans. Then, clearly, the distant cannonading drifted to me on the wind, and on the wind the mist, and I became aware that what I saw was of this world.

Half a mile away a vast mass of water seemed to flow forth from the sky. It was a river, which, having wandered quietly through the forests of Brazil, had come at length to the edge of a great plateau. There, as though it knows that it is soon to die amid the mighty waters of the Paraná, this little Napoleon of rivers girds itself for a grand climax to its career, so spectacular that no one who sees may ever forget that it surpasses all other rivers in the sublime beauty of its last hour and leaves behind one of the wonders of the world.

In order to achieve this glory, the Iguassú takes its time. The campaign is kept in hand. There is no quickly consummated plunge, no single, mad, headlong dive. The river carefully deploys itself into a thousand channels along both sides of the vast cañon that penetrates deep into its heart, and then when every water-drop is ready, with one mighty charge, along a front *ten thousand feet in length* it hurls itself, cheering, over the brink, in superb two-hundred-foot cataracts of foam.

For me to have come at midnight, alone and lost in the wilderness, unwarned and undefended, upon this moon-drenched vision, made me stand, and stare, and marvel—and believe.

Even Niño, curled up on my shoulder. . . . No, it was my mistake. Niño was not believing. Niño was fast asleep.

I have said that the Iguassú was the greatest waterfall on earth. This statement needs qualifying, lest Niagara and Victoria denounce me. Together these three sister giantesses make a trilogy that stand above, and apart from, all competitors. Niagara claims the largest body of water and the best visibility. Victoria is by far the highest, four hundred feet, but the least visible. In times of high water its own spray almost hides it from view. The Iguassú, with a maximum two-hundred-and-thirty-foot plunge, is seventy feet greater than Niagara, and, with a ten-thousand-foot crestline, over *twice* as long.

For artistry and coloring, Iguassú stands alone. There are no bridges, no power plants, no improvements, such as surround Niagara, to deface it. Blue jungle smothers every rock and islet. The seas of snowy foam send their mists into a tropical sky. Here the jaguars still come to drink as they did a thousand years ago. An utterly primeval state pervades the place and gives to it a wild and verdant beauty which Niagara has long since lost.

Two days later, back at the Paraná, Niño and I took another river boat and voyaged one hundred and twenty-five miles farther up-stream to a place called La Guayra. At this point the Paraná itself takes a header, in a series of rapids, off the edge of the great Brazilian plateau and offers a show of its own that is scarcely less spectacular than the Iguassú. These rapids send a volume of water as large as the Mississippi tearing south in a gorge only four hundred feet wide, at an estimated speed of *seventy miles per hour*. The roar of the maelstrom can be heard for miles. Its terrifying violence caused Niño to cling to me in fear, and woke me up at night for weeks after I had encountered it.

Above the rapids one reëmbarks again. La Guayra is considered the end, the frontier. But once every two months a crazy little paddle-wheel steamboat collects about it a brood of barges and labors another thousand miles up-stream to meet the railroad that leads to civilization.

By the grace of heaven Niño and I just caught the departing caravan. Again we had a free ride. The owner of the boat was sending a friend, who was desperately ill from stomach cancer, to a hospital in Rio and, in serious need of some civilized person to assist in transporting him, turned to me, offering a free ticket in payment.

Niño and I were willing. Still clutching our hand-organ we pushed off, our tiny boat lost upon the Paraná which here, and for many leagues to the north, is four miles wide. Our patient suffered horribly. He could retain no food whatsoever. The drinking water was out of the river. There was no ice, no medicine, no breeze. The heat slayed one with its relentlessness.

Two days from La Guayra I began to fear I would never get him alive to the railroad, five days away. I urged the captain to put on all possible speed.

On the third night, about twelve o'clock, the poor man grew delirious. The realization that he was dying first came to me from Niño, who had set up a most doleful wailing and seemed in mental anguish almost beyond endurance. Every groan from the bunk sent the monkey off into fresh whimpering.

There was nothing I could do but look helplessly on. As I looked, the dying man dragged himself from his bunk and staggered toward the open door which led directly on to the black river. I blocked his way and struggled to hold him back. Niño was shrieking from the window-sill. For a moment this horrible wrestling endured, until in the midst of a convulsion he lurched lifeless to the floor.

The captain and I dressed the corpse in what street clothes were available, and laid him, lacking a better place, on our mess table. Candles were lighted at his head and feet. We sat on the mess benches till morning.

Meanwhile the boat had turned down-stream and was rushing back to La Guayra in order that our unfortunate passenger might have a funeral and a burial in his own community.

Then Niño and I embarked again and struggled back to the scene of the tragedy, our free ride still holding good even though I no longer had a responsibility.

At least I didn't know of any on departure. But one soon arose.

On the third day the only woman on board had a baby.

She had planned to reach the town at the rail head before the baby came, and would have, had not our emergency return to La Guayra delayed our boat almost five days and upset all her calculations. Now her time had come and caught her, a friendless and solitary woman, on a little scow in the middle of the River Paraná. But there's no postponing these babies. They're very inconsiderate in regard to the place of their birth.

The woman was a half-breed about thirty years

old, traveling on the deck. I could not bear to see her child born so publicly. After my recent medical training with the cancer victim I felt like an old family doctor, and though the record of my cases so far had been one hundred per cent. fatalities, I did not hesitate to appoint myself obstetrical expert for the good reason that there was nobody else aboard who either would or could.

The same bunk where my first patient had died was commandeered. I tied Niño outside this time. He would only have suffered otherwise, and been in the way.

The only disinfectant we had was cheap soap; the only instruments, my own scrupulously washed hands.

After three hours of travail, just about dawn, the baby, a girl, was born.

Once the mother was reasonably comfortable I washed the baby in a bucket of river water and took her out to show the captain.

We decided to name her Raquel.

That was the name of the boat.

CHAPTER XXIII

FAREWELL TO NIÑO

For several days more, with never a change in the flat, deadly monotonous, jungle-edged banks, we chugged bravely on up the wide, calm stream, tying on to the shore once or twice a day to renew our fuel supply, or shoot a few ducks for dinner, or deliver a box of supplies to a lonely Indian farmer. Indians, slightly touched with Brazilian culture (nothing for them to be proud of), were the sole inhabitants along the river.

Next to the last day (the eighth), we docked at a little half-caste village of some thirty inhabitants and took aboard a renegade Irishman and seven sixteen-year-old Indian girls.

Each girl, barefooted and bareheaded, was dressed in a single screaming cotton dress and reeked to the heavens of cheap perfume.

The Irishman was as dismal a spectacle as I ever saw, but even so, he spoke my tongue, and I'd not spoken it since leaving Buenos Aires.

"Why all the girl friends?" I asked. "Moving day for the harem?"

"Nope. I'm a buyer."

"You mean you *bought* these females!"

"Sure. And now I've got to sell 'em."

"How much are they worth?"

"How many would you want?"

"Not any, just now. I've got my hands full with a monkey. But suppose—later——?"

"I'll sell you the pink one for seventy-five milreis (thirty dollars)—or the green one. Two for a hundred and twenty-five."

"Do you ever rent them?"

"Sometimes—if the market is bad."

"Where do they come from? Who buys them? Is it a good business? I mean I want to know all about it."

"Sure it's a good business. I have the best connections in this part of Brazil. In the country up along the new railroad there are lots of new ranches with dozens of men and almost no women. They want girls—prefer Indians because Indians are cheap to keep and don't know anything."

"But how do you get them?"

"Easy. I take this boat on the down trip, and stop off at that village back there until the boat comes up-stream again. I bring along some rum and knives and tin money, and these colored night-gowns you see, and lots of cheap perfume, and go calling on the Indian families round about. I give the papas the rum and knives and a few milreis, and the pink dresses and perfume to the girls. Nothing could be simpler. The girls are always crazy to get away. They'd join me just to have a ride on this boat—and they're happy enough with their ranchmen—at least they never seem to want to go back home."

"How much profit do you make on each one?"

"That all depends on their looks. The young and pretty ones bring the most. The ranchers don't seem to mind 'em fat. But they've got to have their teeth. They all have good dispositions—don't mind an occasional beating. Sometimes two men will form a partnership and buy a girl between 'em, or one rancher may buy two or three at once. I have orders for all I can get. I'll take the same train you're taking and leave these dames all down the line."

"And then?"

"And then I'll go to São Paulo and spend it all in a week."

But he didn't have to wait to reach São Paulo to have his fling, for the last night before we docked—December twenty-fourth—he got uproariously lit on his own rum. Thereupon, the *Raquel's* Indian crew, realizing that the maidens' Irish chaperon was *hors de combat,* took advantage of the situation to the extent of commandeering my hand-organ and, amid the loud strains of *Valencia,* seeing to it that on Christmas Eve a good time was had by all.

The thousand-mile railroad from São Paulo west to the Paraná is what the Union Pacific was in 1870—crude but promising.

Once on it with Niño and the hurdy-gurdy, I returned to my old practise of concertizing at each station. Nor had Niño lost his skill at extracting alms. Even so, we were fighting a losing battle with the train conductor, when the baggageman, smitten with the monkey's winsome ways, took pity on our traveling circus and gave us a ride in his baggage car for twenty-four hours into São Paulo.

There we worked hard for three days—*Valencia, La Paloma, Marseillaise—Valencia, La Paloma, Marseillaise*—all over this rich and beautiful city. Argentines or Brazilians, it was all the same to Niño. They kept their coins in the same places. But I think Niño preferred the Brazilians—their police didn't arrest you and pack you off to jail.

The moment we had saved up third-class rail fare

When I die I don't want to go to heaven; I want to go back to Rio.

In the capital of Brazil, Niño and I climbed one day to the summit of the Sugar Loaf in the harbor, and there held a concert.

to Rio, away we went to the capital, twelve hours beyond.

When I die I don't want to go to heaven; I want to go back to Rio. It is so unquestionably the most beautiful city in the world I don't see why other cities put up any claim at all. The buildings themselves are commonplace, but you forget that after one glance at the gorgeous harbor with the jungle-covered peaks piling up behind, and the red roofs gleaming in the eternal sunshine, and the tropical sky and the sparkle and splash to everything. Somehow *Valencia* sounded sweeter here, the *Marseillaise* more ringing. The people are even gentler than the Argentines, looser, more tolerant, less successful. Niño reduced the Argentines to children. He reduced the Brazilians to tears.

Our favorite stand was on the Copacabana Beach. It was summertime in Rio, and at this season this beach, five hundred feet deep of gleaming snowy sand, is the favorite playground for hundreds of thousands of Rio's gay untroubled citizens.

The chief difficulty was that even though we needed only to touch the organ handle to have children running up in crowds, they were in bathing suits and innocent of pennies. The streets and parks offered ten times the profit. But for the first few days we couldn't be bothered. Better starve on the Copacabana Beach than prosper away from it.

Later we did make sorties to the top of the Sugar Loaf in the harbor, and up the cog railroad to Corcovado hanging three thousand feet above the town. On one of these occasions we met up with serious competition, a baritone street singer who with a mandolin under his arm made as sweet music as ever came off the sidewalks. And he had a way of getting paid for it too.

As each of us sensed in the other a dangerous rival, we decided to organize a partnership, sharing profits equally. He knew the town, but I had the better show. It worked marvelously. He sang; I played; Niño danced. We simply stopped traffic.

And yet, before a week had passed, I began to realize that my hurdy-gurdy days were numbered. I had done what I had set out to do—made my way overland from Buenos Aires to Rio on the profits of my monkey business. But any prolongation of this escapade would be senseless and ever less amusing. The time had come for me to push north to French Guiana. Niño, much as I loved him, could not continue on indefinitely. It would be winter when I reached America. He had never known, and could not survive, cold weather. The sane thing, the only thing, to do was to give him his liberty—back into the forest, his original, his natural, domain.

So I took a taxi to the jungles that surround the city and, finding a nice wild nut-tree, cut the leather belt from Niño's waist and lifted him, a free, a self-possessing monkey, into the branches.

For me this was a most unhappy moment. Had I been abandoning my own child I could not have felt worse about it. Yet this was the lesser of the two evils. Better to leave him here than to take him away.

I stroked his head one last time, as he looked at me with a most curious and troubled look. What new crime was I up to now? How well I had come to understand his thoughts, to speak his language, and how well he had come to understand my own. He seemed to sense that something ominous was behind this strange behavior of mine and searched my face for an explanation.

But however heartbreaking, I must see this beastly business through. He would be lonely for a day, until he learned to live in his treetops once more.

I shook his hand good-by and hurried toward the waiting taxi. Instantly Niño realized the truth and let forth one wail of despair. He was climbing down from the tree. I began to run. Screeching he ran after me, leaped upon my hurrying knee, climbed in a bound to his usual perch on top my shoulder, and sat there trembling and pleading and sobbing.

There was no escape. His gentle, dependent nature had conquered me long before. Miserable and lost, I surrendered, resigned to the realization that if I had to stay in the tropics the rest of my life for his sake, I'd never leave that ragamuffin monkey.

French Guiana was still in the tropics. Niño would be safe that far. So I took him, still with the hand-organ, aboard my north-bound ship, trusting he would enjoy the voyage.

He did enjoy it. Free of any leash, he ran all over the place, climbed the mast, swung and leaped about in the most hair-raising acrobatics. From the very first moment aboard he was the king and the joy of the boat. The crew loved him; the passengers all sought his company.

This popularity, however, while it may have been deserved, had its penalties. Everybody on the boat wanted to—and did—feed him. The sweeter and more indigestible the morsel, the more greedily he ate it and the more satisfactory the exhibition. His consumption of candy and cookies passed belief . . . with lump sugar and peanuts and beer in between. Such shocking gluttony began to alarm me. But I had always understood that animals, unlike men, eat only as much as they relish and need; and so I supposed Niño was the best judge.

This was a stupid and criminal mistake. As we neared the equator my four-pound monkey ate four or five doughnuts, a large cake of chocolate and three bananas all in one afternoon, and shortly after suffered a sudden and violent attack of acute gastritis. Seeing that he was extremely ill, I carried him, clinging to me desperately, to his box on the lower deck and rushed for the ship's doctor. Together we came hurrying back. Niño lay in his box, his fragile little hands crossed over his face. I called to him. Here was the doctor. Everything would be all right now.

But Niño did not seem to comprehend.

Niño was dead.

We had a very simple funeral. I dressed him in his old red carnival suit, and the red hat that had known so many pennies, and wrapped him in a pillow-case for a burial at sea.

I felt he might like music for his funeral. So I

brought out the faithful hurdy-gurdy that he might depart to the strains of his beloved *Valencia.* Once more I turned the rusty handle; once more, as a number of Niño's friends stood silent along the rail, the old, familiar melody rang forth. . . .

Valencia—in my dreams it always seems I hear you
softly call to me—
Valencia—where the or-ange trees for ever scent
the breeze beside the sea—
Valencia—in my arms I held your charms beneath
the blossoms high above—
You loved me;—in Valencia, long ago, tra, la,
la, la——

There was a very small splash in the vast Atlantic as Niño's body was dropped into its dark waters.

Niño was gone. Yet the organ remained and, as Trudis had said, what good is an organ without a monkey?

So lest the little fellow feel lonely and incomplete on his outward journey, I dropped the hand-organ into the sea beside him.

Thus did Niño depart for the place where all good and faithful monkeys go, where the pennies are all pesos, where the *Valencias* are never ceasing, and the hand-organs are all made of gold. There, in that blessed and happy land, he can eat all the doughnuts his heart desires, and never, never fear acute gastritis.

CHAPTER XXIV

DEVIL'S ISLAND

THE noonday heat rested heavily on the Iles du Salut. Man and beast, the wind and the sea, lay sleeping. It was the siesta hour.

But that day the Iles du Salut were not destined to complete their usual slumber, for they were awakened, suddenly and startlingly, by a strange and terrible roar that fell down upon them from the skies. Was a cyclone coming from the Caribbean Sea, or a tidal wave? Windows flew open. People rushed out into the streets.

The cause of the roaring was soon apparent: a gigantic airplane overhead—the first airplane the Iles du Salut had ever seen.

It was the flying boat *Washington* making its historic, path-finding flight from New York to Buenos Aires.

And I was aboard her.*

* My ocean liner from Rio (upon which Niño had died), did not stop at French Guiana, my destination, but carried me on to Trinidad, eight hundred miles beyond. Here I was taken aboard the *Washington* and brought back to Guiana by air.

At noon that day, flying at six thousand feet, I had descried upon the sea, some miles ahead, three dark blurs. Quickly they grew clearer—islands, small islands, green islands, covered with palm trees and houses. Nearer and nearer, with two thundering engines, we rushed toward them, down upon them, within three hundred feet of them.

An intense excitement seized me, for I knew that this, below, was Devil's Island!

Devil's Island, and its two companions—the Iles du Salut—the most terrible, the most tragic prison in the world! They lie just off the coast of French Guiana. To them France sends her worst, her most dangerous, criminals to die of tropical heat, and fever, and wretchedness, and despair.

Down upon the eight hundred miserable, decaying, victims of this infamous prison, our seaplane swept like a supernatural monster from some other world. Many of the prisoners there had been in captivity twenty years and had never seen men fly before. The excitement was enormous. They poured into the prison courts, or clutched the iron bars that held them back, trying to behold the miracle.

But no prisoner there was half as agitated over seeing us, as I was over seeing them. I nearly fell out of the plane, staring down at these little isles.

I could distinguish each one that makes up the group, Devil's Island, the smallest, completely hidden under palm trees; Ile Royale, the largest, with the big prison on the plateau, and the hospital, and the commandant's house; and Saint Joseph, the terrible island of agonies where, under the roofs of those three long buildings, two hundred men were caged like animals in windowless, special punishment cells, for the expiation of their crimes and the protection of society.

All this I knew because I had informed myself beforehand. And I knew that I was coming back to this place to reside among these outcasts, wear their convict clothes, eat their convict food, live as they lived. I didn't know how all this was to be brought to pass. That outsiders were not welcome I was well aware. But at the same time I was determined to enter there. Absolutely nothing else on earth mattered. I was prepared to take any risk, pay any price, that would get me convicted into the company of *les miserables* on the Iles du Salut.

And I got there, and I did all there was to do, and saw all there was to see. And I have come away to tell the story—to tell it as bluntly as possible. But if I tell only that which is the truth, who shall condemn me?

CHAPTER XXV

DE PROFUNDIS

When we landed in the harbor of Cayenne, the capital and chief port of French Guiana, it seemed the entire population rushed to the dock to greet us. A *fête* was given that night in our honor, and when the *Washington* sped on next morning, and I was left behind, French hospitality continued to be showered upon the one remaining hero.*

It was soon apparent, however, to the official French families that I was not a hero at all, but a disgrace to my country and my social caste, for I very quickly found out that Cayenne is as much of a prison center for the French *transportés* as the islands, and I promptly withdrew from its respectable mulatto citizenry in favor of all the thieves and murderers in town. I wanted to know the *transportés* intimately. That's why I had come so far. To achieve this I had to be, as far as pos-

* The explanation I offered for remaining in Cayenne was that so much extra gasoline had to be taken aboard to reach the next fueling station that it was necessary to sacrifice one member of the "crew" in order to avoid overloading.

sible, one of them. And so from the very first day, I plunged into my new rôle, and for the month I remained in French Guiana scarcely spoke to anybody not in convict stripes. Local creole tea parties held for me no interest. But in the faces and the hearts of those outcast thieves and murderers I found a living, aching picture of much that is wrong with the world.

Before I had been long in town I made a friend of a young French convict-intern in the convent-hospital, where, in lack of a hotel, I was quartered. André was intelligent, an ex-Parisian medical student. True, he was a murderer, and having spent seven years in various Guiana prison cells was now serving out his life sentence as a hospital slave. But these facts only made his friendship of double interest and double value to me.

I talked to him, the first time, during the siesta hour when Cayenne's ten thousand inhabitants sleep. Nothing stirred outdoors but the countless vultures which hopped and waddled unmolested about the sun-scorched streets.

"André, you're a fine young fellow. What are *you* doing in this dismal place?" (I knew what he was doing, but I wanted to have him tell me himself.)

"I'm a convict, Monsieur—*en perpétuité.* But

De profundis.

In Cayenne I donned the prison uniform (right hand figure) and, in order that I might learn the truth about the Devil's Island penal colony, lived as the prisoners lived.

as you see I've received a first-class ticket for good conduct, and can work in private homes and institutions. I don't have to wear the stripes."

"You were sent here for murder, weren't you?"

"*Oui,* Monsieur. I killed my mistress."

"Oh,——" A slightly embarrassed silence, and then: "It must be depressing to look forward to spending all your life in Cayenne."

"If it only *were* Cayenne. I'll probably be sent back to Saint Laurent."

"Saint Laurent? Where's that?"

"That's the real headquarters of the penal colony, but it's only a detestable little town on the Maroni River—the river that divides French Guiana from Dutch Guiana. The biggest prisons are there, and about two-thirds of the prisoners, some three thousand or more. You never see that many, for the lumber camps keep most of them employed."

"But the islands——"

"They have eight hundred. Half on Royale and half on Saint Joseph. Devil's Island, where Captain Dreyfus was imprisoned, has less than a dozen, all political exiles. We have five hundred in Cayenne."

"That makes about forty-five hundred in all."

"Sixty-five hundred, counting the two thousand *libérés.*"

"Libérés?"

"Yes, they are the ex-convicts who have served out their sentences but can not leave the colony. They have to remain as many years as *libérés* as they served as convicts—that is if their sentence is under seven years. Over seven, they have to stay here always. They are the poor old wrecks you see with their wheelbarrows sitting around on street corners, starving to death."

I had seen them, and I was to see many more of them. They are one of the most tragic features of this tragic place.

"What does become of all the *transportés,* André?" I asked. "You say there are sixty-five hundred. But I see numbers on their uniforms as high as fifty thousand. Where have they all gone to?"

André laughed. It was a very bitter laugh.

"To the bamboos."

I looked uncomprehending.

"That's the cemetery. It's enclosed by thickets of bamboos. The French Government has to send new men out fast to keep the prisons filled. The casualties are a thousand a year—dead, escaped, disappeared. One convoy replaces another. The commissary department always plans for fifty per cent. of the new men to die the first twelve months.

Food and clothes are purchased accordingly. I came out seven years ago with seven hundred others. Not one hundred of us remain. Fifty a year are murdered by their fellow-convicts; a hundred die trying to escape. The fever, the dysentery, the food, the heat, the jungles, the despair take the others. France knows when she sends us here that we'll never come back to plague her. One year—five years—ten years! It's all a mockery. Any sentence to Guiana is a condemnation to death. We call it the dry-guillotine.

"But I mustn't intrude too long upon your time, Monsieur." André rose as if to go. "I forgot nobody is interested in convicts."

"Oh, but you're wrong, André. I'm terribly interested. There's much more I want to ask. I understand there's a special ship that brings you out from France. It must be quite an undertaking to transport a thousand rebellious prisoners all at once."

"There's a special ship all right," André said, taking his seat again, "—*La Martinière*. She has the distinction of being the only convict ship left in the world. Leaves the Saint Martin de Ré prison at Marseilles twice a year. It was March when I came over on her—seven hundred of us. We wore heavy gray wool uniforms and wooden shoes. They had us manacled in threes. Squads of soldiers with fixed bayonets all about. It was a half-fearful, half-hopeful moment for me. Out of prison, if only for ten minutes—with a sea voyage ahead. But oh, *mon Dieu,* I did not know—— None of us spoke. Every mouth was closed grimly. All you saw were expressions of misery and malediction. Manacled to me on one side was an assassin who had killed because he was too lazy to work. On the other a bank bandit who had locked his victim in the vault and let him suffocate. Behind the military cordon a big crowd stood and watched. Here and there an old woman, suffering and weeping, caught sight of her boy, and waved a pitiful handkerchief—perhaps he would come back soon—perhaps escape. There was always hope. She couldn't see the thickets of bamboos waving in the hot Guiana breeze. My own mother died long before. I thanked God for it—that day. But my sister was there. She always fights for me. She saw me, and I heard her cry out: '*A bientôt!*'

"*A bientôt!*—seven years gone—seven thousand years ahead——"

Silence.

"Tell me about the convict ship, André."

"Oh, it's a terrible cage, divided up into compartments for fifty men. We slept in hammocks strung so close together they touched. And there were pipes all around filled with steam in case of a mutiny. But there wasn't much chance for a mutiny,—not with sixty-five military police aboard. The food was just prison food—soggy bread and beef soup, like all prisons. Seven hundred of us were crowded together, the good and the bad, the depraved and the innocent, and left to our own devices for three weeks."

"If you were a judge, what would you do about it, André?"

"Well, Monsieur, I'm a convict. I've suffered as the others have suffered. I hate this place with all my soul. Even so, I can understand that many of us deserve all we get. Many are incorrigible criminals who have been sentenced time after time in France until the courts as a last resort send them here to die of fever. I suppose if I were a judge I'd do the same with them.

"But there's another type on the convoy, men like myself, not at all criminal at heart, men who have committed a crime in a moment of blind passion, only to be horrified the next moment at the behavior of their own hands. These men, often of gentle birth and good minds, suffer most from the degradation and torment of prison life. They are the first to die—of broken bodies and broken hearts.

If I were a judge, I'd have to imprison this type, I suppose, but I wouldn't sentence them to be tortured in Guiana.

"And there is the most tragic element of all—the boys, eighteen years old, seventeen, sixteen even, caged on the *Martinière* with its vicious cargo and sent into exile for some youthful madness. They get debauched by the older convicts, taught every form of crime and robbed of all the goodness and honor they ever knew. What boy's heart is truly criminal at seventeen? But his innocence is short-lived on the *Martinière*. I think that the judge who sends *him* to this hell-hole is the worst criminal of us all."

CHAPTER XXVI

CONVICT NUMBER 49,766

THAT evening when André had finished with his hospital duties he came again to my room. All afternoon I'd been evolving complicated schemes to get myself locked up inside the prison walls, and needed his assistance.

"André, here's one hundred francs. I want you to buy me a complete convict uniform. That's enough money?"

"*Oui,* Monsieur—but—if you will excuse my saying so—isn't it a very strange purchase?"

"Not at all. I wish to spend to-morrow night in the prison barrack, and need the proper costume."

Again André would have smiled at my idea, only he saw I was in dead earnest.

"I want to find out the truth about prison for myself."

"Will they let you?"

"The warden won't. But I think the guards will."

"But, Monsieur, you don't know what you're getting into. There'll be eighty convicts in that barrack, Arabs and negroes, murderers and robbers. They will kill you if they think you've any money."

"Then I'll take a knife."

"Somebody will steal it."

"If I'm in danger, André, I'll just yell for you."

Next morning, still playing the rôle of stranded aviator, I gained, through devious channels, the ears—and the pockets—of the two guards who came on duty late that afternoon. They were amused and pleased that a great American flyer like myself should want to spend a night in their prison, and agreed to help me. We must stake our chances on audacity. To ask for official permission would be disastrous. Our plan was simple, but completely bold.

The prison schedule had to be considered first.

At six o'clock in the morning the two hundred and fifty prisoners quartered in the Cayenne barracks went to work (the other two hundred and fifty stationed locally were in punishment cells, in lumber camps, or scattered about the town as servants, interns, watchmen, etc.). They labored in groups repairing the streets, working as stevedores, or a dozen other forms of manual labor, some under guard, some unsupervised. At ten-thirty they returned to the prison court, were fed their noon-day soup and allowed to rest till two, then marched out again, and back at half past five. Between half past five and six they ate supper and assembled in the court for roll-call. Immediately afterward they were locked in for the night.

It was the guards' plan that I should enter the courtyard as the roll-call formation was breaking up. I'd be wearing the uniform just like all the others. The chances were excellent that if I mingled with the crowd of convicts returning to their barracks for the night I could enter the barrack-door along with them and never be noticed. Once inside there'd be no guards to question me—but once inside I'd have to shift for myself. There were at present a few more canvas-strip beds than inmates (the *Martinière* had skipped its last semi-annual voyage while the departures to the bamboos had continued to be as numerous as ever). I could probably find and occupy one of these strips. As for getting out in the morning——? I had no concern over that. My only concern was getting in. If I failed and was caught I promised my accomplices I would in no way implicate them. All the guards had to do was not to see me when I passed from the street through the prison-portal into the courtyard. The hour was to be a quarter to six. We could not see a single hitch.

Next morning André had my uniform ready—cotton blouse and trousers, striped red and white, and the wide straw hat. Stamped across the blouse in big black figures was the number 49,766. I discreetly did not ask André where he got the outfit. Unfortunately it was almost new, so we soaked it in hot water to take the shine and stiffness out.

To rehearse my new part I slipped down behind the convent walls to the seashore during the siesta hour, donned the uniform and hat, and paraded, barefooted, up the main street. Of the dozen people abroad at that moment not one even so much as noticed me. That was good.

Half past five came. Again I went to the shore and waited, this time behind the prison walls which also face the sea. This time I was carrying a small tin bucket. André, now keenly interested in my adventure, had suggested this, for at the supper hour a number of town-quartered prisoners come with their regulation buckets to the prison for their rations. I would be mistaken for one of these.

The roll-call bugle sounded. I waited, somewhat taut, for eight minutes, as the guards had instructed me; then strolled, with what I supposed looked like a very casual gait, toward the front entrance.

There was my friendly guard, standing near-by.

With my head down, trying not to show the pain the rocky gravel was causing my bare feet, I walked straight for the gate. Another convict walked just in front dressed exactly as I was dressed, with a bucket just like mine. I am not sure the guard even saw me, so perfectly did I fit into the habitual picture.

But one point we had overlooked—the search that every convict must submit to as he passes into the courtyard. This oversight might have proved disastrous, had there not been the other convict three feet ahead of me to set the example. I saw the turnkey stop him. Up went his arms mechanically. A quick search, equally mechanical. On my example marched, and I took his place. Up went my arms. Scarcely noticing my face, the turnkey made the usual automatic gestures. Then I too marched on, right for the group filing into the nearest barrack door, through the door, into the ultimate goal.

Still nobody noticed me. New convict faces are seen almost daily in any one of the Guiana prisons, for the prisoners are continually being shifted, or dying and being replaced.

It was only six o'clock, but already the barrack was growing dark. Yet not too dark for me to make a quick survey. The room was about one hundred feet long and twenty wide. An iron railing six feet away from the wall ran parallel to it for the entire length of the building. Between the wall and the railing the canvas-strip beds were stretched, forty on each side. This gave each bed only two and one-half feet. Herring are not packed closer than Guiana convicts.

Seventy-seven men were quartered in "my" barrack. That left three vacant beds. I must find one of these without attracting attention. To be sure it didn't matter, now that the door was locked, and the turnkey departed, whether I was found out or not, except that I preferred to have them ignore rather than notice me. I saw several convicts that had rowed me ashore from our seaplane. If they recognized "the American aviator" in their midst there'd be considerable excitement. I'd be favored and fêted. My comrades would put on their party manners. The news of my adventure would be all over town next day, and the governor would hear of it, and I'd be asked to leave the colony.

No, at any cost, I must remain inconspicuous.

The prisoners did not at once seek each his own bed, as I had hoped. They drifted into groups, or paced up and down the boulevard between the railings. I was standing at the end of the aisle, watching. About six beds distant I saw a canvas strip that I judged was unoccupied because of the lack of personal possessions on the shelf above. On either side lay a convict reading, and when I climbed on to the vacant strip one of them, a hard-faced rogue about thirty-five, looked up and asked profanely what I wanted. He had taken off his shirt to use for a pillow, and his bare shoulders, burned black by the sun and covered with tattoo, revealed that he was a military prisoner from some north African army camp.

"I want to sleep here, if it isn't occupied,"—in my best French.

In a tone that was anything but cordial he grumblingly withdrew his objections, and I climbed on to the strip.

It is only natural that with such crowded quarters a vacant bed beside one is highly prized and reluctantly surrendered. A new convict coming into the barrack sometimes has difficulty finding a berth—that is unless he looks as if he might have money. Then he has no difficulty at all. In fact there is keen competition for his company. The strong and self-assertive take whatever bed they wish, unoccupied or otherwise. But if one is neither rich nor strong—only an average wretched convict, a *cave* is the slang of the prison—he must seek the barrack proctor, himself a convict, and have him use his official powers to commandeer a canvas strip.

These beds are the only furniture. They are the chairs and the tables. On them one sleeps, eats, writes, gambles. The canvas is not renewed until it rots and falls to pieces. The sweat, the grime, the evil odor, of many years, of many convicts who have come and gone are imbedded deep into the warp and woof.

It was completely dark outside now. (Night comes swiftly in Guiana.) The stars shone through the dozen small grilled windows up near the roof. I sat back on my bed and leaned against the wall that I might command a view of the entire barrack.

The air had become rather heavy—nearly eighty men packed so close together. I noted that all the prisoners had taken off their blouses, disdainful of the mosquitoes which had swarmed in for their evening feast, and seventy-odd nude torsos caught the faint rays of the kerosene lamps.

These lamps were in keeping with the rest of the prison—made by the prisoners themselves out of condensed milk tins and filled with fuel, into which they had dropped a wick of cotton bandage. Africa owned one of these little flames, and it was by this that he read. The prison does provide a central lamp, but it is so feeble that without these home-made reënforcements either end of the long room would be left in darkness.

The shelves that support these private lamps run, one on each wall, the length of the barrack just above the line of beds. Upon them is placed all the property belonging to the prisoner—small boxes, bottles, photographs.

At the far extremity of the room is the latrine, reached via a narrow stone passage. I noted that it was placed as close as possible to the kitchen.

By this time idle visiting had ceased, and everybody was occupying himself with something. A dozen or so of the convicts had spread a blanket on the floor by the door and were seated on it cross-legged playing a card game called *Marseillaise*. The proctor held the stakes in a tin box which he shook noisily in an effort to entice more players. One man near to me was mending a pair of shoes; another, tattooed even more flamboyantly than Africa, was carving a coconut; another weaving a crude lace tablecloth out of sisal fiber. In the dim distance a mandolin and a banjo tinkled the popular music of three years ago.

That, briefly, was the setting.

Of the seventy-seven prisoners in my barrack I later learned that forty-nine were serving life sentences for murder. The others were there for various lengths and for various crimes. Of the seventy-seven only forty-four were French—eight Germans, eight negroes, five Italians, four Spaniards, three Poles, three Annamite Chinese, and two Arabs. Some of them were pitifully thin and emaciated, others, like Africa, seemed to have thrived on hard labor and deprivations, and looked as strong as ever. A dozen were young men around twenty; another dozen, old men, incredibly old men, of fifty, who could scarcely remember the crime they had committed. And in between was every age and condition. Some had come out on the last *Martinière;* some had been here thirty years. It was easy to tell how long each had served by the degree of hopeless wretchedness in his face.

And yet they were not all-dead inside. From time to time the spark of life blazes up in a moment of fury against an enemy. This barrack, filled with what seemed completely whipped spirits, had known many a murder. There is a convention that all murders must take place in the latrine. There, left to themselves, the opposing forces fight it out. Nor is there any half-murder. It's always done thoroughly, lest the victim squeal on the victor. Nobody else ever knows anything about it. To bear tales against another convict is unpardonably bad form. Half the murderers in prison go unpunished. (The dead man is a good riddance,—one less convict.) The other half get locked up in close confinement for a few months. Any attempt to escape from prison is an infinitely worse crime than murder in it. *This* may lead you to three years in the bear-pits.

So quiet and isolated had I been all this time, that I am sure nobody except my inhospitable neighbor was fully conscious of my presence. I saw him, out of the corner of my eye, scrutinizing me. My broad accent, my uncropped hair (in the exigencies of travel it had not been cut for a month), my intense interest in the life about, all stamped me as being a stranger and a prison novice.

"What nationality are you?" Africa asked. His curiosity had at last displaced his resentment.

"Dutch," I declared. "I've just come from the islands." This last was true.

"What did they ship you out for?"

"Murdered my mistress," I said, echoing the usual phrase. "What was your crime?"

"Same here," he admitted yawning. "Got a cigarette?"

I did have, and gave him one.

"Would you like to see my pictures?" he asked.

"Très bien."

He reached into his little treasure chest on the shelf behind and grasped a handful of photographs and letters.

"This one is my old lady."

"She's young-looking to be your mother. She's probably given you many a licking."

"Never once. But my old man used to often enough."

"This one—who is this?"

"That's the girl I killed."

"She's very pretty."

"A good pal. I'm sometimes sorry I did it."

In every pocket, in every wallet, on all the walls of every prison in Guiana, there are pictures of women—mothers, mistresses, actresses, queens, fashion plates perhaps in the mode of 1916, nudes from *La Vie Parisienne.*

Woman to the prisoner * in Guiana is always splendid, always provocative. Nine men out of ten are there because of her. All nine blame her for their plight. And all nine yearn for her, and call for her.

The more the memory of the real woman fades, the more the prisoner embellishes her virtues and her loveliness. They forget the unhappy hours.

* The following passage is derived from a letter written to me by one of the convicts in Cayenne.

They remember only the tenderness or the intoxication. They have conserved only a gesture, an attitude; but the gesture is beautiful, the attitude divine.

The betrayals, the hurts, the quarrels, the blows —these have all faded. It is the sweetness of a kiss, the gentleness of a glance, the song of a voice, that moves them and warms them still.

La femme! For the prisoner in Guiana she is not the "calamity," of Hesiod, nor the "instrument of the devil," of Saint Bernard. She is the source of all beauty, all happiness, all goodness—the only refuge.

Africa's women had gone back into his box. But they did not stay there. His lamp had been extinguished; all the other lamps as well. And now all the women from all the seventy-seven boxes came invisibly for a rendezvous with the lovers who had murdered them, with the sons who had broken their hearts. The dreaming convict sees them reach out to him, recovering his heart, recapturing his body, which the law believed it had taken away for ever. Sometimes the visitor is gray, and sad; sometimes she is young, and nude, a temptress, holding her breasts in her hands and waiting for his passionate embrace. . . .

And then the rain fell violently upon the rotting

sheet-iron roof. The flood of water came dripping through. The dreamers stirred and cursed, cursed to realize it was only the old, old dream. There was no pity; there was no tenderness, no lips, no love. There was only the rain and the rats, only the stench of their own wet bodies, only hate and helplessness and despair, only the eternal, tormenting, hunger—only, only—prison.

CHAPTER XXVII

THE BLOCKHAUS

From Cayenne I traveled by means of a small coastal steamer to Saint Laurent, situated, as André had explained to me, some twenty miles up the Maroni River, the river that divided French from Dutch Guiana.

Saint Laurent is the real heart of the penal colony. The administration offices are all here, and likewise, in the neighborhood, over half the convicts. Here too reside a thousand *libérés,* who compose one-third of the town's population.

It is at Saint Laurent that the *Martinière* discharges the major part of her unhappy cargo, and it is beneath the "bamboos" at Saint Laurent that so many of the convicts so soon find a release from their wretchedness.

Naturally no convict believes that the bamboos will be *his* fate. There have been escapes from the colony—several hundred in the last thirty years; and what others have done the new convict believes that he too will do.

The first year nearly half of them attempt it, urged onward by the sight of the corpses of the other half being carried to the cemetery.

But of every twenty-five that run away, only one succeeds in gaining liberty. The other twenty-four are recaptured by the ocean and the jungle. They are the two omniscient, omnipresent *surveillants*. They never sleep. They never relent. They are the savage watchdogs into whose keeping the prison has entrusted its victims. The military guards themselves are only there to receive the defeated convict on his delivery by the jungle, and to impose upon him new torments in punishment for his rebellion against the old.

And yet though the escaping prisoners starve in the forest, feed the ravenous insects, go mad, suffer unspeakably, before they stagger home; though the sea devours their hollow log and washes them ashore crazed with thirst and sunstroke into the hands of the Dutch officials; though the penalty for all this sacrifice is a fresh sentence of three years of silence and solitary confinement in a torture chamber on the islands, the desperate struggle for liberty via these two terrible routes is never-ending. What stronger indictment against the penal colony of French Guiana can there be than

The "bamboos" in St. Laurent. The grave-digger has little time to rest.

Convicts in St. Laurent at work in the lumber yards.

Les Iles du Salut, generally known as "Devil's Island." Devil's Island itself is the smallest of the three, at the upper right. Only a handful of political prisoners are quartered here. Ile Royale, at the upper left, is the largest of the group, containing the administration buildings, the commandant's house, the hospital, the galley slaves' prison, and barracks for two hundred *transportés*. St. Joseph, with its infamous punishment cells, is in the foreground. This island-group is twelve miles from the mainland. The picture was painted, with surprising accuracy, by a prisoner.

that the prisoners, to escape from it, are willing to face all these torments, feeling that no matter how great the agony ahead of them may be, it can not be so bad as that which they have left behind.

Sometimes they do succeed. Sometimes by a miracle they endure the six hundred miles of sea that separates them from Venezuela. (Dutch and English Guiana, the two logical asylums, are not asylums at all, for every convict caught there is sent back ruthlessly to Saint Laurent.) Or even more likely they hoard their miserable earnings, winnings, thievings, month after month, until they have the five hundred francs necessary to bribe a fisherman to smuggle them away in his sailboat to Cuba or Para.

A convict has difficulty preserving this fortune while it accumulates. He can not keep it in the Bank of France. Convicts are not allowed to possess money. Nor in his hip-pocket. It would be seized at the daily pocket inspection. Nor in a box on the shelf above his bed. It would be stolen by his neighbor in less time than it takes to tell it. No, he has only one depository that is safe, the only one that remains—his own body. In this vault, in a large aluminum capsule called a *plan*, he safeguards the price of freedom.

This sounds so easy—just save up, till you have five hundred francs, and then book passage on a departing ship. But where is the money coming from? Certainly not in payment for his prison labor. Yet there must be other ways, for the necessary sum from time to time *is* attained. One way is to get yourself hired out as a *garçon de famille,* in the household of a military guard. Here you earn twenty francs a month—eighty cents—and maybe save half of it. In four years you will have the price.

Or you can murder a fellow convict for the money he has stolen from some one else. It's fatal to reveal, even to your best friend, that you've money in your *plan.* The desperate and hardened ones will scheme unceasingly to get it, will threaten you, will garrote you. The weak and the timid convict is afraid to resist. He knows that his attackers have no fear of the consequences of murdering him. The penalty is only a few weeks in a reclusion cell. He knows that they know that he won't dare squeal even if they carve his *plan* out of his body with a kitchen knife. Squealing won't get his money back. It will only bring fresh revenge.

And there is always prostitution. If you are young enough and appealing enough, the wives of the guards, as a diversion from the miserable monotony of the place, will pay you well for an occasional clandestine embrace.

The story is told of one lusty young gentleman who with a face handsomer than his morals was in such demand among the local ladies that he earned a thousand francs before he'd been in town three months, and bought a de luxe passage outward on a trading schooner. His departure was greatly lamented by half the wives in Saint Laurent.

No, escape is not so easy. If it were there would not be four thousand convicts rotting away this instant in a Guiana gaol.

The first evening I reached Saint Laurent I left my lodging about midnight for a stroll around the little town. There was a moon and the avenues of palm trees formed black vaulted aisles above the deserted streets. I passed the silent prison—the great prison—and knew that inside five hundred men were sleeping on canvas strips dreaming the same dreams, enduring the same pain, as their fellows in Cayenne. Beyond lay the river, all silver in the moonlight. I found the pier where the *Martinière* ties up, and aimlessly walked out upon it, avoiding the holes in the rat-eaten and dilapidated planks.

At the far edge I noticed the flicker of a small lamp, and on approaching found a man barefooted and in convict clothes leaning against a broken post. The faint light emphasized the deep shadows of one of the most bitter faces I've ever seen. That is, it was as bitter as a young face can be, for the convict was not over twenty-five. The bitterness was in his mouth. In his eyes one might have seen keen sensitiveness. It was a face that rarely spoke, never smiled—only suffered.

"*Bon soir, mon ami.* Do you sleep on the dock?"

"No. I'm the watchman."

"You must get lonesome by yourself here all night."

He shrugged his shoulders in a detached, indifferent way, and remained silent. But his very reserve distinguished him from the other garrulous prisoners I had met, and made me all the more curious to know his history.

I handed him a cigarette and a match. He seized them eagerly. This is the key to every *transporté's* good will.

"I say you must get lonesome here. It's so still and melancholy."

"It's better than the barracks."

More silence. Then presently . . . the cigarettes were softening him a bit:

"Aren't you a stranger in Saint Laurent, Monsieur?"

"Yes. I'm an American. I've come to visit your prison."

He looked at me in amazement. I must be mad, coming to this ungodly place when I didn't have to.

"What brought *you* here?" I asked, getting to the point.

It was the old story—an eighteen-year-old boy desperately in love with a more worldly and less honest woman. He must have money lest he lose her. He went to rob a restaurant—his first crime; was surprised, and in terror fired his pistol at the gendarme who was about to arrest him.

Traveaux forcés en perpétuité.

"Two times I've tried to escape."

He was talking now with more and more willingness. I gave him another cigarette—I gave him the whole package. Escape. That was exactly what I wanted to hear about.

"And you've always failed."

"Yes. The first time I tried to go via Albina."

Albina is the Dutch town on the river directly opposite Saint Laurent. Though a mile distant across the water its intensely white houses are conspicuous by day in the tropical sunlight, and by night its dock lights twinkle upon the wide Maroni (we could see them clearly at the moment). When the *Martinière* first steams up the river with her seven hundred prisoners they notice Albina waiting and beckoning, and the idea that this village will soon be their means of escape becomes fixed in their minds. There is liberty. They need only cross the river. The repeated disastrous failures of other convicts does not discourage them. They must fail for themselves.

And so, the first two or three months after arriving in Saint Laurent, dozens of convicts cross the Maroni, carried over by the bush negroes in their canoes. From Albina there is a road plunging fifteen miles straight through the jungle to an Indian village where one buys a dugout and, taking the streams, drifts the hundred miles to Paramaribo. From here there are ships to Europe.

"Sounds so easy," I said when my convict friend had explained all this to me.

"Well, it isn't," he insisted. "The Dutch have a small army of police at Albina to take care of us. On my first *évasion* they grabbed me an hour after I landed, and shipped me home next morning. I got a month in a dark cell.

"The second time, a year later, I tried again—with three others. We had stolen two revolvers from the military guards and got across the river easy enough. This time we slipped past the police and found the road. But we didn't know they'd established a guard house about ten kilometers out of town, and almost ran into it. We thought it might help to get hold of the soldiers' uniforms —there were four of them too—so we held up the Dutchmen with our revolvers and took their own guns and clothes away. Then we put on the uniforms and got to the Indian village unchallenged. Of course you know they are not Indians at all —they're bush niggers whose ancestors were runaway slaves. But they're about as near wild men as you can find—go around naked except for a few brass bracelets.

"They recognized us as convicts all right. They're a rather kindly lot though—gave us a grass house to sleep in and some food. But they wanted us to pay and pay well. We turned our pockets inside out to show we didn't have any money. It didn't work. They were wise niggers. They knew all about convicts, and that each one of us was carrying a *plan*. And we didn't get one banana till the *plans* were produced.

"We shouldn't have gone on to Paramaribo. At least not with our Dutch uniforms on. But we were damned fools. We took a canoe and sailed right into the police who were waiting for us. The guards at the sentry box had reached Albina and reported our doings to headquarters. The police put us in irons for two weeks and then back we went, chained together, to Saint Laurent.

"The Dutch are absolutely merciless with escaping French convicts. But I suppose they've been driven to it by the crimes the convicts commit trying to get away.

"Our *évasion* came right on top of the Coutancot affair. That made them doubly severe."

"What was the Coutancot affair?" I asked.

"Oh, he was a *brave garçon* doing twenty years for robbery. He escaped via Albina too, and headed for Paramaribo. But a few miles this side he got hungry and broke into a Chinaman's shop. The Chinaman put up a fight. Coutancot knocked him unconscious, pillaged his goods, stole a pistol, got drunk on the whisky supplies, set fire to the place and burned it to the ground with the Chink inside. The police went after him, and he shot one of them through the head. But they caught him, and executed him. The death penalty which had been suspended in Dutch Guiana ten years before was reëstablished just for Coutancot.

"Then a few days after his execution *we* came along!"

"What did they do to you when you got back here?" I asked.

"They put us in the *blockhaus.* That's where they put everybody who commits a crime in prison —and next to striking a guard, *évasion* is the worst crime of all. In the *blockhaus* we have to wait till the tribunal meets to try our case. It meets only three times a year, so sometimes we have to wait four months."

"It's different from the other barracks?"

"Oh, yes. It's much worse. There are no beds —only two wooden platforms against the walls. You sleep on the planks as best you can, side by side.

"The day I was thrown into the *blockhaus* one of my four companions was with me. The turnkey was an Arab. He pushed us through the door and slammed it.

"The odor—oh, *ya, ya!* It nauseates the poor devil sent there the first time. The place is suffocating. Everybody is completely naked—the heat, sweat, latrine, stench—but you get used to it; you may as well. . . .

"We began to look around for a berth on the planks and found a vacant space at the end. The planks were rough and uneven. It would be difficult to sleep here, but we knew we'd fare better if we kept together than if we got separated.

"The *gardien* brought us our soup about half past five. Soon after he came back and cried out '*Pousse!*' and everybody ran through the door to get his *baquet*. Jean and I followed."

"What's a *baquet?*"

"It's a small wooden bucket for sanitary purposes. Everybody is chained to the boards all night, so they give us a bucket apiece. There never are enough to go round. Of course Jean and I didn't get one.

"In the *blockhaus* again the turnkey fastens the iron manacles on our feet. A military guard counts the men. The door is locked, and there we lie for twelve hours.

"For the first night neither Jean nor I could sleep. We almost suffocated even though we had taken off our clothes. There's no modesty in the *blockhaus*. The boards bruised us. You can't lie very comfortable with the manacles on your feet. Every time a convict stirred the chains clanked and scraped. The mosquitoes tormented us. The only thing that brings any comfort to the men in the *blockhaus*—tobacco—we didn't have. If we'd only had that, we could have endured so much better.

"About eight o'clock when the lights were out somebody—in the midst of this filth and tears—began to *sing*. We all listened. It was Ranard—we called him Blackpool—a singer from a café in Paris.

"He sang well—a song called *Le Demon du Jeu*. At the end everybody called for *le jazz band*. He sang that too, and we shouted the refrains with him, beating the time with our chains against the iron clamps. Our gaiety wasn't very real. But it was better than weeping.

"Ten weeks crawled by in this miserable place. The stench became more foul, the meat and bread more revolting. I couldn't eat the bread, so I exchanged it for tobacco.

"Of course I fell sick. The doctor on his weekly visit prescribed quinine without looking at me—and I was dying of starvation.

"But I wanted to die and get it over with. I weighed forty kilos (ninety pounds), when they finally ordered me to the hospital. They saw to it there that I lived. They weren't through tormenting me.

"The tribunal met, and Jean and I got six months *en reclusion* on Saint Joseph. Jean died there. And I?—My soul died there too. My body is night-watchman on the dock at Saint Laurent du Maroni."

The moon had sunk behind the black jungle tops, and clouds blotted out the light of the stars. I walked home in the darkness, desolate over the inhuman things that man has done to man.*

* I want to express here my appreciation of Blair Niles' book, *Condemned to Devil's Island.* Its authenticity, the searching truth of its portrayal of the *transportés* and their prison life, make it the final word on French Guiana. It seems to me inevitable that her book will awaken the conscience of those in whose hands lie the powers of reform.

CHAPTER XXVIII

LES ILES DU SALUT

DEVIL'S ISLAND and its two companions had first become visible to me from the air. They now became visible from the sea. I was going back to them, as I had promised myself when I first sailed over them in the seaplane *Washington.*

I had no authority to go there. In fact I had been denied permission very bluntly. But again luck was with me. I had addressed an envelope to the commandant of the islands, and when we anchored off the quay of Ile Royale I jumped into the big life-boat rowed by the galley slaves and brandished my letter before the military guard, demanding that he take me ashore in order that I might deliver the weighty document to the commandant himself.

Such a favor was very much against the rules. But it was night, and groups of arriving and departing convicts were causing so much confusion that the guard had no time to argue me out of the idea. Along with a dozen prisoners I was rowed to the landing.

The commandant happened to be on the quay. I greeted him with the information that I was the American aviator who had flown over his island some days before. I added that I'd like to visit his domain at closer range.

Napoleon could not have been given a heartier welcome. The commandant escorted me to his own home, invited me to be his house guest and opened a bottle of his best champagne.

And the next boat back to the mainland was two weeks hence!

Probably no visitor in history, French or foreign, ever saw the Devil's Island group as thoroughly as I saw them, or ever will again. As the visiting aviator, as the commandant's protégé, I was *persona grata* wherever I chose to go. And I chose to go into the darkest corners and to inquire into the unhappiest hearts that I could find.

First of all let me explain again that Devil's Island itself has never been used as a prison except for a handful of political *déportés*. It is only because Captain Dreyfus, whose sensational case twenty-five years ago attracted international attention, was confined for his four terrible years on this island that its name has become so familiar; that it has, in fact, given its name to the entire penal colony of French Guiana. The dozen prisoners there now live not uncomfortably, each in his own little two room house. They have the same food as the soldiers. They have adequate furniture—even mosquito nettings. They have gardens and dense groves of palm trees and complete freedom to wander about.

True, these de luxe living conditions are post-Dreyfus innovations. *He* suffered barbaric cruelties. The tiny stone hut that was his shelter still stands, a monument to French inhumanities in the past, and a source of hope that the reformations which have come to Devil's Island will spread, as they have already, very, very slightly, to the island's two distracted neighbors.

On Ile Royale where I landed, one finds prison barracks similar to those in Cayenne and Saint Laurent, containing some three hundred convicts. They are the incorrigibles, the irredeemables, who have been sent here for repeated offenses and *évasions* on the mainland. There is no *évasion* from Royale—no Albinas, no friendly Indians, no fishing-boat captains to bribe, no money to bribe them with. There's only one deliverance from Royale. . . .

A few days after I landed at the islands I was allowed to go to Saint Joseph, the third of the group. Here I knew I was to find the complete depths, nor was I disappointed, for on Saint Joseph are the hideous *reclusion* cells that are the wages of insubordination, murder, and above all, *évasion.* Nothing that the convict has endured before prepares him for this ordeal. This is the rack designed to break his spirit and his body. It operates successfully.

Before arriving in Guiana I had heard stories of brutal floggings of the *transportés.* This is not true. I had heard that they were bound fast in the jungle to be tortured by insects, and were killed on the slightest provocation. These stories are all the absurdest inventions.

But there is no invention in regard to the agony on Saint Joseph.

The same boat that delivered me from my ship took me across the channel that separates Royale from its neighbor. It was manned by the same six galley slaves.

These slaves number twenty in all. Almost every one is a military murderer convicted in some African post. They are the huskies from among the local prisoners and are quartered in a special barrack near the quay. No emaciated bodies here. They are all of magnificent physique. The life-boat communication must be kept going across the violent currents that race between the islands, and these slaves are the only power. It takes strong and enduring oarsmen. Therefore the administration sees to it that they are amply fed and considerately treated.

In their company, locked up in their barrack, I spent the second evening of my residence on the islands. They all knew I was "the aviator" and gave me what little hospitality they could. Our evening meal consisted of the usual beef soup, to which, however, for *these* men were added several pounds of fish and turtle they had caught themselves, and a large quantity of beans and rice. The bread, if very bad in quality, was of sufficient quantity. The meal had heat and strength in it . . . and left me not unmindful of the starvation diet endured by the prisoners whose services were not necessary to the administration.

After supper somebody suggested the inevitable game of *bilote*. They drew up a home-made table between two of their bunks (these, built double-decker, similar to the bunks in the fo'castle of cargo ships, were not uncomfortable), lighted a kerosene lamp and sat around stripped to the waist. (They all disdained to wear shirts, day or night—bad form among galley slaves.) I took my place in the circle, but being unfamiliar with the game, was content to watch. Everybody had a little money, and won or lost it like good, though very noisy, sports.

Outside the wide grilled door the waves were bursting on the quay. The palms rustled incessantly in the steady night wind from the sea. Inside, twelve bulging torsos leaned upon the table, slapped down their grimy cards and shouted out their bids in heathen French. The restless little lamp, imperiled by every gust of wind, cast its yellow rays upward against the encircling wall of tattooed brawn, and hard, strong faces.

At nine o'clock I had to go. But I was well-sped on my way. Over half the galley slaves gave me presents (the other half had nothing to give), a hand-carved paper knife, a sisal-fiber tablecloth, a bit of tortoise shell, the jaw-bone of a shark, a copy book filled with crude crayon pictures of fancy ladies, a post-card greeting from home, a photograph of a twin brother in jail in Lille. Rarest of all, Lopez, the Spaniard, gave me a small cup made of a steer's horn, on which, while I watched the game of *bilote,* he had engraved a crude picture of an airplane and my name, and the name of Ile Royale, and the date of that extraordinary evening.

These were the men—all old friends now—who rowed me across the channel to Saint Joseph Island.

The galley slaves on Ile Royale. These prisoners, chosen because of their physical strength, man the boats which ply from island to island and offer the only means of communication. They are better cared for than the other prisoners. Most of them have been sent to Guiana for murder committed in colonial army camps in Africa.

A typical convict and his dog on Ile Royale. His costume, only a pair of cotton trousers, is all he needs in the equatorial climate. In the background is Devil's Island.

These four galley slaves asked for this special picture. The pose was their own. Lopez, at the extreme left, is a Spaniard; Hans, at the right, a German.

Outwardly the island is like the other two, high and covered with palms, and undeniably beautiful. But on the plateau at its crest there is a grim silent building that is like nothing else in the world.

The building consists of three very large iron-roofed sheds each three hundred feet long and fifty wide. Inside each shed eighty cages are arranged in two parallel lines. A central wall twenty feet high, reaching half-way to the roof and running the length of the building, separates the two lines. The cages, twelve feet long, twelve high, and seven wide, are solid concrete. There are no windows. The door is solid iron with an aperture a foot square which can be opened and closed by a sliding steel shutter. It is through this aperture that the food and the *baquets* are passed. The cells have no roofs—only grills of heavy bars. Four of the cages once used for special punishment have boards on top the bars, so that no light whatsoever enters in. But outraged public opinion in France caused these to be abandoned a few years ago. Along the top of the wall that divides the two lines is a railed runway. Here the guards walk their beats back and forth looking down on either side through the bars into each bear-pit, and upon each of the caged animals. There is no escape from the gaze of the passing officer. Nothing can be hidden.

Inside each cage there is one wooden bench six feet long, two small wooden buckets, one blanket and one man. That is all.

High over everything arches a vast iron roof that keeps out the sun and the rain—and the light. On very bright days it is dark in the pits. On dark days there is almost no light at all.

With the chief warden I entered one of these great tombs. Beneath this particular roof eighty men were quartered, forty of them mad.

One goes mad in these pits—no vision but the blank cement wall, no thought but the yearning for relief, no sound but the beat of one's own pulse . . . slowly, slowly, the mind, like the body and the soul, gives way. Then when the prisoner begins to howl and weep and beat his head against the iron door he is dragged from the sane half of the line of cells and put into the mad half. The cells are all alike.

It seemed impossible that there was life in the vast, somber barn—it was so deathly still. But as I walked down the line of iron doors I saw on each a name, a date, a crime. Three out of four were marked *évasion*.

We came to the iron steps at the far end. I climbed them torn between a desire to see these poor caged beasts for myself, and a repugnance against staring down morbidly upon the agony and filth of my naked, defenseless fellow-men.

But I had come to seek the truth. I must not dodge it now.

I moved along the railed walk. I looked into the first cage. A man completely nude sat on the cement floor, his head fallen forward, his disheveled hair covering his face, his noon-day meal spilled across the bench. In the next cell a very old prisoner lay sleeping with a kitten on his chest. The third gazed with open mouth and imbecile blankness up at us. Another beat his hands together and distorted into hideous expressions the muscles of his face. A fifth looked up so quietly and so sadly I was impelled to stop and speak to him:

"How long have you been here, *mon vieux?*"

"Six days, Monsieur."

"He's been here four years," said the warden.

If one must be mad, this is a happy form.

The next man was a particularly tragic case. He had been a galley slave, and one day went for a bath in the sea just off the quay. That the water swarmed with sharks he was well aware . . . but he didn't mean to swim out far, and anyway he held the belief that it was only upon corpses—not live men—that they fed. The water was soft and cooling. He turned on his back to float motionlessly. To the sharks he looked like one more corpse. They seized him, and by the time his companions had frightened off the brutes, all the flesh had been shredded from his hips and thighs. By some miracle he lived, but has been a madman ever since. This pitiful, gnawed creature stood up totteringly at our overhead approach, and smiled, and saluted us. I gave him all the cigarettes I had—and looked away.

Tragedy followed tragedy. One man thought he was a monkey, and when we passed, howled out what he believed were monkey howls. Another called up beseechingly to me:

"Monsieur, look, I am naked. They give me no clothes to wear."

"He appeals to everybody," explained the warden. "We give him clothes and he immediately tears them to pieces."

"And I am thirsty. They give me no water."

"The moment we fill his water bucket he flings it against the wall."

Another at sixty years old had been liberated. He had received a pardon. He wasn't a convict or even a *libéré* any more. He was *free*. But he was very old and very weak. He had no friends, no money, no means of departure, and nowhere to go. He was found on the streets of Saint Laurent a month after his liberation, starving and raving.

And so he's back home in a mad-cell now.

Sick at heart I passed on across the line that divides the insane from the sane.

There was little difference in their aspect. Among the sane the same unclothed state prevailed. Most of them, hearing our footsteps at an unusual hour, and seeing me, a civilian stranger, looked up or stood up, out of curiosity. The others were dejected beyond being curious any more. They paced, paced, like caged tigers or lay on their benches like dead men. A few were reading in the half-light; one or two had papers and pencils, but the great majority had only the four hateful walls, and a bench, and a blanket, and two small wooden buckets.

By the time my visit to all three of the barns had ended, I had gazed down upon two hundred of these helpless souls—old men and young men, strong bodies and haggard bodies, Chinese, negroes, Poles—the same cross-section of convicts I had seen in the prison dormitory in Cayenne. One thing they had in common—their sunken expressions of exhaustion and defeat . . . just waiting in chains for a thousand hours every day, for six months, twelve months, five years, waiting to go back to Saint Laurent, and try to run away again, and fail again, and again come back to suffer through more eons of this hell.

This cruel state of affairs has promise of reform ahead. At a recent date a new system has been introduced, on trial. For three months the convicts *en reclusion* are kept constantly in their cells as heretofore, and then for three months they are given work as gardeners and road-menders about the island. The fifty-year-old system of the bear-pits has received its first blow. Others, God willing, will follow, until all three of these cursed barns have been, like the Bastille, razed to the ground, and the wreckage burned, and salt scattered on the spot.

As I returned to the small pier where the life-boat moored, I met the commandant coming ashore to hold a special tribunal in the chief warden's office. I followed to listen in.

The first case was a young, untamed-looking convict who had called his fat red Corsican keeper "*mon chéri.*"

The keeper came in blustering.

The commandant, who was a kindly old fellow with gray hair, looked at the culprit very gravely: "Georges, did you call Monsieur Fiquot '*mon chéri?*' "

"*Oui, mon commandant.*"

"You know the penalty for impertinence. I'll have to give you sixty days *en reclusion.*"

The boy tossed his head unrepentently.

I liked his spirit, and I thought *mon chéri* a fitting name for the old owl of a guard. I came to Georges' rescue.

"Please don't lock him up, Monsieur—as a favor to me. I promise you he'll be orderly henceforth."

The commandant was not without a sense of humor.

"All right," he said. "As a favor to my friend, you're dismissed, Georges."

The boy's eyes danced with joy, and as he turned to leave the room I caught a twinkling glance from him that indicated he had already thought up a fine string of new insults to call the fat *vache* if there ever were occasion.

CHAPTER XXIX

LIBERTÉ—ÉGALITÉ—FRATERNITÉ

Convicts *en reclusion* have found, after fifty years' experience, that there is only one way of gaining relief from its terrible blight, and that is to get sick enough to be sent to the hospital on Royale. The problem involved is how to mistreat one's self so that the damage will not be obviously self-inflicted, and yet guarantee an illness dangerous enough to insure a removal.

If you can get a horse's hair, and run it through your flesh, you might get tetanus.

The bean from the castor plant, forced into a leg sore, will cause a first-class inflammation.

But horsehair and castor beans are not always available to a man in the bear-pits. There is, however, a home-grown way.

First you get scurvy. That's easy. All you have to do is eat the food they give you for a month or so and sleep on the damp concrete floor of your cell which is no harder than the bench. Everybody gets it anyway, sooner or later. Then when your teeth are falling out and your gums filled with pus, you rub a bit of this pus into a self-made wound. Infect yourself three days before the doctor's weekly visit, and your arm will be a proper purple when he calls. One or two days before are unsafe. The wound might not have grown angry enough to arrest his attention, but will kill you from blood-poisoning before he comes around again the following week.

In my life-boat going back to Royale there were two convicts being sent hospitalward with scurvy —and infected arms.

The doctor at the islands was my particular friend. He was responsible for the health of over eight hundred people, and had only the most antiquated equipment and only convict assistants. His hospital buildings constructed in 1870 were being carried off bodily by the rats. When I showed sympathy for this disgraceful state of affairs he conscripted me into his service and every day for a week I worked with him in the convict operating room.

In the beginning I was of little use, for the place, reeking with the filth of legions of convicts long since dead or soon to die, made me seasick. But after a day or two I became more or less indifferent to it.

The very first convict operative case I assisted in was that of an Arab who had been stabbed four inches into his kidneys . . . cauterize and bandage while he screamed with pain; rush him out and make room for the next one—abscess in leg . . . open and drain. The third man, a tattooed giant, our assistants carried in on the stretcher. (We had only one stretcher. It was used for everybody, every disease. It brought in the dying and carried out the dead.) He was to receive a fresh dressing on a terrible neck wound that had half-severed his head from his body. Five nights before in the Royale prison barrack he had brutally mistreated one of the younger convicts who, waiting till his tormentor was asleep, had plunged a knife into his throat and tried to kill him—and all but succeeded.

Only one more case—an old *libéré,* sent over from Saint Laurent, and dying of pleurisy. He had been ill three months, and now, yellow and dry, was ghastly to look at. No hope, but we punctured his lungs anyway, one last time.

And every day, for the week I worked in the hospital, this procession of tormented humanity passed under our operating knife.

Each morning I made the inspection rounds with the doctor. He had to supervise one hundred patients in an hour, one patient every thirty-six seconds. It was a mad race. Unless the convict was groaning with pain, or unconscious, he got little or no attention.

Fully a third of the *malades* had dysentery. This kills off one quarter of each convoy the first year, attacking the younger men particularly. A third had tropical fevers, and the other third tuberculosis, typhoid, and infections.

No American farmer would have quartered his cows in the dormitories. Floored with jagged, uneven boards, and ventilated by barred windows without panes, the wards made a mockery of the name of hospital. Each ward contained fifty men, without any attempt whatsoever at segregation, except that the tuberculars were "isolated" behind a small partition because they coughed so much nobody else could sleep.

The hospital cots were delivered from France in 1870. Rust had eaten so deeply into every one of them that it was a wonder they stood at all. The mattresses looked as old as the cots. There were no sheets, only a single blanket. The patient slept on the mattress, and at night used the blanket as covering, for in these wind-and-rain-swept rooms the nights are always cool. When there is a death, the mattress is left in the sun for a few hours, and put back in its place, immediately to serve, along with the reeking blanket, for the next victim. Once in four months the blanket is washed in cold water. Nothing happens to the mattress till it rots from its own filth, falls to pieces, and is thrown away.

Upon these evil cots the sick men lie, green, unwashed, unshaven. There may be soap in the hospital. I never saw any. Cotton nightshirts are provided, but nakedness is preferred. The men lie so still, so uncomplaining, so hopeless, sunken eyes staring into space. When the battalions of flies and vermin crawl over their faces no attempt is made to brush them away.

The sanitation system is the inevitable wooden bucket, one for each man. The dormitory door is locked at night, and there is no access to the latrine. The nurses are convicts who have chosen this occupation because it is easier than the lumber camps. The food is in keeping with the other conditions.

It is not to be wondered that the mortality in such a place is appalling.

—Or that the most desperate attempt at *évasion* in the history of Ile Royale was from this hospital.

A convict named Lounay had been locked up in *reclusion* on Saint Joseph. By means of the usual castor bean, or scurvy pus process, he had infected himself, and been transferred to Royale. He carried a *plan,* but in it instead of bank notes he had secreted, months before while in Saint Laurent, small instruments for picking locks. The moment his blood-poisoning enabled him to be about, he picked the lock of the hospital dormitory door late at night and with the help of an accomplice actually carried the planks and ribs of his own cot down the steps and into the courtyard. A wall topped with broken bottle-glass surrounds the yard. The gate to this wall was guarded, but by throwing his blanket over the glass he surmounted the wall on the unguarded side, had the boards passed over to him, and carried them down to the seaside only a few feet away. He tore the blanket into strips, and tying the planks together with them, made a crude raft. Then he bound himself to the raft.

He could not swim one stroke!

And put to sea.

For five days and nights the currents carried him south and west. Half-dead from exhaustion and thirst, he was cast up with his raft on the shores of Dutch Guiana, only to be arrested by the Dutch police—and sent back to Saint Laurent.

Three more years in the bear-pits.

But Lounay was not the man to surrender. Again, by faking appendicitis, he got transferred to the hospital on Royale. This time the doctor naturally distrusted him. They watched him day and night and gave him no chance to make the break. Even so, he continued to simulate great pain, and went on the table believing that during his period of convalescence the opportunity would come.

Again he failed.

His health had been so undermined by his previous *évasion,* and by the fresh weeks in *reclusion* which followed, that he had not the strength to withstand the shock of the—unnecessary—operation, and died soon after from its effects.

Death is no cause for lamentations in the hospital on Royale. In this chamber of horrors they mock at it.

This is how our pleurisy case died. I heard the details next day.

He came out from the chloroform with a very weak pulse. He could scarcely speak or lift his hand.

That afternoon the doctor prescribed for him the unheard-of luxury of two soft-boiled eggs. He did not touch them. A neighbor rolled a cigarette for him from cut tobacco, lighted it and put it between his lips. Quietly he smoked. Presently it was noticed that the burning cigarette had dropped from his mouth to the mattress, and that the old man's head had fallen forward.

Somebody called out: "I believe the old boy has kicked in."

All the other patients who could stand made a rush at him to pillage his few possessions before the interns got there first. One seized his knapsack hanging on the wall; another got his shoes at the foot of the bed; a third grabbed the uneaten soft-boiled eggs; a fourth snatched for the half-burned cigarette. One man took the blanket, only to put it back. This would be detected. They would like to have taken the old man's *plan,* but there was no time. They heard the intern approaching.

The corpse was shown to him. He brought the familiar stretcher and had the body carried out to the undertaking shed.

The undertaker is also a convict. This is considered the prize office on the island. It pays fabulously, for what convict is there who does not carry a *plan?*—And who but the undertaker has the opportunity to appropriate it?

This operation over, the corpse is wrapped in a cotton shroud, put in a box and carried down to the quay.

It is part of the galley slaves' duties to row the corpse out into the harbor, and to cast it overboard. (The box is always saved.) A heavy attached stone assures submersion. Instantly the water swirls with sharks. I wondered when I first witnessed this lugubrious ceremony why the sharks seemed so ravenous. They have no reason to be. They are fed almost every afternoon.

The day after the burial of the pleurisy victim, I asked to be shown the guillotine.

This terrible instrument of execution waits patiently for its diet of human heads. It is kept well oiled, ever ready.

I found it in a small high room next the death cell. The room was only large enough to hold the guillotine and the wicker basket which carries out the body.

Guillotine machinery is simple enough. A vertical track, twelve feet high, allows a three hundred-pound ax to be raised to that height. The victim is placed face down on a horizontal sliding steel plate and pushed forward until his neck is directly in the path of the knife. A wooden collar fastens his neck firmly to the spot. The rope, which, over a pulley, had elevated the ax, is released. The ax falls twelve feet, and severs the neck as if it were made of chalk. The head falls into a well-placed bucket.

This method of execution is very bloody, but instantaneous and infallible.

In Guiana it is no longer frequently used, and only in punishment for the murder of a guard or a civilian.

My next move was to see the official executioner.

There is only one for all the colony prisons. He travels from place to place when in demand, but lives on Royale. He is himself a convict.

I found him occupying a tiny hut on the remotest slope of the island. Nobody ever goes near him. Nobody ever speaks to him. He is a pariah among his fellows.

On my approach up the path toward his hut he went inside and closed the door . . . unclean.

But I wanted to talk to him, and insisted that he admit me.

He seemed inoffensive enough—a man about forty with a heavy mustache. His is the only convict-mustache allowed. The executioner always wears one. It is the convention.

"I've just been to see your guillotine," I said by

way of opening a conversation, "and want to compliment you on the neat way the 'widow' works."

"The engine in Saint Laurent is much better," he said, overcoming his embarrassment at my visit. "This one is old and out of date."

"You've operated that one too?"

"*Mais oui!* In 1923 I beheaded two men on the same day in Saint Laurent."

I started a bit at his casualness.

"One was my predecessor. He had beheaded *his* predecessor."

"So I suppose you're prepared to die that way yourself," I said. "Seems to be the custom."

"It's a superstition," he admitted, smiling.

"What had your predecessor done to merit the guillotine?"

"Killed a turnkey who tried to prevent his escape. The other execution that day was a convict who had killed a civilian. Haspel—that was the executioner—tried to get a pardon from the President of France, but they turned him down. He was a brave fellow all right—a little mad, I think. He asked permission to set up his own guillotine—didn't trust me. Said I was an amateur. He never did become downcast—defiant to the end. Climbed the scaffold shouting: 'See how the administration thanks me for my services.' And

A group of prisoners on Ile Royale. The two end figures are Frenchmen burned black by the sun. The second figure from the right is a negro. St. Joseph lies beyond.

Les Iles du Salut are not all tragedy and despair. To them the guards are allowed to bring their families, and one may see groups of children like this. Their special friend was the convict candy-man.

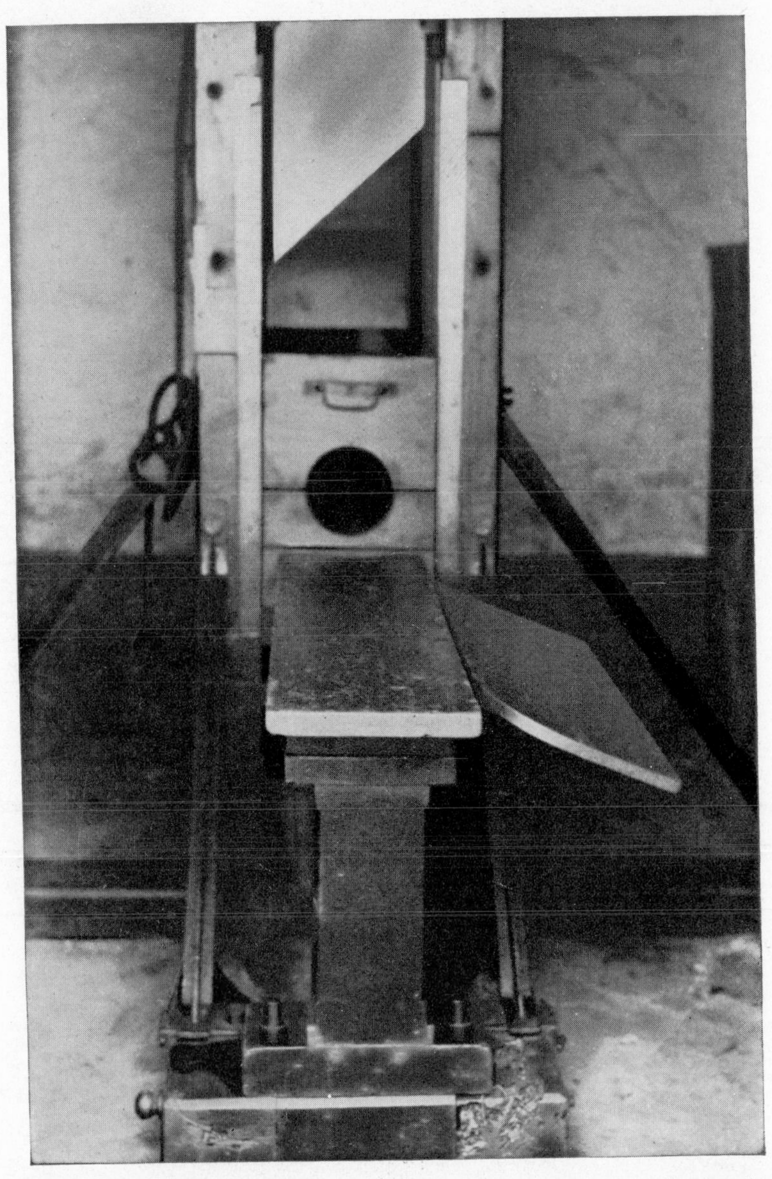

The guillotine on Royale. This terrible machine is used only to execute prisoners who have committed a capital offense during their imprisonment. The victim is strapped face-down on the steel plate, with his neck fastened in the wooden collar. The three-hundred-pound knife is raised twelve feet up the wooden groove, and falls with terrific force.

turning to me: 'Be sure you do it right. No blundering now. And you'll be next. I'll wait for you in the executioner's private hell.' He waved his hands at the crowd—there were a lot of guards and officials watching:—'Bon soir, everybody, bon soir!' "

"Are you paid well for your work?"

"Well enough. I get a hundred francs a head. That day in Saint Laurent a friend of the civilian who had been murdered by the second man I executed gave me two hundred francs. So I made four hundred in all. I sent it to my wife and child in France."

He paused and looked out over the sea. His dog came up and licked his hand.

"This is my only comrade," he said. "It gets lonely at times, just waiting. . . ."

Each day added new names to my list of friendships among the *transportés*. I won my way into their confidence with sympathy and cigarettes. It wasn't altogether the cigarettes that they were grateful for. It was partly my recognition that they were human beings, who suffered and starved—my recognition that they were not, despite all efforts of the administration to make them so, just beasts with numbers. They responded like children, because, with the exception of the artful or the confirmed criminals who were always in evidence, most of them *were* children.

Of my special friends the two that moved me and interested me most were Henri Frenoy, a Belgian, and Antoine Duval from Bordeaux. By a coincidence it happened that Henri was very nearly the youngest convict on the islands (the extremely young ones are not sent here), and Antoine very nearly the oldest. Henri was twenty-one, Antoine over sixty. Henri had served four years; Antoine thirty-four.

Henri at sixteen had been an accomplice to three others in a shop robbery in French territory. His profits from the crime were thirty francs—one dollar and twenty cents. All four had been caught and sent to Guiana. Henri had turned seventeen on the *Martinière,* and though very young, was one of the rare exceptions who had the physical strength to defend himself against aggression. The initial victory had carried him through, and after four years of existence in this sink of iniquity, had enabled him to maintain a strange combination of independence and ingenuousness. He had never resisted prison. It had become his home. He made himself as comfortable there as possible, and saw no reason to be miserable. The criminal atmosphere the others breathed had never touched him. In fact he seemed not even to be aware of it, and though surrounded by depravity, had remained the most virginal spirit I've ever seen in a grown man. Nobody ever thought of locking Henri up with the other prisoners. Completely trusted, he was allowed to live alone in a hut by the sea. There the children of the military guards could always be found in crowds. They adored him, because he made candy for them, could play tunes on a cane flute, and was clean and clear-eyed. Wherever he went they followed after. All the world loved Henri—and he was the only person on the islands who was perfectly unconscious of the reason why.

If Henri was the most naïve personality I met in French Guiana, Antoine was the most experienced. His hair was snow white, his strong, sun-blackened face a mesh of lines that spoke eloquently of the years of deprivation and pain he had lived through by sheer will-power. He had known Guiana days when the convicts were made to work naked in the jungle, drawing, under the lash of the slave-driver, the logs and timbers. Four times he had tried to escape. Four times he had failed. Of his thirty-four years in captivity *eight* had been spent in the bear-pits on Saint Joseph. For two years—seven hundred and thirty days and nights—he had never beheld the light. He had been punished for reporting wanton thefts from the convicts' food supplies by the prison guards and clerks, a custom still notoriously in vogue. (The officials could hardly be expected otherwise to live on the salaries they receive.) He had witnessed thirty-four years of murders, injustices, inhumanities. He had been shot through the stomach while standing at attention at roll-call by a negro guard who had become enraged at Antoine's "insolence." A whole year in the Royale hospital had followed. *Thirty-five thousand convicts* had gone to the bamboos and the sharks since he arrived. Of his convoy of seven hundred men, he alone remained.

And there was life in the old man yet. His eyes still burned with rebelliousness. He still mocked the prison and its thieving officers. He was still defiant, still untamed, an unquenchable individualist after thirty-four years of brutalities. If God ever made a courageous spirit that deserved to live, it was Antoine Duval of Bordeaux.

Late afternoon of my last day on the islands, these two friends and I climbed a wind-swept hilltop on Royale to watch the sunset. This spot had once been the location of the madhouse, but it had burned, and only a circle of stately palms remained. We could look down on Devil's Island, hidden under its dense groves; and across to Saint Joseph where the roofs of the *reclusion* barns caught the last red rays of the sun. From the *grande terre* we could see my little steamer approaching, and knew that I had not much longer to remain.

All three of us were very dejected. I was the first and only person who had ever spoken a kind word to Antoine since he came to Guiana . . . and now I was going away. . . .

In the gathering darkness Henri made no effort to disguise his depression.

"Don't you suppose the commandant would let you take me away on the boat if *you* asked him?"

"I've already asked him, Henri. He would like to, for your sake. But he hasn't the power."

"Then have I got to stay here always? Will they never let me leave? They said I was a thief. But I'm not a thief. I don't understand at all. I only want to go home."

At the moment of departure my two friends came to the commandant's house to escort me with a lantern to the quay. Henri carried my duffel-bag, Antoine the lunch basket. As I stepped into the life-boat to be rowed by the galley slaves out to the ship, Henri handed me a box. It was full of small presents—his badge of good behavior, his reed flute, his small crucifix his mother had given him when he was sent to prison at sixteen. They were all the things of value he had in this world.

And Antoine, what did Antoine give me?

Antoine, who had been exiled from the old country four and thirty years, who had suffered such everlasting hell in her national prison, who had been shot and beaten and persecuted by the guardians of her brutal laws, who had reason, above all other men, to feel only hate and shame for his native land—Antoine gave me a small piece of tricolored silk, a flag—the flag of the Republic of France.

CHAPTER XXX

POOR RICHARD CRUSOE

(With Apologies to Daniel Defoe)

I WAS born in the early part of the present century, in a small city situated in the state of Tennessee, of a good family, my ancestors having migrated to that state from England six generations previously. After several unsuccessful attempts at naming me I was called Richard after the town's chief patriarch whose life had been so distinguished for wisdom and prudence it was hoped that I in receiving his name might also receive his virtues. Considering the story I am about to relate it is clear that this hope was not to be fulfilled.

My childhood profited from every comfort and advantage, but as I grew older it became apparent to my father who had planned for me the life of a gentleman that I was of a restless and rebellious nature, and not likely to follow his wishes. Books of adventure and geography were my chief delight. I read *Robinson Crusoe* till I knew it almost by heart and this story more than all else filled my head very early with rambling thoughts.

Having turned eighteen, my desires prompted me to follow Crusoe's example and run away from home, not that I had the least reason to run away, for no boy ever enjoyed happier surroundings or more generous sympathetic parents than mine. Not daring to take counsel with my parents, knowing that I would not be able to withstand their wise and sober arguments against departure at this stage of my schooling, I made up my mind to leave secretly.

And I carried out this resolution, disappearing from my home—a home in which any rational boy should have been supremely happy. But nothing, God knows, not Buckingham Palace itself, would have made me either rational or happy, except the sea. Without waiting for my father's blessings, without any consideration for circumstances or consequences, in an ill hour I traveled to New Orleans and sought employment as a seaman.

Never did any young adventurer's misfortunes, I believe, begin sooner or continue longer than mine. In New Orleans a seamen's strike disrupted all shipping. I joined the strike-breakers and found myself in a hospital with a badly broken head and a violent calenture within the week.

My distressed father learning of my state sent me a ticket home in case I wished to reconsider my course, though he by no means urged me to. But I tore up the ticket in an effort to shake off all irresolution, and applying myself, upon deliverance from the fevers, to drink and seaman company, as I supposed all adventurers should, I got as complete a victory over conscience as any young fellow that resolved not to be troubled with it could desire.

At last a ship, a very small and unseaworthy one, signed me on, to my indescribable delight. The other members of the crew were the most hardened rogues one could ever have met with, though at first, to my inexperienced and romantic vision, they seemed like knights. No sooner was the ship out of the Mississippi but the wind began to blow, the waves to rise in a most frightful manner, and as I had never been to sea before, I was most inexpressibly sick in body and terrified in mind.

The seamen, also, very quickly turned out to be not knights at all, but savages who made my life doubly miserable. I began seriously to reflect upon what I had done, and now, seeing plainly the wisdom of my father's observations, resolved that at the first port I would abandon this mad career and like a true repenting prodigal go back to my parents.

And I did just that. They had gone away to the Virginias; and by good fortune my ship put in at Hampton Roads. I asked leave of the captain, meaning never to return, and he gladly gave it to me, hoping I never would.

Looking very ill and feeling very chastened I sought my mother and father, anticipating their great joy over my safe return. After greeting me affectionately, to my dismay they informed me I must go back to my ship, that what I had undertaken I must complete, that if I surrendered this first time to adversity I would lose all respect for myself and never again have the courage to take charge of my own destiny. My father would have weakened and bade me remain, but my mother's composed and unselfish judgment this time overruled his sentiment, and I was sent off again to that cursed vessel, feeling that there was no youth in the world whose misfortunes could equal my own.

The captain grudgingly took back his incompetent seaman, and I sailed away resolved to pity my condition no longer but to fight for my rights and to establish a position of respect aboard by outdrinking and outblaspheming any sailor on the ship. To make short this sad part of my story I went the way of all sailors and in wickedness drowned my repentance.

Though I did, in time, come back to receive a university degree, I never really turned my face from the sea, and the moment I was at liberty, once more gave myself up to it.

Ships and dreams and fortune took me off to Spain and Egypt, the Indies and Japan, back again to Italy and Greece, and at length to the New World of the Spanish discoverers. For a year or more I followed Columbus and Cortez, Balboa and Pizarro, up and down Latin America until at length I came to the Devil's Island prison colony in French Guiana, where I spent a month in the company of the unhappy convicts imprisoned there.

With liberation I felt very much inclined to travel homeward, but on reaching British Guiana and the nearest port of size, it was my lot to find that no packet whatsoever was sailing toward North America for fourteen days. With ill-reasoned impatience I besought a fisherman to take me in his sailboat up the coast to Trinidad three hundred and eighty miles away, with the hope that in this place I might find more immediate transportation.

I sometimes wonder if experience really teaches us anything; at least it seems never to have taught me, for I had once vowed after a four hundred mile voyage in a fishing smack out to Selkirk's Island in the Pacific that I would never again go cruising in such a boat. But my memory being short and my impatience great, again in an ill hour I ignored the dictates of my sounder judgment and sailed away.

My craft, of about six tons' burden, carried a crew of two, and a large and stupid dog belonging to the captain. We had taken aboard ample provisions for a fortnight, though we expected to make Port of Spain, Trinidad, in four or five days' time with the prevailing winds. I brought along a pistol for security not being too well acquainted with my sailing companions; likewise a sisal-fiber hammock to sleep in on deck.

The same day we left the Guianas behind, we stood away to the north-westward with design never to leave the coast out of sight. Very good weather prevailed, only excessive heat, all the way till we came to the mouth of the Oroonooko River. Here a sudden and violent storm coming from the south took us quite out of our course; it blew in such a manner that we could do nothing but drive, so that we lost sight of land and became not a little concerned as to our safety. I was shamefully seasick, yet not half so much as our dog Adam who, though he was a sea-going dog, this time lay prone upon the deck with a pale green visage.

In this distress, the wind blowing very hard, the captain gave over all hope of making Port of Spain, and decided to steer for the island of Tobago which, if the direction of the storm did not change, lay right in our present path. And indeed, on the fourth morning after our departure from the Guianas, just at dawn the captain cried out, "Land!" and we judged upon looking at our charts that the land could be no other than Tobago.

The storm having somewhat abated we anchored off the beach, launched our tiny skiff and rowed to the shore of what I knew was the island where Defoe had cast away his *Robinson Crusoe.*

Having solaced my mind with the first aspect of my condition, I began to look around me to see what kind of island I was on, and what was next to be done, for I saw no indication of inhabitants. Also I began with a heavy heart to consider what would be my lot if there were any ravenous beasts in this country, and was relieved to remember the pistol and cartridges aboard.

A shelter offered itself in a broad chalk cave in the bluff which rose up from the shore. From the sailboat I fetched my pistol and hammock, and strung the latter in this grotto. Then having been excessively fatigued I fell fast asleep and slept as comfortably as, I believe, few could have in my condition, and awoke to find myself well rested.

The beach before my cave, which I shall call mine since it seemed to have no owner, was of the purest white sand, and shaded with palm trees, very high and slender. While my boat's crew repaired our sails and tackle, I went for a bath in the surf and found it so pleasant and refreshing, and the whole aspect of the place so delightful, that I resolved to let my sailboat depart and leave me behind to dwell in solitary exile just like Crusoe on Crusoe's island.

CHAPTER XXXI

CRUSOE'S ISLAND

I ACQUAINTED the boatmen with my decision and offered to purchase from them all the provisions and gear aboard their boat that were not already my own. They agreed for a good price to sell me the extra sail, the rope, the tool chest, the boxes and barrels, the small iron stove, their lamp and knives, the cooking utensils, all the fishing tackle—and Adam. Adam seemed in no way loath to quit his seasickening sailboat, nor his owners to be rid of him, for he was indeed the stupidest creature that ever I have seen.

These things along with the food supplies and my duffel-bag, I stowed in the little skiff, and then as a final purchase I bought the skiff itself.

When our sailboat put out to sea again it was completely destitute of equipment, but the Port of Spain was now no more than thirty-six hours distant, and there the boatmen planned to refurnish anew with the money I had given them.

With my property piled about me, and the skiff

pulled upon the beach, I found myself very well disposed to eat. I discovered a box of crackers in the provision barrel, and a keg of rum that had belonged to the captain. Of the rum I took a large dram, after which I was in high spirits and encouraged to go beyond what I should have been able to do upon another occasion.

At the top of the bluff above, I found a thicket of bamboos. With a great deal of labour I felled a number of these with my hatchet and erected a shelf or two inside the cave on which to store my provisions against the rains, it raining almost every day in this season.

The provisions proved to be more ample than at first I had hoped. I found that I had all the food prepared for three men for fourteen days, less the five days' supply we had consumed.

My most valuable prize, I soon realized, was my chest of tools, for it contained a saw, a hammer, an iron mallet, a hatchet and a big sack of nails. Thus I was prepared to build for myself whatever was needful.

The next thing of importance was to devise some sort of calendar, otherwise I should lose my reckoning of time, and forget the Sabbath day from the working days. To prevent this, in imitation of Crusoe, I cut the date of my arrival, May thirtieth,

I went to work to build me a chair and a table, but my cabinet craft was constantly interfered with by Adam, Kitty, Susie and Listerine, the white kid. They sat on my saw, on my head, climbed on the table and over my tools, spilled the nails and made my labours generally difficult.

I set up my dairy and had plenty of milk, though Quelques Fleurs and Listerine always competed simultaneously for their share and more of the provision. Polly usually observed the operation from my shoulder.

into a board, planning to add a new notch for each new day.

Now that my house and my calendar were in order I went out to acquaint myself with what the island produced. Adam was left behind as guard, though he was a poor watchman since he slept all the time and could have been carried off by the thieves along with my property had they been so minded.

After wandering about half a mile I came upon a grass-grown road leading inland from the groves of coconut palms that grew in dense ranks along the shore. I also perceived that there were goats on the island, for I passed a flock of them attended by a negro boy. My domain was not uninhabited then. I asked the boy in English if there was a village on the island, and in English he replied, yes, that its name was Scarboro, about three hours distant, with the road all the way.

The journey proved trying for I had no hat and the sun was excessively hot. But at length I reached the village and found it settled almost entirely with black men. I examined the few shops for Robinson Crusoe equipment, since, as it was, I did not have one tenth the possessions my original example enjoyed.

First of all I needed a gun with which to shoot

birds, Crusoe's gun having been his staff of life. Then I must have a Bible if I were to be his true disciple. Both of these things I found without difficulty. Also a spade, an ax, needle and thread, a bottle opener, extra kerosene for the lamp, several old copies of *Punch,* and a netting against the mosquitoes which were very bad. Likewise I found a very large and elegant printed calendar advertising the Society of Scottish Mechanics, and even though I had just spent the morning contriving my notch calendar I took the paper one along for it might be more accurate and certainly more decorative.

Then there arose the problem of a cat and a parrot. Cats were plentiful. I was showered with cats by the natives, but kept my supply down to a single gray kitten. As for parrots there was only one on the island, owned by an old negro woman as a pet. But this too I inveigled away from its owner in exchange for a dollar. The bird's name was Susie, and this name it shrieked at everybody. I laboured many hours afterward in the effort to teach the parrot to call me Poor Richard Crusoe and not Susie, and at length succeeded.

All these new possessions put me in mind that I could not convey them back to my cave now that I had them. In this dilemma a strange, rusty, and very noisy vehicle rolled up driven by a young black man. I asked him what this archaic machine might be, and he said it was The Ford which had been on the island beyond the memory of the oldest inhabitant, and was the only machine of its kind in Tobago. It occurred to me that this machine might get me and my purchases home, which indeed, with great bumping and rattling, it did. I resolved to engage the vehicle and direct it myself, for I quickly saw its virtues in assisting me to range the island for food, a thing I planned to do more or less every day. It could stand in the grass road at night. True, the rain would pour in torrents but that could in no way hurt what had been rained on already for many years.

I now began to consider seriously the circumstances I was reduced to, and I drew up the state of my affairs in writing so as to deliver my thoughts from daily poring upon them. In order to distinguish my case from worse, I stated impartially the comforts I enjoyed against the miseries I suffered.

EVIL	GOOD
I am cast upon a remote island two thousand miles from Tennessee.	But Providence could not have given me an island more rich or beautiful.

EVIL	GOOD
I am divided from mankind.	But I like it. I can read and sleep all I want to for the first time in my life. For a good part of each day I can go without clothes which has always seemed to me to be an ideal though unattainable state.
There are mosquitoes.	But no radios.
My friends and family can not reach me.	But that must be a great relief to them.

Upon the whole I came to the conclusion that there were worse modes of life than this, and that the good in it quite offset the evil.

Having now brought my mind to relish conditions, I applied myself to making life comfortable. I remembered that Crusoe had a flock of goats which provided him with meat and milk. Consequently I bought a female with two kids from the young negro goatherd I had met with, and annexed them to my household. One of the kids was spotted gray, the other snow white. I named the gray one Quelques Fleurs, the white one Listerine. The mother I called Hyacinth.

Each morning I attempted to milk Hyacinth and to draw the milk into an iron kettle taken from the sailboat. But as I had no idea how to begin or what stroke to use, and as Quelques Fleurs and Listerine always competed simultaneously for their share and more of the provision, I made little progress in providing myself with milk. The problem was finally solved by cutting a number of bamboo poles and with them walling up the entrance to a large fissure in the rocks near my cave. This I called the dairy. Here I kept my flock of goats penned at night, and here I learned to imprison the two kids while I led Hyacinth forth for the ordeal.

Freed from the interference of the greedy children, I learned at length to milk as well as any man. To this contribution from Hyacinth I added chocolate, and cooking the whole in my iron pot, I was able to prepare for myself a nourishing meal.

Coconuts grew all around me and provided both food and drink. No matter how hot the day the juice inside a green coconut is always cool and refreshing. In fact as there was no spring of fresh water near-by, my animals as well as myself had no other drink but this during my entire sojourn in the cave, nor did we ever regret the substitution.

The food problem solved momentarily I began to turn my attention to such necessary things as I found I most wanted, as particularly a chair and a table, for without these I was not able to enjoy what I did have; I could not write or eat or do several things with so much pleasure without a table.

So I went to work. I had never handled a tool in my life any more than I had milked goats, yet in time by labour and application I contrived a table and a chair out of planks taken from the ruins of a house a mile distant, that had been razed by a hurricane some years before and left deserted. My furniture was neither good nor beautiful, only clumsy and crude, but it answered its purpose and I was satisfied, thanking heaven that I need not hew down a whole tree, as Crusoe had to do, and from the trunk laboriously hack a single board for my carpentry.

Crusoe, however, had an advantage over me in that he was a better animal trainer than I. My cabinet craft was constantly interfered with by Adam, Kitty, Susie, who sat on my saw, on my head, climbed upon the table and over my tools, spilled the nails, got under my feet, and made my labours generally difficult.

Susie was particularly tyrannical in her disdain for my personal rights. Her favorite perch when I was trying to milk or saw, was on the back of my neck, and if I did not conduct myself to her taste, I got a sound scolding and a peck on the ear.

Each night, snug in my cave with the waves

I made it my business to teach Toosday everything that was proper to make him handy and helpful. He soon learned the use of the firearms and accompanied me on my hunting excursions. (The bamboo fence enclosed the stockade where I kept the goats.)

I stood like one thunderstruck at the sight of footprints in the sand.

rustling outside and Adam asleep at my feet, I took Susie's education in hand and endeavored to instruct her in the English idiom. As was the case with Crusoe's pet, results came not immediately but later. When I had given her up as a moron parrot incapable of any speech beyond her own name she suddenly burst forth with, Poor Richard, poor Richard, poor Susie, nice polly, damn you get off my neck, lie down Adam, and other phrases I had spoken aloud in her presence; so that I became discreet thenceforth in my conversations with this chatterbox.

CHAPTER XXXII

O SOLITUDE!

If I were going to play Crusoe in any sort of realistic manner, I must get myself into a more Crusoe-like costume than the loin-cloth which was, at the present stage, my chief garment. In my cave, in the surrounding coconut groves, bathing in the sea, clothes were unnecessary and uncomfortable so hot was the weather. But being an easy victim of sunburn which always gave me a prostrating calenture, I never went far abroad without complete protection from the sun.

All the protection I had was the wardrobe brought ashore from the sailboat, viz., two white linen suits, a few shirts, and a neckerchief. One of the suits had been ripped to shreds during my labours as carpenter and milkman; and the second suit I wished to preserve against the day of my deliverance.

In this condition I remembered Crusoe's use of goatskins, and again I made a purchase of goats, half a dozen of them this time, from my friend the herdsboy. I promised him that if he would slaughter the animals for me and bring me the skins I would make him a present of the meat. This he was very glad to do, and thus was I saved the bloody business of butcher which I had no mind for.

With the six skins well dried in the sun, I set myself a-tailoring, but if I was a bad carpenter I quickly found I was a worse tailor. However, I made shift to make a great cap for my head, with the goat's hair on the outside to shoot off the rain. For many months I had possessed no hat, but in Tobago the heat of the sun beat with such violence as to give me a headache, which if I covered my head would go away.

The making of the cap I performed so well that after this I made me a coat reaching half-way to the knees. The sleeves, which took me hours of labour to cut and attach, were made very short. I had no buttons or hooks, yet did contrive a broad belt of canvas which held my coat together and offered a holster for my pistol.

Next I undertook to make breeches to match the coat. This proved entirely beyond my skill, and after cutting up two of my best skins in the attempt, I gave it over as too intricate. The linen breeches, torn and ragged though they were, would have to suffice. Shoes, or rather slippers, turned out to be not as formidable to manage as I had anticipated. I merely sewed a skin into the form of a sack with a flap for my heel and shaved one side clean with my razor for the sole.

After this I spent a great deal of time to make me an umbrella, also of skins. I was indeed in great want of one as I was obliged to go abroad every day and needed it as well for the rains as the heats. I took a world of pains but spoiled two or three before I made one to my mind that answered indifferently well. The main difficulty I found was to make it let down. Crusoe's umbrella did let down, but again my skill was not equal to his and I had to be content with one that remained spread. With the hair of the skins upward it cast off the rains like a penthouse and kept off the sun so effectually that I could walk out in the hottest weather. In my cave its widespread state consumed a vast amount of space until I contrived a hook in the ceiling by which I could hang it out of the way.

I had been cast upon Tobago Island more than a week when I came to realize that my supply of victuals was not inexhaustible and that I must replenish it by means of my rifle. In the interior of the island were jungle-covered hills, and thither

I traveled in my vehicle (which I had christened Victoria), as far as the road would take me, in quest of game.

It greatly diverted me to walk through these jungles with my gun and pistol, for the green depths were always cool and bedecked with flowers. Some of the trees grew very large, and one called, I believe, the cabbage palm, reached an exceedingly great height, overtopping all others.

Here I found no end of birds and small animals. Many of the birds were carrion and not fit for food, but occasionally I brought home a dove or a wood pigeon. Hares also abounded, and I never had to wander far to find all I wanted. Adam, having proved himself inferior to Susie as a watchman, always accompanied me on my hunts, though was so lacking in enthusiasm that his services were of little value beyond that of companion.

About twice a week I spent the morning fishing from my little skiff. The owners of the sailboat left me with an embarrassment of tackle, for I had their entire equipment. Trolling from my boat just off the cave was usually rewarded with a large catch, but I could never keep more than a small part of it, for I had no way of preserving sea food beyond a few hours, because of the terrible heat. On fish days Adam, Kitty and Susie, always banquetted royally as they much preferred fresh-baked perch to any other delicacy I could offer them.

In this quiet and simple manner I lived mighty comfortably with my faithful family, my mind being entirely composed by resigning to the will of God. When I began to regret the want of conversation beyond the squawkings of Susie, I would console myself that there was no longer any such thing. Thus removed from all the distractions and all the wickedness of the world I continued to lead a most virtuous life.

As might be expected, my appearance daily grew more extraordinary. Had any one in North America met such a man as I was, it must either have frightened him or raised a great deal of laughter; and whenever I stood still to look at myself, I could not but smile at the notion of my traveling through Boston or Charleston with such an equipage and in such a dress. Be pleased to take a sketch of my figure as follows:

On my head was the high shapeless hat, made to keep the sun from me and to keep the rain from running down my neck, nothing being so hurtful in these climates as the rain running down one's neck.

I have mentioned the jacket, very heavy and stiff, and the tattered linen breeches. Stockings and shoes I had none, except the pair of sack-somethings I have already described, of the most barbarous shape, as indeed were all my clothes.

On my shoulder I carried my gun, and over my head the clumsy goatskin umbrella, but which, after all, was the most necessary thing I had about me next to my gun. As for my face, the color of it was usually scarlet from the sun and wind, as one might expect from a man not at all careful of it, and living within nine degrees of the equator.

My chief pride and joy was my beard, for I suffered it to grow long in order to have it look like Crusoe's beard. I must say, however, that even after two weeks it was not very formidable, being soft and pale in color. But after considerable experiment with tonics to make it grow, I hit upon a can of ox-blood shoe polish discovered in my duffel-bag. A generous application of this dark red paste upon the feeble beard gave it a most frightfully vigorous appearance. True, the paste was made of ink and turpentine which burned like fire, but my vanity, very pleased over my Mohammed-like visage, would not permit me to wash away the discomfiture.

In this kind of figure I went sometimes into Scarboro causing great amazement among the inhabitants who stopped from their work or play to stare with open mouths at the ghost of Crusoe returned into their midst.

Feeling that I should record for future reference the events of my daily life, I began soon after my arrival on the island to keep a journal of which I shall give you a copy.

THE JOURNAL.

May 30th. I, poor Richard Crusoe, being storm-driven, came for refuge to the shore of this island of Tobago. The rest of my company having departed I was left in solitude.

May 31st. Spent two hours arranging my possessions on bamboo shelves, and eight hours bathing in the surf upon my private beach.

June 1st. I have found that there is a village, eight miles distant, and that it is called Scarboro. Arriving at this village only to-day I bought many things necessary to my comfort, the most important items being a cat, a parrot, a Bible and an automotive machine. Arriving home after dark I lighted my lamp in order to read my new Bible, turning to the Psalms which I found very diverting. The Twenty-third Psalm is my favorite, being the only one I know.

June 2nd. This day is Sunday which Crusoe kept as a day of rest. But I have decided to improve on his observance and have *every* day in my week a day of rest.

June 3rd. (Written on June 8th.) This morning I spent three hours in the skiff with my trolling lines. Being a great fool I had no hat and no shirt upon me, so that the sun blistered my skin painfully. In the afternoon I suffered a violent calenture which caused me to lay a-bed all next day ready to perish with thirst but in such miseries of mind and body I had not the will to climb a coconut tree for drink. The second night it rained very hard which refreshed me greatly and I awoke the next morning weak but alive.

June 5th. This day I went for a walk in the hills with my gun. I came to the top of a ridge from which I had a good view of the sea to the south and west, and it being a very clear day, I fairly descried land laying very high, extending from the west to the S. W. at a great distance; by my guess it could not be less than fifteen leagues off. Whether it was an island or a continent Crusoe did not know, but I knew that it was the island of Trinidad, the three peaks which caused Columbus to name it Trinidad being visible.

June 6th to 9th. Spent in making goatskin clothes against the sun, and furniture for my cave. While the clothes are a success sartorially, the skins have been only sun-cured and consequently the odour of goat is so strong upon them that they are not pleasant companions. I feel, however, that if Crusoe could bear it I can. Even so, I am not obliged to him for establishing the vogue, for if there ever were an inappropriate costume for equatorial climates it is one made of goat's furs.

June 10th. To-day I have been a castaway for twelve days, and except for one evening spent reading a few Psalms in my Bible, I have not had a godly thought. This neglect makes my copy of Crusoe a poor copy indeed for he was a devout and prayerful man. I have, alas! no divine knowledge; what I received by the good instructions of my father and from the Presbyterian Sunday-school catechism has become by this advent well worn out by eight years of seafaring wickedness.

But now being very solitary I have begun to have religious thoughts, and to realize that I have good reason, no doubt, to be grateful to Providence, casting me up on this delightful and abundant island instead of some barbarous place.

Consequently I have decided to become a Christian, and shall read my Bible resolutely upon this instant for an hour.

June 11th. My religious activities of last night were only partly successful. Having opened the book casually, the first words that occurred to me were these, "And the man whose hair is fallen off his head, he *is* bald." I put my hand to my crown in sudden alarm, but found no need for any anxiety. Again I read, "And Aaron took Elisheba, daughter of Amminadab, sister of Naashon, to wife; and she bore him Nadab, and Abihu, Eleazer, and Ithamar." Stuttering I stumbled on; "And Obadiah, *he* died, and Ezekiel, *he* died." Discouraged I put aside my book and kneeled down to seek consolation in prayer. Again I was defeated in my earnest efforts to do right, for Satan came to torment me with a plague of mosquitoes, and they attacked me so venomously that I was once more diverted from devotion to blasphemy, and driven to seek refuge in my hammock over which I have hung a net against the insect demons. Still persevering in my Christian resolutions I sought to attain a kneeling position in my hammock in order to petition forgiveness for my transgressions, but again, Satan caused the hammock to swing slightly so that I lost my balance and fell out most disgracefully upon my head, which accident put an end to any more religious observances for several days.

The above extracts will give you a sample of my journal.

Shortly after my encounter with the Bible, as if in reward for this recognition of Providence, a most extraordinary adventure befell me, an adventure that was to introduce an entirely new scene in my life. Returning from a hunting expedition in the hills I was exceedingly surprised with the tracks of a man's naked feet in the sand on my beach. I remembered that Crusoe had likewise found a footprint, though only one, and that the print turned out to be made by one of a cannibal tribe of Carib Indians which came over from Trinidad to feast upon their prisoners of war. I also remembered that it was one of these prisoners which Crusoe rescued from hungry enemies, who became his devoted servant, and almost as celebrated by posterity as Crusoe himself. During my entire fourteen days here I had seen no other human being on my beach, for it was indeed well removed from all habitations, and now to come upon these tracks leading to my abode and back into the sea and out again in the direction of the palm grove, filled me with agitation. I rushed to the cave expecting to find it plundered, if not by cannibals or pirates, at least by thieves who had found out my secret. Every box and book was in order.

But Adam, who was with me, also noted the tracks, and for the first time in his life became aroused, running up the beach into the palms and barking. I followed and came upon a Carib Indian—or rather he *might* have been a Carib Indian with his dark brown skin—standing under the trees in a sort of Mother Hubbard suit of dripping wet underwear about six sizes too big.

And thus did I find Toosday.

CHAPTER XXXIII

THE MAN WHO WAS TOOSDAY

HIS appearance was so absurd I broke into laughter, forgetting that my own appearance must have been infinitely more absurd. Then I noticed that this Carib was no savage but the negro boy who owned Victoria.

What are you doing here, I demanded. Ise waitin' t' see yer, he said, and I breathed a sigh of relief—he was not being pursued by cannibals from which unhappy state I'd have to deliver him as Crusoe delivered *his* man. The boy's wet condition was explained by the fact that he had just been for a swim in the surf, wearing the ridiculous costume in guise of a bathing suit.

Why are you waiting to see me? I asked. You owes me twenty-fo' shillin's on my Fo'd, says he. So I do, says I. You sho looks crazy, suh, says he; that is to say he thought I looked very odd in my goatskins, as no doubt I did; enough to make any one stare with wonder. It entered my mind, however, that though my habit looked crazy it was more artistic than oversize wet underclothes. Yet artistic or otherwise here was certainly Providence's answer to my prayers for a Friday.

Can you cook, boy? I asked him. Sho can, says he. Then you're going to be my slave till we're rescued, says I. But get off those underclothes and put on a grass skirt such as a really respectable savage should wear; and when you have it on come prostrate yourself before me and lift my foot on to your head. Otherwise you wouldn't be truly my man Friday.

The poor boy was now quite convinced I *was* crazy. Even so, he obeyed all that I bade him do, either through a sense of amusement or because he dared not cross a maniac. The original Carib himself could not have put his head beneath Crusoe's foot with any better grace than my new servant put his head beneath mine, though it took several attempts before we got the pose to look natural.

Then it occurred to me that I could not call him Friday, after all, because the day of my finding him was not Friday. What day *is* this? I asked of him, not being at all certain. Ain't it Toosday? he said. Indeed it was, and so henceforth I called him Toosday for the memory of the time.

Toosday's appearance rather pleased me; he had a slender but strong figure, and an agreeable open countenance, being, as I reckon, about twenty years of age. His hair was very short and curled like wool, the color of his skin not quite black but rather dark brown. Immediately I taught him to say Master, and let him know that was to be my name.

Returning to the cave I fed him a drink of rum, left over from the sailboat. The problem of sleeping quarters now arose. I did not possess a second hammock, but we managed to contrive a pallet, on the sand floor, of the canvas sail and several more goatskins. Toosday was loath to occupy this couch since the skins had by no means lost their odour, nor indeed would he do so until I had persuaded him that just as I had become used to my clothes he would become used to his bed.

The day after my new manservant's introduction into my household he inquired of me how long I wished for him to wear his grass—or rather rope skirt. I replied, only until I could make him a goatskin costume like my own. At the thought of having to wear clothes like mine he groaned with anguish. On the other hand, I felt he would not be a true Friday if he continued to go around in his underclothes. Consequently I made him a jerkin of goatskin, since I had now grown a tolerable good tailor, and cap to match, but he insisted the sleeves of the jerkin galled his shoulders, and pres-

At home with my family. Each evening I diverted myself by giving language lessons to Susie. Adam rests at my feet; Hyacinth waits patiently for her two kids; Kitty, on the table, looks jealously up at Susie; Toosday is holding Listerine; Quelques Fleurs is in the basket. On the wall may be seen the Scottish Mechanics calendar. My day's catch of fish hangs from above.

In order to make our boat we pitched upon a tree and felled it with the ax. How bravely we worked from dawn till night to make it hollow. I had visions of sailing in our finished craft majestically across to Trinidad, or maybe even New York.

ently refused to wear it at all, pleading that the nights spent next the evil skins were enough. Realizing that I wore my own coat only as a protection against the sun, and that Toosday was not in any danger of being burned as I was, I gave over trying to civilize him in this respect, though he had to continue wearing his skirt.

It was soon evident that Toosday, with a little direction, would be a most serviceable companion. His statement that he could cook was not an exaggeration, and as he seemed to enjoy it, and as I did not, I let him prepare every meal, which left me extra hours to ponder over Deuteronomy and Lamentations. Also as he was able to get more milk out of Hyacinth than I could, he became the family dairymaid. Of course his favorite rôle was pilot to Victoria, and in this capacity, with Adam and me in the back seat, he was grand indeed.

Among the island's simple-minded black population my own figure had caused enough commotion from the start, but now that I was seen accompanied by one of their own tribe naked except for a short rope skirt, such riots were precipitated that the native constable had perplexities as to what should be done with us. On the night of the weekly movie, leaving Adam and Susie behind to guard our cave, Toosday and I in all our glory drove up in Victoria and took front-row seats. The manager had to appear personally to restore order enough to allow the picture to be shown.

On the way home that night I felt somewhat concerned lest this visit to the movies might be an unpardonable departure from my impersonation of Crusoe, and to ease my conscience I took over Toosday's evening dairy duties and solemnly milked Hyacinth before going to bed.

But to return to my new companion; I became daily more delighted with him, and made it my business to teach him everything that was proper to make him useful, handy and helpful. Yet withal you may be sure I was not wanting to lay a foundation of religious knowledge in his mind, for I remembered that one of the features in *Robinson Crusoe* was the master's conversion of Friday from cannibalism and worship of old Benamuckee to the understanding of the true God. However, the moment I approached the subject I found that Toosday's literal faith in heaven and the devil, in angels and hot fire and brimstone, in salvation and the life everlasting was so much stronger than my own, nay, so much more vivid than mine, that he was in a good way to convert me to Christianity rather than my converting him. Very evidently Toosday needed no rescuing from the clutches of old Benamuckee, so I gave up being a missionary to the heathen and let the matter drop.

The prospect of Trinidad's three peaks rising to the southwest, that I had seen from the hilltop had filled me, ever since the day I saw them, with the hopes of reaching there in a boat made with my own hands. And now that I had Toosday to help, I resolved to go about it.

I was so fixed upon my design that we shortly went to work to find out a great tree proper to fell, and make a large periagua to undertake the voyage. There were trees enough on the island to have built a whole fleet of periaguas, but the main thing I looked at was to get one near enough the water.

At last Toosday pitched upon a tree, along the shore several miles from our cave, on the side of a hill which sloped into the sea. I do not know to this day what name to call the tree except that its wood was not as hard as some others. Having felled it we set to work with our ax and hatchets as it lay, cut off the branches and then faced the great labour of making it hollow. How bravely we worked from dawn till night, assisted by small burning logs that helped us eat out the core. We cut and hewed the outside into the true shape of a boat, and made it very handsome by rubbing it with sand. She could have carried twenty men with great ease, and consequently was large enough to carry me and all my cargo.

After a week of constant work and many a weary stroke we called our boat finished. And I was excessively delighted with it, for the boat was really much bigger than I ever saw a periagua in my life. I had visions of sailing majestically across to Trinidad, into Port of Spain—all the way to Charleston maybe—or even New York. Everything was ready now for the triumphant launching.

Summoning all our strength we gave one mighty push together. We may as well have tried to push Saint Paul's Cathedral or the Tower of London. The terrible truth was soon made clear to us—we had built a boat in weight a hundred times beyond our ability to stir it. I cursed myself over this stupidity, which indeed seemed doubly stupid, for did I not have Crusoe's own unhappy example in doing exactly what I had done to warn me? I thought of every possible device to overcome the difficulty. We could not dig a canal from the sea to the boat since the tree had stood forty feet above the water. Perhaps we could dig enough dirt from under the boat to start it rolling down of its own weight. All of another morning with a prodigious deal of pains we worked at this idea until at length it did begin to totter, and presently gave one great groan and rolled not toward the water but merely upside down—and there the damned thing rests to this day, so far as I know.

Late that afternoon as we plodded homeward down our beach, very weary and dejected over the loss of all our labour, I heard Toosday suddenly give a shout of joy and surprise. I looked up to find a schooner riding at anchor not two hundred yards from shore. I gazed at her scarce believing my eyes, but indeed she was a real and not a phantom ship.

With the greatest excitement we rushed to our skiff, and trusting the schooner was not a pirate vessel, rowed out to her. The crew and captain thought, no doubt, that we were escaping madmen, and at first would not let us come aboard, but my brief explanation that I was only a voyager marooned by ill fortune on this island and not as wild as I looked overcame all fears, and I was invited aboard. The schooner was making a survey of reefs and shoals, and that night would be sailing for Port of Spain, to which port the captain agreed to take me.

Somewhat dazed at this sudden turn of fortune I returned to our cave wondering what to do with my family. Susie I resolved to keep as a relic of my life as a castaway, Adam and Kitty could remain as pets for Toosday who, with Victoria already on his hands, must stay behind. Hyacinth, Quelques Fleurs and Listerine would be given back to the goatherd from whence they came. All else I bequeathed to my manservant. The umbrella I greatly prized, but as it would not fold up I had to leave it, with a tear, behind. We piled everything mountain high into the automotive machine, and amid a bedlam of barks and baas, Toosday drove Victoria away into the night.

Lonely, and jealous of the surrendered solitude, I stood, with Polly on my shoulder, in the empty cave. The moon was shining on the sea outside and all the slender palm trees waving as if in farewell.

Thus I left Robinson Crusoe's happy island, the twenty-seventh of June, after I had been upon it nine and twenty days. And on the same month ten years that I had run away to sea to act the rebel to my parent's authority, I came penitently home to my father's house, proudly bearing my scars of battle, and a parrot named Susie, and a contentment that in my conquest of adventure I had sought the New World and met a land of romance, face to face.

THE END

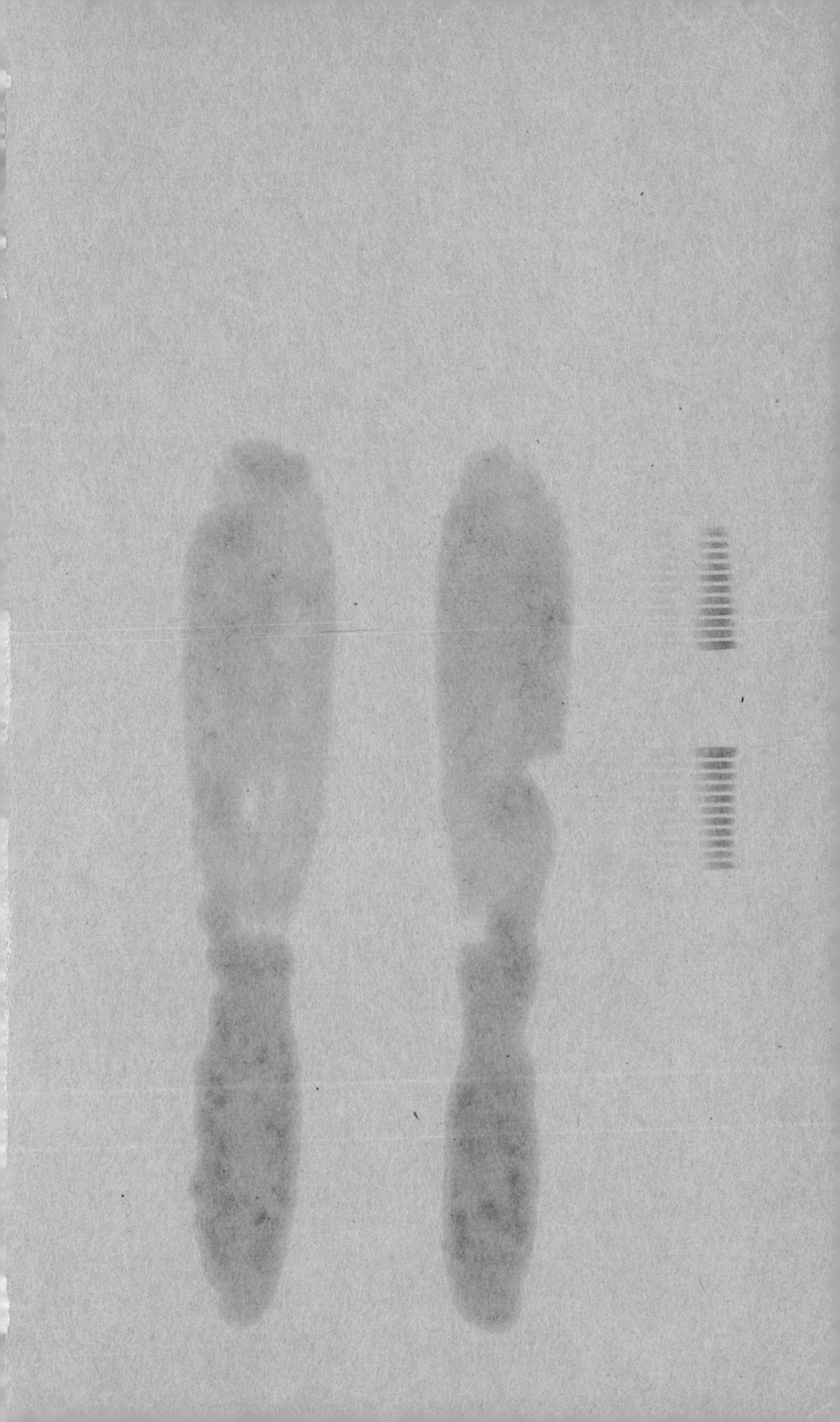

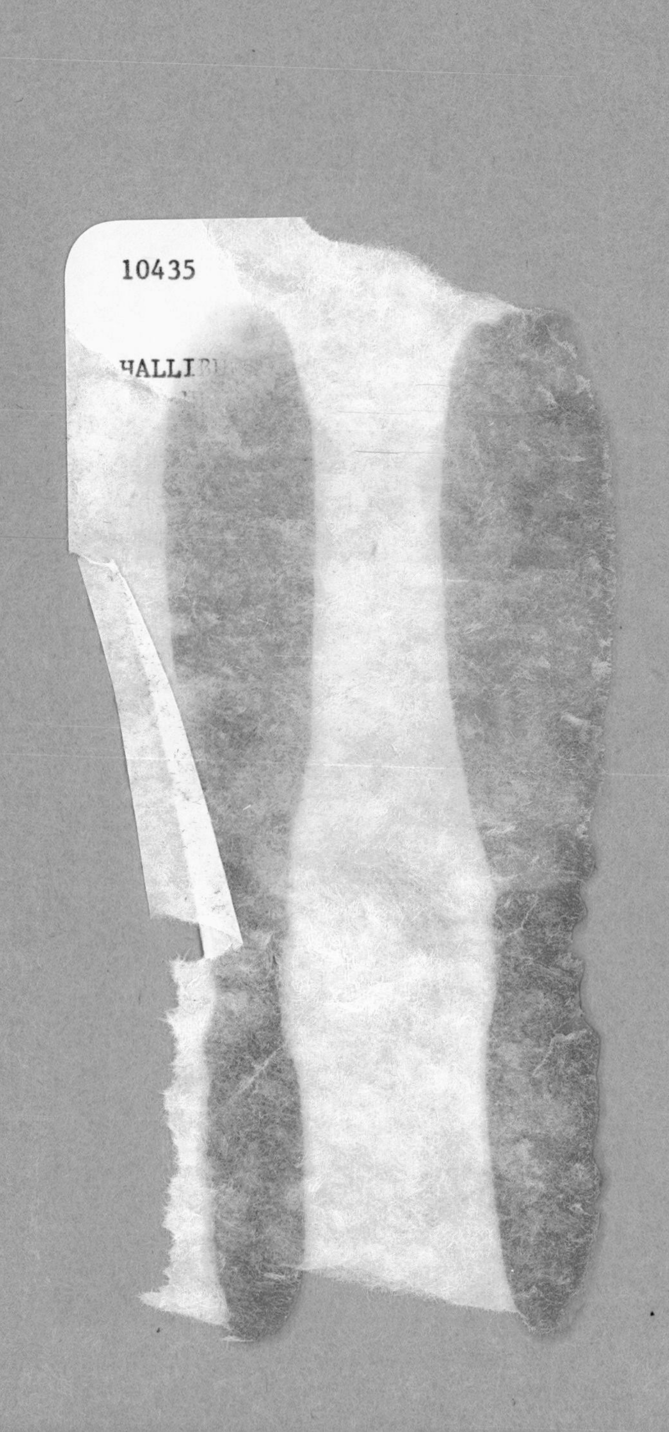

10435
HALLIB